An Introduction to Fully Integrated Mixed Methods Research

I dedicate this book to one of my high school English teachers, Naomi Manning. Increasingly aware of the advantages that came to me from attending a very strong high school in the suburbs of New York City, I want to give a "shout out" to the teacher who first introduced me to research and an appreciation for absorbing work in a quiet college library. It is from her that I learned a low-tech method for note taking on three-by-five index cards that I subsequently used in every article and book I have ever written.

An Introduction to Fully Integrated Mixed Methods Research

Elizabeth G. Creamer

Virginia Polytechnic Institute and State University

Los Angeles | London | New Delhi
Singapore | Washington DC | Melbourne

FOR INFORMATION:

SAGE Publications, Inc.
2455 Teller Road
Thousand Oaks, California 91320
E-mail: order@sagepub.com

SAGE Publications Ltd.
1 Oliver's Yard
55 City Road
London EC1Y 1SP
United Kingdom

SAGE Publications India Pvt. Ltd.
B 1/I 1 Mohan Cooperative Industrial Area
Mathura Road, New Delhi 110 044
India

SAGE Publications Asia-Pacific Pte. Ltd.
3 Church Street
#10-04 Samsung Hub
Singapore 049483

Acquisitions Editor: Leah Fargotstein
Editorial Assistant: Yvonne McDuffee
Production Editor: Olivia Weber-Stenis
Copy Editor: Erin Livingston
Typesetter: Hurix Systems Pvt. Ltd.
Proofreader: Jennifer Grubba
Indexer: Rick Hurd
Cover Designer: Karine Hovsepian
Marketing Manager: Susannah Goldes

Copyright © 2018 by SAGE Publications, Inc.

Printed in the United States of America

Library of Congress Cataloging-in-Publication Data
Names: Creamer, Elizabeth G., author.
Title: An introduction to fully integrated mixed methods research / Elizabeth G. Creamer, Virginia Polytechnic Institute & State University.
Description: Los Angeles : Sage, [2018] | Includes bibliographical references and index.
Identifiers: LCCN 2016045086 | ISBN 9781483350936 (pbk. : acid-free paper)
Subjects: LCSH: Education—Research—Methodology. | Mixed methods research.
Classification: LCC LB1028 .C72 2018 | DDC 370.72—dc23
LC record available at https://lccn.loc.gov/2016045086

This book is printed on acid-free paper.

SFI® Certified Sourcing
www.sfiprogram.org
SFI-00453

17 18 19 20 21 10 9 8 7 6 5 4 3 2 1

BRIEF CONTENTS

DETAILED CONTENTS

PART 2 • EXECUTING FULLY INTEGRATED MIXED METHODS RESEARCH

PART 4 • CONTROVERSIES AND FUTURE DIRECTIONS

LIST OF TABLES AND FIGURES

PREFACE

I begin with a confession. I first started teaching mixed methods in an undergraduate course in the late 1990s, finding that Creswell's (1998) dialectical approach of "turning the story" fit well within the interdisciplinary context that was my academic home. Five years later, my disciplinary affiliation shifted to one in education and I started teaching mixed methods research design courses at both the masters and doctoral level using a foundational set of textbooks well known to the mixed methods community.

My confession is that despite teaching and doing research with mixed methods for more than twenty years, I have struggled to apply some of the most fundamental concepts that have been used to distinguish the timing and priority of studies using a mixed method design. I have never been able to figure out, for example, if the term *concurrent* applies to data collection or to data analysis or to both. Similarly, the idea of a sequential design suggests a distinction between qualitative and quantitative strands that I do not find characteristic in the most innovative studies. To further compound the matter, I have never been sure if the term *mixing* has been used principally in reference to types of data or to types of analytical techniques.

Remaining under the illusion that the error in thinking was mine, the thought of undertaking the task of writing a textbook did not occur to me until I launched an initiative to design an introduction to mixed methods research class that would be delivered online. As I developed the materials for that class, I found that none of the widely adopted textbooks seemed compatible with my goals and paradigmatic orientation. One of the available options seemed too narrowly focused on a philosophical orientation and offered too little guidance for the novice researcher. Another was decidedly more prescriptive and positivist. So much space was devoted in most chapters to an explanation of quantitative and qualitative approaches that little space was actually allocated to uniquely mixed methods ways of accomplishing a particular task, like sampling. This approach was incompatible with my growing conviction that the distinctions between qualitative and quantitative approaches in practice are far more difficult to disentangle than the rhetoric implies. I was surprised to discover how little attention was devoted in most textbooks to exploring ways to mixing and to the attention that was lavished to prescribing set designs, which at this point in the development of mixed methods could be interpreted to actually discourage rather than promote meaningful interaction between data from different sources.

In addition to mixed methods, I have long taught a graduate-level course in qualitative research. My enthusiasm for the power of qualitative research, particularly in theory generation, is evident in a number of ways in this text. One way is a repeated emphasis about the contribution to explanatory power of a genuinely inductive approach to analysis and to mixing. A second way my qualitative orientation is evident is in the conviction that opportunities for innovation are largely unplanned and in the space I devote to mixed method approaches to content analysis, grounded theory, and case study research.

CONCEPTUAL FRAMEWORK

As I pursue in further detail in the first chapter, leaders in the field are still lobbying for different definitions of what constitutes mixed methods research and, most particularly, what exactly is mixed. There is general agreement that the mixed methods labels suggest that different types of data are collected and that the two are engaged in some interactive fashion. Some leaders in the field offer the conservative suggestion that mixing or integration should occur in at least one phase (e.g., Creswell & Plano Clark, 2011), while others, most notably Greene (2007), are proponents of a paradigmatic stance that embraces a more thorough saturation of the intent to engage qualitative and quantitative strands throughout the research process.

Without suggesting that such an approach is mandatory to warrant the designation of being mixed methods, I join Teddlie and Tashakkori (2009) by adopting the terminology of *fully integrated mixed designs* or *fully integrated mixed methods* to refer to research studies where the qualitative and quantitative strands are engaged in a dialectical manner at *all* stages of the study. Fully integrated mixed method studies are executed through an ongoing iterative exchange between the qualitative and quantitative strands that invites an engagement with the unexpected and often paradoxical that cannot emerge when the mindset is driven by a singular hypothesis testing framework and a linear approach to analysis. One way I maintain the focus on integration is by illustrating different ways that this can be accomplished at each stage of the design and execution of a mixed methods study.

PURPOSE

The centering of ways to integrate qualitative and quantitative data through all phases of a research project is reflected by the title for the book, and the framework of this practical textbook is intended for use in an introductory graduate-level mixed methods research course. In part because I have largely adopted terminology that is already used widely, this textbook will be useful in setting the stage for a more advanced course in mixed methods research.

The primary purpose of the text is to provide novice researchers and those new to mixed methods the tools to design, execute, and evaluate a mixed methods research study. For a class with an enrollment of master's-level students, I envision the principal task of the text to provide a systematic way to evaluate a mixed methods publication in order to determine its contribution to knowledge and/or practice. In my experience, doctoral students bring an interest in learning how to design a credible mixed methods study to the class.

The goals for the book include the following:

1. To provide an introductory textbook for graduate students in applied disciplines in the social and behavioral sciences that reflects contemporary views, such as that mixed methods requires integration of different data sources in multiple phases of the research process.
2. To provide novice researchers and those new to mixed methods the tools to design and execute a fully integrated mixed methods study.
3. To provide supplemental materials that will assist instructors in teaching an introductory mixed methods course.
4. To introduce the terminology associated with the methodology.
5. To illustrate ways that the qualitative and quantitative strands can be integrated at all stages of the research process.
6. To provide an extended discussion of data transformation as an analytical strategy to mix qualitative and quantitative data.
7. To propose a rubric to evaluate the quality of a mixed methods research publication.
8. To illustrate key concepts by weaving references to a set of exemplary publications across chapters throughout the book.
9. To explore the use of mixed methods approaches to grounded theory, content analysis, and case study research.

I find that almost every student who enrolls in my mixed methods class does so with an intuitive enthusiasm about the potential for collecting multiple sources of data and that their principal interest is finding models that will help them design their own research study. They want help with writing a purpose statement and research questions and with setting up a study in ways that promote the meaningful integration of their data. Experience has taught me that students appreciate a relatively jargon-light, practical textbook that is dotted with multiple real-world examples that make it possible for them to apply what they have learned to their own research interests.

AUDIENCE

The primary audience for this textbook is graduate students in applied disciplines, including all fields of education, health-related disciplines, and human development. The book also is addressed to more advanced researchers, such as postdoctoral fellows, research associates, evaluators, and those whose route to mixed methods is the product of unexpected results or the challenge to integrate qualitative and quantitative data. Regardless of the reason(s) for pursuing mixed methods research, the identification of criteria to evaluate quality at each stage of a research project and the emphasis on illustrating ways to build in methodological transparency will be instructive to those seeking to design a persuasive mixed methods research proposal or report.

As I have written this textbook, I have tried to keep my eye on graduate students as my principal audience. When faced with a decision about what to include and what to exclude, I defaulted to the question: Is this something a newcomer to mixed methods would need to know to launch a credible mixed methods study? With this in mind, I avoid lengthy detours to synthesize and cite a large body of literature about key topics, preferring instead to acknowledge key pieces from the literature and to use exemplars to illustrate key design features.

Because I do not use a framework that first reviews the fundamentals assumptions about the different approaches taken in qualitative and quantitative research approaches at each phase of the design and execution of a research study, this book will be most useful in a course where the focus is on mixed methods or in a survey course where it is one of several required textbooks. Those who bring at least a foundational knowledge from an introductory research course will be in the best position to benefit from this book. It is less critical that readers know the ins and outs of the two approaches than it is to understand what is required to design a credible research project that has the potential to generate knowledge and/or contribute to practice.

DISTINGUISHING FEATURES

A number of features distinguish this text from other textbooks that might be selected for an introductory course in mixed methods research design. First is the repetition and expansion of the uniting metaphor of the architectural arch to represent the potential to maximize the benefits of a mixed methods approach by considering innovative ways to integrate the qualitative and quantitative strands at all stages of the design and execution of a study. Switching from an emphasis on process to product in the last chapter, the arch also proves helpful to visualize the types of conclusions that are drawn in a mixed methods study.

Secondly, the book turns repeatedly to the question of how to produce and report on high-quality mixed methods research, including by devoting a separate chapter to consider ways to evaluate the quality of a mixed methods research publication. In this chapter, the Mixed Method Evaluation Rubric (MMER) is introduced to help the novice single out models worthy of replication. In addition to items related to transparency of the rationale for using mixed methods and a way to assess the methodological grounding, the MMER contains one item to measure the amount of mixing across the phases of the research process and a second to evaluate the engagement with diverse perspectives.

A third feature of the textbooks reflects an intentional decision to avoid introducing a whole new, complicated lexicon of mixed methods terms and designs. Instead, I offer a bridge to other methodological texts by relying on terminology that is already well ensconced in the discourse about mixed methods.

Fourthly, the text is unusual in that it provides a discussion of strategies to accomplish mixing of qualitative and quantitative data during analysis, including through the process of data transformation that extends across chapters. This is a much more detailed discussion than is available elsewhere.

A fifth distinguishing feature is that I have woven repeated references to a small set of readily available journal articles from a wide variety disciplinary journals as exemplars. I have prioritized methodological transparency in their selections. I selected the exemplars with the intent of providing models of studies worthy of replication and doable within the time frame and resources typical for a doctoral student. They were not selected to illustrate a specific set of mixed methods designs but were situated in chapters in order to provide examples of different ways to accomplish a procedure like sampling or mixing during analysis. The presence of so many examples with a qualitative priority reflects my own constructivist mindset and offsets the criticism that mixed method approaches are most adaptable to a quantitative mindset. The fact that the exemplars appeared in a diverse set of journals demonstrates that while a staple in educational and health-related research, mixed and multimethod approaches have been adopted in a remarkably broad range of academic fields.

None of the final set of articles featured as exemplars is authored by a figure well known to the mixed methods community. Two of the exemplars report on the results of dissertation research. This supports my contention that while foundational knowledge is an advantage, advanced expertise in mixed methods is not required to execute innovative work. This furthers the argument that it is feasible for a novice researcher with foundational knowledge of the literature to design a credible mixed methods study.

In chapters that lack a reference to an exemplary research publication, I have provided examples of some innovations reported in popular literature. The suggestions for supplemental class activities in several chapters involve developing research questions or a proposal for a research topic that has surfaced in the popular media, including an example about the use of robots to promote learning in autistic children. I have included examples from the popular media not only to pique interest but also to demonstrate the ingenious ways that researchers from multiple disciplines have come together to solve real-world problems in a collaborative manner.

ORGANIZATION OF THE BOOK

The book is organized in four parts. The first part explores foundational issues that are well known to members of the mixed methods community. The contribution of this portion of the text is framing the discussion relative to fully integrated mixed methods designs. Part 1 includes a chapter about the defining characteristics of mixed methods research and a second that reviews a classic typology of rationales that have been offered for using a mixed methods approach. The third chapter offers an original approach to framing the discussion about paradigms. Rather than linger on what now seems an outdated argument about the incompatibility of qualitative and quantitative approaches, it identifies four strains of paradigmatic reasoning that are compatible with mixed method approaches and reflects about the role each might play in how research is designed and conducted. The fourth chapter explores distinguishing characteristics of mixed methods research designs, giving more attention to priority and less to timing than has normally been awarded. As compared to subsequent chapters, the first four chapters are firmly rooted in foundational material that marked the emergence of a community of scholars that self-identified as mixed methods researchers.

The original contribution of the text begins to emerge most clearly as the discussion turns in Part 2 to the topic of mixing. The contribution of this section is to provide a more extended discussion of mixing, with many examples, than has been previously available.

The first chapter in Part 2 considers strategies for mixing prior to analysis, particularly during sampling and data collection. The remaining two chapters in this section provide an in-depth exploration of mixing during analysis, including through data transformation.

The third part of the book contains two chapters devoted to issues of quality. This section addresses practical dimensions of mixed methods and includes a chapter about how to evaluate the quality of a mixed method publication and suggests approaches to designing a mixed method research proposal or dissertation.

The last part of the book is devoted to addressing some lingering controversies about mixed methods, including the long-standing emphasis on a prescribed set of designs. It deconstructs the logic of combination that underlies so much of the discourse about mixed methods. Further innovation is evident in this chapter in suggestions about ways to capture the centrality of mixing in figures and flowcharts. An additional contribution of the final chapter is the introduction of the idea that attention to meta-inferences provides a window into how a study was designed.

ORGANIZATION OF EACH CHAPTER

Each chapter is organized in a similar manner. They begin with a list of goals that could quickly be translated to serve as a study guide. The chapters end with a bulleted summary of key points, a list of the terms that were introduced in the chapter, suggestions for supplemental activities to use in class, and recommendations for assigned reading to accompany the chapter. The glossary terms are highlighted and followed by a definition, which appears in italics. A glossary summarizes the terms that are introduced in the chapters.

TAKING ADVANTAGE OF THE TEXT

In addition to the recommendations for supplemental activities and readings and the exemplars, several additional features of the text are designed to support the goal of providing novice researchers and those new to mixed methods with the tools to design, execute, and evaluate a mixed methods research study. These features include the use of a template to summarize the exemplars, a list of key points at the conclusion of each chapter, and supplemental materials that are available through the book's website.

Templates. In many chapters, I offer an extended analysis of either a single or multiple exemplars to describe options for different procedures, such as mixed method approaches to sampling or ways to mix data during analysis. In place of the more widely used flow chart that visualizes design elements of a study but fails to consider the outcomes or inferences produced, I use a standard template to succinctly summarize key features of each of the chapter exemplars. The template contains the following information about each of the exemplars: (a) the rationale or reason for using mixed methods, (b) if the article reflects a qualitative, quantitative, or mixed priority, (c) timing of data collection, (d) timing of data analysis, (e) phases where mixing occurs, (f) inferences derived from the qualitative phases, (g) inferences derived from the quantitative phases, (h) meta-inferences, and (i) expressed value-added of using a mixing methods approach. Completed templates for all of the chapter exemplars appear in Appendix D.

The template used to summarize key features of each of the chapter exemplars offers a way to structure a summary of an article that is more inclusive than the conventional flowchart. The template maintains a balance between an interest in dissecting key facets of the way the data for the research project were collected and analyzed with an interest in the type of inferences and meta-inferences produced. This draws attention to the value-added to a mixed methods approach and what insight is actually gained by linking conclusions from the qualitative and quantitative strands.

The article template will be useful on several fronts. It can provide a useful way to facilitate discussion about additional articles that might be assigned. It is also useful as a form to collect a structured set of data that would facilitate cross-case comparisons in a content analysis or literature review.

A list of key points appears at the end of each chapter. These are listed in a chapter-by-chapter summary that appears in a document in the appendices. The key points will prove useful as guides for classroom discussion, for review of course content, or to structure formative and summative evaluations in the form of multiple-choice quizzes or short-answer and essay exams.

Additional supplemental materials. Additional materials to support course instruction are available on the book's website. These include a sample syllabus with a recommended list of assigned reading. This also includes sample quiz questions for each chapter and a list of recommended individual and group assignments that can be used as class activities.

RELATED ASSIGNMENTS

The organization of this text into ten chapters creates an opportunity for instructors to tailor the course in ways that suit their interests and the students' skill levels. For a semester-long course that contains fifteen weeks, instructors might find it beneficial to end the course by allocating time to mixed methods approaches to different quantitative traditions (such as the randomized clinical trial) or to qualitative traditions (including case study, grounded theory, content analysis and systematic reviews, the critical incident technique, action or participatory research, and/or evaluation and assessment).

Several additional assignments are compatible to the sequencing of information in the text. For doctoral students, the supplemental activities are interlinked in a way that is conducive to an assignment that I use regularly in the classes I teach: to prepare a content analysis of the use of mixed method approaches in journals in a single disciplinary area such as math education, higher education, leadership, nursing, or library science. An annotated bibliography or literature review about how mixed methods have been used to study a particular topic, like playground safety or active learning, would be suitable for a class containing largely master's students. Further exploration of examples of mixed method and interdisciplinary research appearing in the popular media would be appropriate for master's students as well.

There may be an advantage to not being one of the first generation of scholars to pioneer the development of mixed methods as a field of study. I have learned that there are other authors of more recent works who have spotted the same ambiguity in language about mixed methods designs that has troubled me for such a long time. I envision this text as a bridge between the first generation of foundational textbooks that had such a profound impact of practice and the next generation of researchers using technology and mixed methods in ways that could not possibly have been imagined by combatants in the 1980s who underscored the distinctions between qualitative and quantitative approaches. This textbook aspires to move the conversation forward by de-emphasizing a set of prescribed designs and by accepting the challenge to center attention on the explanatory power gained from the meaningful integration of different sources of data and analytical procedures.

ACKNOWLEDGMENTS

Undertaking a textbook like you will find unfolding in the subsequent ten chapters is not possible without the support of many layers of personal and editorial support. My spouse of thirty-five years, Don, receives the first round of kudos for bearing with me in the endless conversations I no doubt initiated to help unravel the logic of each and every chapter and, eventually, to tolerate my travelogue about the many rounds of revisions and copy editing. He is still wondering if I will ever actually finish the text!

I have benefited beyond measure from the guidance of two editors at SAGE. The first, Vicki Knight, guided me through the proposal stage and the writing of the first six chapters of the book before she was lured away to her next life as a retiree. Vicki was the one who taught me to look at a set of reviews and consider all the things that might have been said that weren't (e.g., the organization is poor, instrumental pieces of information are missing). I miss her sage advice and wicked sense of humor but feel fortunate to have been assigned to a second editor, Leah Fargotstein, with the experience to guide me through the steps in the process of moving from a manuscript to a final product. I have relied heavily on both Vicki and Leah for practical guidance about how to interpret reviewers' comments and how to translate those recommendations into revisions that keep to the major themes of the text. It was their network of connections that produced the list of the reviewers.

An Introduction to Fully Integrated Mixed Methods Research has benefited from the insight offered by reviewers that teach in very diverse settings. Some approach mixed methods as part of a survey course, while others teach it, as I do, in a stand-alone course. One set of reviewers stuck with me through the first six chapters, while a second set agreed to come on board to provide feedback about the remaining four chapters. After the manuscript was completed, a dedicated set of reviewers took on the even more challenging task of evaluating and providing feedback about the document as a whole. The contribution of these reviewers cannot be overstated. They have fueled many exciting ideas for additions and revisions and reinforced the value of some of the features that most distinguish this text. While it has not been possible to fully take advantage of all their suggestions, my brain continues to churn as I look to the future and think of where my mind might travel next.

My deep gratitude to the time and dedication of the following set of reviewers who gave permission to be recognized in the acknowledgments:

- James A. Bernauer, Robert Morris University
- Julie A. Cowgill, Benedictine University at Mesa

- Shannon L. David, North Dakota State University
- Mark A. Earley, Bowling Green State University
- Joan Engebretson, University of Texas Health Science Center at Houston
- Rhea Faye D. Felicilda-Reynaldo, Missouri State University
- Tina L. Freiburger, University of Wisconsin–Milwaukee
- Diane Gavin, University of Phoenix
- Leanne M. Kallemeyn, Loyola University Chicago
- Laura J. Meyer, University of Denver
- Arturo Olivárez, Jr., The University of Texas at El Paso
- Elias Ortega-Aponte, Drew University
- Juan D. Rogers, Georgia Tech
- Margaret F. Sloan, James Madison University
- Pamela Whitehouse, Midwestern State University

Elizabeth G. Creamer
September 5, 2016
Blacksburg, Virginia, and Beaufort, South Carolina

ABOUT THE AUTHOR

Elizabeth G. Creamer is a professor of educational research in the School of Education at Virginia Polytechnic Institute and State University, where she has balanced administrative and faculty roles since 1980. Beginning her career as a high school reading and English teacher, once at Virginia Tech, she initially moved into teaching courses at the undergraduate level, including nearly ten years in the women's studies program where she taught courses in feminist research methods in the Center for Interdisciplinary Studies. An inclination to interdisciplinary thinking is what led her to teach her first mixed methods research course in the late 1990s. A person with broad-ranging interests, including about writers and the writing process, Creamer has maintained a long-standing research agenda that centered on women's interest and success in fields in engineering and information technology. Actively engaged in a series of interrelated research projects funded by the National Science Foundation, she is coauthor of a 2007 volume, *Reconfiguring the Firewall: Recruiting Women to IT across Cultures and Continents* and in 2010, *Development and Assessment of Self-Authorship: Exploring the Concept across Cultures.* Creamer teaches both an introductory online mixed methods research design course and an advanced mixed methods research design course at the graduate level as well as an advanced qualitative research methods course with an emphasis on constructivist grounded theory. Her interest in mixed methods studies with a robust qualitative component is evident in her selection of exemplary publications for this textbook.

FOUNDATIONAL ISSUES

PART ONE

DEFINITIONAL ISSUES

PRINCIPAL PURPOSES OF THE CHAPTER

1. To introduce foundational terminology used in the mixed methods literature
2. To review several definitions of mixed methods
3. To present fully integrated mixed methods as the conceptual framework for the book

EXAMPLE FROM THE POPULAR MEDIA: LOCATING THE BONES OF RICHARD III

A team of researchers at the University of Leicester in the United Kingdom made a remarkable discovery in 2012. Struck down in the Battle of Bosworth Field, the bones of one of the monarchs of England, Richard III, had been missing for more than 500 years. Richard III was depicted as a villainous hunchback in the play by Shakespeare by the same name, where he was claimed to have yelled, "My kingdom for my horse!" before he met an ignoble end after a mad dash on foot across the battlefield. Analysis of the skeletal remains in the unmarked grave convincingly identified it as Richard's because of the pronounced curvature of the spine. He was not a hunchback, as Shakespeare portrayed him, but suffered from a scoliosis, among other ailments. Analysis of the bones revealed that Richard suffered multiple blows that could easily have accounted for his demise.

The team of researchers from the United Kingdom provide a contemporary example of how the use of multiple research methods from a variety of disciplines can unlock a mystery. The search for the bones of the long-lost monarch frustrated generations of scholars and adventurers (see Figure 1.1.). Members of the team of researchers mapped references to the location of the bones found in historical letters, diaries, and newspaper accounts to historical maps of the period and later transposed them to contemporary maps of the area. They then used map regression analysis, a statistical procedure, to pinpoint the location of the unmarked grave. Their strategies

FIGURE 1.1 ■ Discovering the Bones of Richard III: A Contemporary Example of Triangulation for Convergence

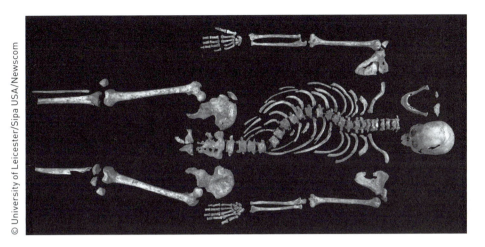

proved effective, as the long-missing bones were discovered under a parking lot in the town of Leeds.

Mixed methods researchers would label the procedure used to solve the mystery of the unmarked grave as a stellar example of one of the principal reasons for using mixed methods: to enhance validity through **triangulation**. *Triangulation involves corroboration or verification through multiple data points or multiple types of data about the same phenomenon.* In the case of the discovery of the long-lost skeletal remains, locations identified in historical accounts were converted to quantitative map coordinates for further analysis. It was the triangulation of the data that ultimately led to the discovery of the unmarked grave.

The concept of triangulation is a foundational construct in mixed methods research. It is a concept that illustrates that rather than having entirely distinct methodological assumptions, there are areas of overlap in the philosophical assumptions between qualitative and quantitative research methods. Greene (2007) argued that triangulation provided an "olive branch" in the waning days of the "paradigm wars," as researchers engaged in heated disputes about the legitimacy of the newly emerging qualitative movement. Greene maintained that the mixed methods movement formally began to emerge in the mid-1980s as qualitative and quantitative researchers found common ground by endorsing the contribution of triangulation to the credibility of research findings.

PURPOSES AND GOALS OF THE CHAPTER

In this chapter, you will be introduced to many of the foundational terms used in the mixed methods literature and that you will find in the glossary. There's a description of various perspectives about the definition of mixed methods research and a discussion of different ways to distinguish qualitative and quantitative approaches and methods. The conceptual framework for the book is presented next. The chapter closes by identifying some of the controversies associated with the foundational issues introduced in this chapter.

The goals of the chapter are to

1. review different perspectives about the definition of mixed methods research,
2. distinguish mixed method research from multimethod and quasi-mixed methods research,
3. consider some challenges in distinguishing qualitative and quantitative approaches,
4. describe a mixed method way of thinking as a logic that undergirds mixed method approaches, and
5. acknowledge concerns that are voiced about mixed method approaches.

DIFFERENT PERSPECTIVES ON THE DEFINITION OF MIXED METHODS RESEARCH

The defining characteristics of mixed methods research have continued to evolve since it first emerged as a methodological movement in the late 1980s. While consensus has yet to coalesce about all aspects of the definition, there is general agreement among mixed methods researchers about the core elements of a definition of mixed methods research. This includes the centrality of mixing as a distinguishing feature of mixed methods research and the assumption that it is both a method and a methodology. Diverse viewpoints exist, however, about the paradigmatic foundations of mixed methods as well as about the type and extent of mixing that is required to satisfy a baseline definition.

The definition of mixed methods research supplied by Creswell and Plano Clark in their textbooks (2007, 2011) sidesteps the issue of paradigms but characterizes mixed methods research as having a set of guiding philosophical assumptions and a method where a qualitative and quantitative strand are mixed at some point in the study. According to them,

> Mixed method is a research design with philosophical assumptions as well as methods of inquiry. As a methodology, it involves philosophical assumptions that guide the direction of the collection and analysis and the mixing of qualitative and quantitative approaches in many phases of the research project. As a method, it focuses on collecting, analyzing, and mixing both quantitative and qualitative data in a single study or series of studies. Its central premise is that the use of quantitative and qualitative approaches, in combination, provides better understanding of research problems than either approach alone. (Creswell & Plano Clark, 2007, p. 5)

Creswell and Plano Clark's definition situates mixed methods research as both a method and methodology. According to Greene (2008), a **methodology** consists of *a coherent framework of philosophical assumptions, methods, guidelines for practice, and sociopolitical commitments*. A number of philosophical assumptions undergird mixed methods. One of these is that qualitative and quantitative data and qualitative and quantitative methods are not incompatible. A second is that there is added value by the combination of qualitative and quantitative approaches to produce more robust findings. A third is the assumption that the corroboration of multiple types of data or multiple data points (i.e., triangulation) enhances validity. A fourth philosophical assumption undergirding mixed methods is referred to as the **complementarity argument**, which *claims that the use of a combination of methods can offset the weaknesses inherent in any method*. Each of these philosophical assumptions is discussed more thoroughly in the chapter about purposes (Chapter 2).

The definition Creswell and Plano Clark supply also refers to mixed methods as a distinct **method**. A method *consists of a systematic and coherent set of agreed-upon practices and procedures for conducting empirical research*. As a method, their definition stipulates that a study should contain both qualitative and quantitative strands and that these strands are mixed or integrated at some point in the study. As an additional element of methods, Creswell and Plano Clark champion the position that one of the core characteristics of mixed method research is the use of a taxonomy of research designs for planning and conducting a study. As will be discussed more thoroughly in Chapter 4, not everyone shares their enthusiasm for using a prescribed set of models or designs as a guide for designing and executing mixed methods studies.

THE CENTRALITY OF MIXING TO THE DEFINITION OF MIXED METHODS RESEARCH

While agreement has yet to coalesce about each and every aspect of the definition of mixed methods research, there is little disagreement about the centrality of mixing or the integration of qualitative data or strands as being a defining element of mixed methods research. The term *mixing* is part of the specialized language of mixed methods researchers. **Mixing** *is the linking, merging, or embedding of qualitative and quantitative strands of a mixed methods study*. It is not present when the strands of mixed methods study are kept parallel or distinct.

Creswell and Tashakkori (2007) share the following view about the centrality of mixing to the definition of mixed methods research: "Mixed methods research is simply more than reporting two distinct strands of quantitative and qualitative research; these studies must also integrate, link or connect these strands in some way" (p. 108). Teddlie and Tashakkori (2009) label a study containing *both a qualitative and quantitative strand but lacking any point of interface between the two* as **quasi-mixed methods**.

The centrality of mixing to the definition of mixed methods research is one fixture that distinguishes it from **multimethod studies**, which *occur when more than one qualitative approach or more than one quantitative approach is used in a single study.* This might be the case, for example, when two deductive (hypothesis-testing) or two inductive (hypothesis-generating) approaches to the analysis are used. Multimethod research is not restricted to combining qualitative and quantitative approaches (Hunter & Brewer, 2015). Yin (2006) maintained that the more mixing that occurs across phases of the research process, the more easily the research can be distinguished from what should otherwise be labeled as multimethod.

DISTINGUISHING QUALITATIVE AND QUANTITATIVE APPROACHES

It is surprisingly difficult to pinpoint a workable distinction between qualitative and quantitative research that holds up under scrutiny. By *workable*, I mean useful in determining if a study meets at least a minimal expectation to warrant the use of the label *mixed methods*, regardless of the label affixed to it by its authors. Most markers put forward to distinguish the two do not hold up in practice. While frustration with identifying ways to distinguish the two is so powerful that it has led more than one author to dismiss the distinction as meaningless (e.g., Maxwell, 2010; Newman & Hitchcock, 2011; Ridenour & Newman, 2008; Sale, Lohfeld, & Brazil, 2002), it is so embedded in the rhetoric and practice of day-to-day work of social scientists that it cannot be waved off for philosophical reasons.

Greene (2007) proposed a concrete rule of thumb for distinguishing between qualitative and quantitative approaches that requires little judgment from the reader. She took the position that a principal way to distinguish is during data collection: The data in qualitative research are words; in quantitative research, the data are numbers. Some take this straightforward dichotomy one step further and distinguish quantitative research by its use of statistical procedures and quantification and qualitative research as the absence of that.

Bryman (2004, p. 448) agreed that the word–number distinction is the most basic way to distinguish qualitative and quantitative research but acknowledged that the distinction is not a clean-cut one because it is simply not accurate to characterize qualitative research as being devoid of quantification. Bryman observed, "There is clearly some confusion concerning whether the quantification of qualitative, unstructured data is indicative of a quantitative or a qualitative approach" (2004, p. 100).

Many other strategies have been used to distinguish quantitative and qualitative approaches. Focusing on the design phase of a research project, Ercikan and Roth (2006), for example, argued that quantitative and qualitative research tends to be associated with different types of purposes and research questions. In their perspective, both methods can be used to answer descriptive questions. The qualitative strand is more likely than the quantitative strand to be used to answer *what* and *how* questions about a process.

Some of what can be seen in the published examples of mixed methods research demonstrates the complexity of using a simple dichotomy such as words versus numbers to distinguish qualitative and quantitative approaches. Nowhere is this more evident than in the fairly sizable body of content analyses that have examined the use of mixed methods in all kinds of different disciplinary areas (e.g., Hart, Smith, Swars, & Smith, 2009; Hauser, 2013; Powell, Mihalas, Onwuegbuzie, & Daley, 2008). An example of how the word–number dichotomy does not hold up in practice is evident in a recent content analysis of research articles in distance education by Hauser (2013). Hauser was reflexive about the struggle she encountered when she tried to classify the methods used in each article by applying the tried and true qualitative–quantitative distinction of words and numbers. She observed,

> In [my] review of the literature for this study, [I] found articles that stated that they were quantitative but did not perform statistical analysis and reported no statistical results. [I] also found articles that were declared to be qualitative and collected data using open-ended questions but reported results using statistical methods only and did not include any qualitative analysis or report data in a descriptive format. (p. 156)

The quantification of qualitative data accounted for a good deal of the struggle Hauser experienced in discerning the differences between a qualitative and quantitative approach. She simplified matters by reducing it to a matter of quantification. She categorized any method that reported statistical results as quantitative and only considered the study to have a qualitative phase if the qualitative data were reported without quantification. She applied the mixed methods label without any expectation that the two types of results could be integrated.

QUALITATIVE AND QUANTITATIVE APPROACHES AS DIFFERENT ANALYTICAL STRATEGIES

When I am trying to determine if a study described in a publication meets my minimal definition of mixed methods research, I find it most helpful to first assess if the analytical procedures in a mixed method publication include a deductive and an inductive element. Although this viewpoint is not without its detractors, I consider a deductive and an inductive component to be the baseline, minimal standard to warrant the designation as mixed methods. The two approaches to analysis are sometimes distinguished as moving from the general to the specific (deductive) or the specific to the general (inductive). The borderline between the two can be surprisingly murky.

I find that many graduate students have trouble escaping their methodological socialization and incorporating an inductive or emergent approach that is free as it is humanely possible to be of preconceptions. Similarly, when analyzing a pool of articles flagged as mixed methods, it is not uncommon to discover that many authors approached the analysis of both types of data deductively. A deductive analytical strategy can be framed to test the constructs or relationship proposed in a theoretical framework. The predilection to a deductive mindset may explain why researchers applying the tools of content analyses to a body of mixed methods articles often conclude that the quantitative strand was given priority.

Although this foundational assumption is often violated, inductive reasoning is most often associated with an emergent or qualitative approach. In this approach, a researcher approaches his or her data with an open mind and without imposing a comprehensive theoretical framework. An inductive approach generates hypotheses rather than confirms them. Inductive analytical strategies are much more likely to be missing from a mixed methods study than deductive ones. It is my experience that the emergent strand of a mixed methods study is most likely to produce unexpected findings. It invites further exploration of the unexpected and thus, I argue, is most likely to produce innovative insight.

The description of the research strategies used to pinpoint the location of the bones of the impulsive king illustrates that like many things methodological, the distinction between the deductive and inductive phases of a mixed methods project is not always obvious. The emergent or inductive phase occurred as the researchers analyzed a variety of written narratives identifying the location of where the king had been unceremoniously dumped in an unmarked grave after defeat in battle. The accounts were so contradictory and were relative to such a variety of landmarks that repeated efforts by prior teams had not been successful. The quantitative or deductive phase of the research occurred as the team of researchers linked the accounts in credible historical documents with map coordinates. Mixed methods researchers refer to the process of turning words into numbers as *data transformation*. In the case of the missing king, a statistical procedure subsequently was applied to the transformed data to finally pinpoint the exact location of the skeletal remains.

CONCEPTUALIZING QUALITATIVE AND QUANTITATIVE APPROACHES ON A CONTINUUM

Teddlie and Tashakkori (2009) were not the first to conceptualize qualitative and quantitative approaches not as polar opposites but as a continuum with points that overlap at the center. The extreme points on the continuum might be taken to reflect a "purist" stance. The depiction of qualitative and quantitative approaches intersecting at the center of a methodological continuum communicates that the boundaries between the two approaches are not impervious. It provides a counterpoint to the argument taken by purists that qualitative and quantitative approaches are so different that intermingling the two is impossible. The notion of a continuum highlights that there is significant variability in the paradigmatic assumptions of researchers using

TABLE 1.1 ■ Potential Contributions of Qualitative and Quantitative Approaches to a Mixed Methods Study by Phase		
Phases of the Research Process	**Quantitative**	**Qualitative**
Design	Variable oriented (offers breadth)	Case oriented (offers depth)
	Addresses *what* and *why* questions	Process oriented
		Can also address *how* questions
Data collection	Numbers	Words
Sampling	Allows for generalizability	Can pursue negative case or exemplary case
Analysis	Deductive	Context bound
	Confirmatory	Inductive and sometimes emergent
	Used to test theory	Exploratory
		Used to produce or modify theory
Inferences	Interpretations that extend the data	Interpretations that extend the data

different types of either qualitative or quantitative approaches. Purists at either end of the continuum are the groups of researchers most likely to find the idea of integrating qualitative and quantitative approaches as an anathema to their philosophical standpoint.

Rather than reinforcing the idea that qualitative and quantitative are starkly different approaches, I have organized Table 1.1. to illustrate the potential contribution of each to constructing a well-designed mixed method study. Table 1.1 lists the potential contribution of combining different aspects of qualitative and quantitative approaches at each phase of the research process. I put a different spin on the complementarity argument in this table. While it is often argued that one reason to use mixed methods is to offset the weaknesses of each method, I have set up the table in such a way as to emphasize the potential gains of using both qualitative and quantitative approaches in a single study.

Table 1.1 offers some ideas about how a researcher might borrow strengths from each approach to build a stronger study. The table is not meant to represent a menu or to imply that it is likely that, even at the design stage, a researcher should or could incorporate all of the listed elements. It does endorse the idea that some of the strengths of each approach can be incorporated in a well-designed mixed methods study.

Quantitative and qualitative approaches are each acknowledged as having their own distinct baggage of weaknesses. Qualitative research, for example, is often criticized as if the small, nonrepresentative sample means the results are anecdotal. Quantitative research, on the other hand, may be questioned for its inability to explain why or how an intervention succeeded or failed or why differences in outcomes between groups occurred. In response to these criticisms, in the process of laying out the plans for a mixed methods research project, a researcher might choose, for example, to bolster the representativeness of the sample used in the qualitative strand of a study by employing some quantitative sampling strategies and by ensuring that data from some members of the sample are used in both the qualitative and quantitative strands.

Even as I have found over the years that the inductive/deductive distinction is a workable baseline for distinguishing qualitative and quantitative strands of a mixed methods study and appreciate its emphasis on the analytical phases of a project, I recognize that it might well be argued that it is too simplistic to distinguish qualitative and quantitative methods by concentrating on a single phase of a study. This is one of several areas where there is a considerable gap between academic rhetoric and actual practice.

Quite a number of authors have used relatively strong language to voice their objections about the simplistic assumption that qualitative and quantitative methods are distinct and always readily distinguishable in practice. Ridenour and Newman (2008) labeled it a "false dichotomy." Ercikan and Roth (2006) pointedly observed, "Polarization of research into qualitative and quantitative is neither meaningful nor reflective of the realities of research" (p. 20). A British researcher, Bryman (2004), took a similarly forceful stand when he wrote, "We should be wary of assuming that in writing and talking about quantitative and qualitative research, we are referring to two absolutely divergent and inconsistent research strategies" (p. 446). Creswell (2011) called the two methods "a binary distinction that doesn't hold in practice" (p. 272).

MIXED METHODS AS A LOGIC OF INQUIRY

Two influential academics, Maxwell (2004, 2010) and Small (2011), are among those who refrain from using the term *method* to distinguish quantitative and qualitative research and argue that it is too simplistic to distinguish them by methods alone. This is consistent with the views of an early adapter of mixed methods, Jennifer C. Greene (2007), who argued that mixed methods are not simply the combination of methods and types of data but a different way of knowing or making sense of the world. Small (2011) used the phrases "ways of knowing" and "logic of inquiry" to characterize a dialectical stance.

Greene (2007) coined the expression "a mixed method way of thinking" to refer to a dialectical way of thinking or mindset that deliberately engages complexity and multiplistic mental models. This is a perspective shared by interdisciplinary researchers who begin a project with a mindset that the disciplines will introduce different perspectives. Greene's mixed method way of thinking involves a philosophical mindset along with a valuing of diverse voices, which probably emerges from Greene's involvement throughout her career in issues of social justice and the evaluation of social programs designed to promote equity as well as her axiological commitment to respecting diverse viewpoints.

Johnson, Onwuegbuzie, and Turner (2007) endorse the view of mixed methods as an approach to knowledge that deliberately sets out to consider multiple viewpoints. This axiological commitment is evident in Greene's position: "A mixed methods way of thinking aspires to better understand complex social phenomenon by intentionally including multiple ways of knowing and valuing and by respectfully valuing differences" (2007, p. 17). The view of reality as multiple is part of a paradigmatic view about the nature of reality.

Another way to conceptualize Greene's mixed method way of thinking is a holistic Gestalt that frames an entire research project from the first glimmer of an idea through to its final phase of execution and delivery. That is quite different from the practical reality that many researchers come to use mixed methods without much forethought but as the result of a search for a research approach that might explain unexpected or contradictory results or the failure of participants in a funded project or evaluation to achieve the desired outcomes or gains.

Greene's dialectical stance about mixed methods is about the deliberate engagement of paradox and difference. It is what I am calling a *logic of inquiry*. She positions it as being at odds with one of the principal justifications that has been put forward for using mixed methods, which is to enhance the credibility of results by triangulating multiple sources of different kinds of data. Rather than privileging convergence, consensus, and corroboration, Greene's position places equal priority on divergence, dissonance, and contradiction. This position shares with the scientific method a value awarded to weighing multiple competing hypotheses. At the same time, it recognizes the value-added that emerges from confirming results across settings and with multiple types of data.

Evaluation and Mixed Methods

Mixed method approaches to evaluation are a case in point of how a logic of inquiry can inform all phases of the design and execution of a research project. **Evaluation research** *is focused on program development. It "involves the triangulation of qualitative and quantitative methods to examine acceptability, integrity, and effectiveness of intervention methods as both a formative and summative process"* (Nastasi et al., 2007, p. 166). Data gathering during the formative phases of an evaluation is geared to find ways to improve the effectiveness of the intervention or program. Summative data provides evidence of gains or outcomes that measure the effectiveness of the intervention.

Evaluations are meant first and foremost to be useful and to improve the effectiveness of the implementation of a new program in a specific context. Their commitment to engage different viewpoints makes them highly compatible with a mixed method way of thinking. Despite their usefulness, reports generated from an evaluation often do not see the light of day or reach a wide audience because they are so context specific.

CONCEPTUAL FRAMEWORK—FULLY INTEGRATED MIXED METHODS RESEARCH

As with Greene's mixed method way of thinking, the conceptual framework that is woven throughout this book is presented as a logic of inquiry. I distinguish it from a paradigm because it does not explicitly address assumptions about the nature of reality (i.e., ontology) or the nature of knowledge and how it is constructed (i.e., epistemology). It is an overriding mindset that finds the practice of keeping the qualitative and quantitative strands as parallel but not converging unthinkable. It provides a way of thinking about mixed methods research that is not a prescriptive model for how the research should be conducted. My conceptual framework places equal priority on the qualitative and quantitative strands. As compared to Greene's way of framing mixed methods research, my conceptual framework shifts the emphasis on exploring contradiction and paradox out of the center.

I extend Teddlie and Tashakkori's (2009) expression, **fully integrated mixed methods research**, to refer to an overall Gestalt or holistic perspective that weaves throughout the phases of a research project. Teddlie and Tashakkori defined this as "a family of mixed methods designs in which mixing occurs in an interactive manner at all stages of the study" (2009, p. 335). I define it *as an approach to mixed methods research where there is the intention to mix or integrate the qualitative and quantitative strands of study throughout each of the stages or phases of the research process.* That means that strategies are used to weave together qualitative and quantitative strategies throughout each of the five **phases** or **stages** of a study (*the steps in the process of completing a research study: planning and design, data collection, sampling, analysis, and drawing inferences*). This involves sustained reflexivity about the contribution of both the qualitative and quantitative strands of a study. A commitment to this type of perspective is based on the belief that isolating a mixed methods way of thinking to one stage of the research process does not optimize the potential value-added of mixed methods.

The approach to fully integrated mixed methods research as a logic of inquiry places qualitative and quantitative approaches on equal footing as different but equally legitimate ways of knowing and understanding complex social phenomenon. One of the challenges researchers face when using mixed methods is to maintain, rather than sidestep, the differences between accepted philosophical assumptions and the procedures of each qualitative and quantitative approach.

The value-added of a fully integrated approach to mixed methods lies primarily in the potential of integrating or mixing the qualitative and quantitative strands, including the tenacious pursuit of differences in interpretation that arise during the qualitative and quantitative analysis. My approach in this textbook is to identify strategies that can be used to facilitate the integration of the qualitative and quantitative strands throughout the research process. As this is part of the logic of inquiry I present, my approach is both philosophical and practical.

THE ARCHITECTURAL ARCH AS A METAPHOR

I have found it helpful to visualize my conceptual framework through the metaphor of an architectural arch and to use the keystone that appears at the apex of ideal arches to represent **inferences**. In mixed methods, these are *conclusions or interpretations drawn from the results of the analysis in the quantitative, qualitative, and mixing strands.*

Through conversations with engineers, I have become aware how the qualities of the ideal arch match what I see as the full potential of mixed methods.

There are parallels between how an ideal arch is constructed and the execution of the two strands of a mixed methods study. This kind of arch is built from the ground up with two sides. In my conceptual framework, this represents the unique contributions of qualitative and quantitative approaches. One side cannot stand without the other. In a perfect arch, each of the building blocks are wedge shaped and added one by one, working toward the apex that is added as the last step. This is like the systematic, step-by-step process of executing a research procedure, such as occurs by using the constant comparative method to develop a grounded theory. This is consistent with a constructivist paradigm or view of knowledge that maintains that rather than being discovered in one fell swoop, knowledge is built from the ground up, generally one small increment at a time.

An ideal arch has qualities that also characterize the outcomes of paradigm-shifting research. These can be seen in Figure 1.2. This is a photo of an arch in a remote location at Lake Titicaca in Peru that I happen to have visited.

FIGURE 1.2 ■ Freestanding Arch at Lake Titicaca, Peru

© iStock/Jarno Gonzalez Zarraonandia

Two salient characteristics of an ideal arch are that they are durable while at the same time often aesthetically pleasing. Some still survive in the aqueducts built during Roman times throughout Europe and the near East, such as the example shown in Figure 1.2, which can stand independent of a surrounding structure. When there is a surrounding structure, such as the famous Arche de Triumph in Paris erected after World War II, it is the arch that is supporting the structure around it. The structure is not the mechanism holding up the arch.

Another direct connection between an ideal architectural arch and the essence of a fully integrated approach to mixed methods lies with the keystone. Hidden by decoration or in plain sight, a keystone is the apex of the ideal arch. Figure 1.3 is a photo of an ideal arch with a keystone.

A keystone is a wedge-shaped piece of building material that is the last piece slipped into this kind of arch. It is not a part of all arches. The wings of an arch create perfect tension by resting against the keystone. Once the keystone is set in place, each side is equally strong because each wedge-shaped piece shares the load equally. This makes it a highly efficient structure. This is like "pure" mixed methods, where the

FIGURE 1.3   ■   Ideal Arch With a Keystone

© iStock/Claudia Lusa

qualitative and quantitative strands are given equal priority (Johnson, Onwuegbuzie, & Turner, 2007). To stand, arches do not need the building material that is added above it, to the sides of it, or behind it to form an archway in a building. When it is well designed and the tension is equally distributed and supported, an arch can stand indefinitely, even as the building around it topples in the face of time.

I see parallels between the role of a keystone in an ideal arch and role of inferences in high-quality mixed methods research. *Inferences* are generalizations or interpretations constructed by the researcher that go beyond the results, participants, context, and sometimes theory and that vary by level abstraction (Ercikan & Roth, 2006). Inferences have many attributes; some, for example, pursue implications for future research, practice, policy, and/or theory. There are additional types of inferences in mixed methods that are not found in other research approaches.

A **meta-inference** is a type of inference that is unique to mixed methods. According to Teddlie and Tashakkori, meta-inferences *are inferences that link, compare, contrast, or modify inferences generated by the qualitative and quantitative strands* (2009, p. 300). It introduces an additional layer of abstraction by weaving together two or more inferences. A meta-inference is closely tied to the results of the analysis but is constructed in such a way that it links or merges results from the qualitative and quantitative strands. The keystone serves as a metaphor for different types of inferences, including those that link results from the qualitative and quantitative strands and those that merge them. Examples of these different types of inferences are presented in Part 2 of this book.

Arches can be built more cheaply by omitting the keystone and using a horizontal beam. A horizontal beam is a more common link between the vertical supports, but it is not as durable or aesthetically pleasing as the circular arch. Figure 1.4 is a photo of this kind of arch, also ancient and also in Peru. It is called Gate of the Sun and was constructed 1,500 years ago from a single piece of stone. It shows that the weak point of this kind of nonideal arch is at the center of the beam. This is where, without a keystone, the horizontal beam introduces pressure that is not offset by other elements of the design.

To me, the kind of nonideal, horizontal beam we see in Figure 1.4 represents a particular kind of mixing when drawing conclusions. There is a bridge between the qualitative and quantitative strands of a study, but this is often done in a way that merely juxtaposes them. This form of mixing presents results or findings from the two strands of the study as independent conclusions or inferences, without any superordinate inference that intermingles them. There is a telltale signal for this kind of mixing. You can see it in the results discussion section of a research article that is labeled with separate sections to summarize the qualitative and quantitative results without providing an additional section that brings together the two results to introduce an additional layer of meaning. On occasion, this kind of organizational strategy can allow two contradictory findings to remain unaddressed.

At this point in the evolution of mixed methods as a distinct methodological tradition, the idea of fully integrated mixed methods studies is more of an ideal than a reality widely evident in the literature. It is still very common to come across a research publication broadcasting a mixed methods label but this is no acknowledgement

FIGURE 1.4   ■   Gate of the Sun

of the body of methodological literature that supports it. As much as I value the resourcefulness of researchers using mixed methods to pursue unexpected results, I find it hard to imagine that a researcher could achieve a fully integrated study (i.e., create a perfect arch) without familiarity with the methodological literature and without deliberately setting out to do so.

"MIXED UP" METHODS

Despite the explosion of the use of mixed methods across many academic disciplines, there is no doubt that a group of academics object, sometimes vociferously, to the use of mixed methods. Some of their reasons are philosophical; others are practical. One overriding concern deals with the assumption that there is no logic of inquiry in mixed methods.

Those with the most deep-seated concerns about mixed methods are probably those that are the most reflexive about the paradigmatic assumptions underlying their use of either a qualitative or a quantitative tradition. In my experience, these are most likely to be researchers that have a strong preference for qualitative methods. Among the group voicing objections would be those, perhaps who might be appropriately labeled as "purists," who see qualitative and quantitative research as being conducted with entirely different paradigmatic assumptions about the nature of reality and how knowledge is constructed. Members of this group might have difficulty imagining a mind so nimble as to be able to simultaneously value insight gained from the perspective of a single case study with those derived from sophisticated statistical procedures. The view that mixed methods researchers are attempting to merge clashing paradigms is pursued in further detail in Chapter 3.

Others who express strong reservations about mixed methods may do so with practical concerns in mind. There is no question that some mixed methods studies are ambitious in design. Often, research about the effectiveness of an educational or health-related activity or program can involve multiple stages, researchers with diverse areas of expertise, and a far more ambitious time span than can realistically be undertaken by a graduate student. This is not always the case, however. There are some standard templates for the design of mixed methods studies, such as the basic triangulation design, that are not overly ambitious for a master's thesis or dissertation. In this type of design, qualitative and quantitative data might be collected simultaneously in a single questionnaire through the inclusion of both close-ended and open-ended questions. There is an extended discussion of designs that are realistic for dissertation research in Chapter 9.

Probably the greatest accusation behind derisive references to "mixed-up" methods is the suspicion that mixed methods provides an endorsement of wholesale piracy of analytical and sampling strategies without concern for the methodological and philosophical assumptions that accompany them. This kind of piracy is not particular to mixed methods, however. Misuse of labels to characterize research is not an uncommon feature of the published research, particularly in journals without a strong methodological interest. It occurs, for example, when so-called ethnographic interviews do not emanate from fieldwork or when the label *grounded theory* is inappropriately affixed to research that is conducted to test a preexisting theoretical framework.

The issue here is not pointing to a weakness inherent in the foundational assumptions about the purposes of mixed methods research but the often-uninformed application of the label to research that has not had the benefit of being embedded in the foundational literature about it. This would be the group of researchers that are mixed up about appropriate uses of mixed methods.

Mixed methods should not be taken as an excuse to violate the foundational philosophical assumptions (i.e., logic of inquiry) of either the qualitative or quantitative tradition. In quantitative research, this includes relatively large sample sizes and sampling strategies designed to provide support for claims that the results are generalizable to other settings. In qualitative research, foundational assumptions include concern for capturing the lived experience of participants and for recognizing the interplay between individual attitudes and behavior and the environmental and cultural context. There is no lack of elegant mixed method studies that manage to effectively incorporate the strengths of both perspectives without violating their foundational assumptions.

CONTROVERSIES INVOLVING FOUNDATIONAL ISSUES

Methodologists writing about mixed methods often do so with the goal of advancing the quality of the design and execution of mixed methods studies in practice. Not surprisingly, with growing consensus about key elements of the definition of mixed methods, standards applied to evaluate the quality of these studies have grown more exacting over time. Some types of studies that might have once been accepted as meeting some minimal definition of mixed methods no longer fit comfortably in that mold. One of these is what I might call "eternally parallel" studies, where the qualitative and quantitative strands are never considered in tandem. A second is where there are multiple sources and types of data, but these are analyzed in isolation of each other. I have already discussed the problem of studies that lack a genuine inductive or emergent strand.

Some of the most substantive advances in thinking in mixed methods involve the topic of mixing. As noted earlier, while there seems to be strong agreement that some form of mixing is mandatory to meet any minimal definition, there is still a pull and tug of what this should look like and the strategies that can be used to execute it. Growing consensus about the centrality of mixing to the definition of mixed methods brings into question the legitimacy of the claim that a study is mixed methods when the qualitative and quantitative strands are kept parallel and never genuinely engaged except in a perfunctory way with a sentence or two at the inference stage. These studies might more accurately be classified as another type of multimethod study.

There are plenty of good examples of research envisioned that, for very practical reasons, unexpectedly turn to mixed methods. There are multiple legitimate reasons for this. It is not uncommon, for example, for authors completing a quantitative study to unexpectedly find it expedient to add a qualitative phase to explain contradictory or puzzling findings or to explore why an intervention did not have the intended effects.

I do not share the objection to applying the label of mixed methods to studies that evolve into mixed methods but were not initially conceptualized that way. While not realistic for research designed to meet the requirements of a dissertation, the complex nature of the phenomenon being studied and the years of time and resources devoted to multiphase studies are probably two of the forces that led to the emergence of mixed methods as a distinct methodology. Often supported by external funding, the continued growth of these large-scale projects and their increasingly interdisciplinary nature make it difficult to keep up with their creative introduction of different ways to apply mixed methods.

We close the chapter with a summary of key points and a list of the terms introduced in the chapter.

Summary of Key Points

1. Just because someone completes a qualitative and quantitative phase does not necessarily mean it is a mixed methods study.

2. Mixed methods are both a research method and a research methodology.

3. A study is not mixed methods if there is no mixing or integration of the qualitative and quantitative strands.

4. Deductive and inductive analytical procedures are required to meet a minimal definition of mixed methods research.

5. The contribution of triangulation to enhancing validity is one of the key rationales for using mixed methods.

6. Because qualitative researchers often use numbers to report their results, the word–number distinction between qualitative and quantitative methods is only marginally useful.

7. One of the challenges researchers face when using mixed methods is to honor the fundamental philosophical assumptions of qualitative and quantitative approaches.

8. Fully integrated mixed methods take place when interaction between the qualitative and quantitative strands occurs at all stages of the study.

Key Terms

- Complementarity argument
- Evaluation research
- Fully integrated mixed methods research
- Inferences
- Meta-inference
- Method

- Methodology
- Mixing
- Multimethod studies
- Phases or stages
- Quasi-mixed methods
- Triangulation

Supplemental Activity

Create a table that summarizes similarities and differences in the definitions of mixed methods offered by various researchers in Table 1 in the article by Johnson, Onwuegbuzie, and Turner (2007).

Recommended Reading

Johnson, R. B., Onwuegbuzie, A. J., & Turner, L. A. (2007). Toward a definition of mixed methods research. *Journal of Mixed Methods Research, 1*(2), 112–133.

CATEGORIZING THE PURPOSES OF MIXED METHODS RESEARCH

PRINCIPAL PURPOSES OF THE CHAPTER

1. To explore a range of different reasons for using mixed methods
2. To distinguish six different rationales for using a mixed method approach

MIXED METHODS RESEARCH FEATURED IN THE POPULAR MEDIA

Now director of a center dedicated to the application of science to the human good, Dacher Keltner is credited with being the first to study facial markers of social–moral emotions, such as embarrassment and altruism. He began what was to become a model for an academic career in 1992 as a postdoctoral student conducting research in an experimental lab. His assignment was to test the application of a facial recognition coding system developed by Paul Ekman designed to capture the movements associated with unconscious facial displays. These are two- to three-second bursts of unconscious but highly coordinated movements of facial muscles that occur in response to some generic human emotions (Sapolsky, 2013).

From his first experiments, Keltner and his associates found that subjects consistently displayed a common set of features following experiencing or describing a situation (i.e., an antecedent) they found embarrassing. These include averted eyes, face angled down and to the side to reveal the neck, and puffed or tightened lips. These facial mannerisms serve a social purpose as the more embarrassed a person looked, the more others assessed them to be likable, trustworthy, and forgivable.

In his first days in the lab, Keltner joined others wanting to explore some of the theories posed by influential thinkers of the early 1950s, including those of Erving Goffman, one of the founding theoreticians of sociology and social psychology. These theoreticians proposed what grounded theorists call grand theory. *It was their conviction that emotions are not simply a psychological and individual phenomenon but also serve important social purposes. From what had been learned by others observing the behavior of primates such as chimpanzees and bonobos, who are close to us on the evolutionary ladder, leaders in the field speculated that the visual displays associated with emotions such as embarrassment are strategies of appeasement. They are an acknowledgment that the social order has been violated and an attempt to redress the violation through actions that reaffirm social cohesion. The downcast eyes and tightened lips are involuntary actions and a gesture of reconciliation.*

Over the course of the last twenty-five years, Keltner and subsequent generations of scholars have used an ingenious arsenal of research methods to confirm and extend their double-barreled assumption that consistent visual displays occur in response to certain emotions and that displays serve a social purpose. Studies published in 1996 (Keltner & Buswell) and 2012 (Feinberg, Willer, & Keltner) are similar in their strategy of using a two-phase multimethod design to confirm their theoretical framework. Both studies had what could be characterized as a qualitative phase, where participants were asked to describe a situation where they had done something embarrassing. Coding of this type of response in the 1996 study confirmed that embarrassment was often caused by the perception of the violation of a social norm for propriety, such as farting loudly in the middle of a solemn social ceremony like a wedding or funeral. The second phase of the 2012 study added to the evidence by demonstrating that the more embarrassed participants were judged to be by trained observers, the more generous they were in sharing resources in economic games.

The use of multiple methods for confirmatory purposes was deeply and explicitly embedded in the way Keltner and his colleagues designed each of these and related studies. The purpose is a classic reason for using mixed methods and one of the principal arguments put forward to justify its use: to triangulate or confirm results. Over the course of Keltner's career, he not only triangulated results by using multiple methods and observers within a single study but also constructed a substantial body of evidence by triangulating across a long line of studies with slightly different designs.

Keltner's experiments have practical applications that are relevant today. They can be used, for example, to explain why airport screening devices widely implemented after the terrorist bombings in New York City and Washington, DC on September, 11, 2001 have not proven particularly effective in detecting terrorists. The theory can be used to explain what methodologists call the negative case. *In the early studies, researchers concluded that while observers could consistently detect embarrassment and shame, guilt was far more challenging to identify. This is because some individuals, namely sociopaths, are indifferent to social mores. These individuals do not recognize their criminal acts as a violation of a social order. Others may have an ideological agenda to destroy a social order and, thus, would also be immune to feelings of guilt or shame. Pursuit of unexpected results is a tremendous advantage of multistage mixed methods research.*

© iStock/lillisphotography

In the first chapter, I introduced the architectural arch, evident since pre-Roman times, as a metaphor for the integration of qualitative and quantitative strands in a mixed methods study. The embarrassment example derived from Keltner's work and described with multiple engaging examples in his book, *Born to Be Good: The Science of a Meaningful Life* (2009), expands the metaphor by illustrating how an individual can contribute to a body of scientific knowledge through a series of related studies that confirm and build on each other. A long line of research that grows to become someone's life work often starts small with a hunch or intuitive insight about something unexpected. One study leads to the next and the one after that; the conceptual framework is often built by trying new methods for data collection or analysis or by testing its application to a new population or unstudied setting.

Through its multilayered architecture, the picture of the Roman aqueduct (Figure 2.1) illustrates how the kind of research agenda Keltner built is constructed one study or arch at a time. For the purpose of this discussion, each arch represents a single research study and the bridge represents a series of interconnected studies linked by the same purpose. The single study is the unit of analysis we will be working with as we consider the classic reasons for using a mixed methods approach.

PURPOSE, GOALS, AND CONTRIBUTION OF THE CHAPTER

In this chapter, I explore a range of different reasons for using mixed methods and offer an expanded version of a typology of purposes first put forward in 1989 by Greene, Caracelli, and Graham. For some, the discussion will serve to legitimize a study that has already been completed by providing a label and a body of literature in which to nest it. For others, the review of the different reasons mixed methods has been used will serve as a source of inspiration by which to model a study.

The goals of the chapter are to

1. expand the discussion of the concept of triangulation as a fundamental reason for using a mixed methods approach,
2. consider the advantages of organizing types of mixed methods studies by their purpose rather than by the features of their design,
3. review a typology of purposes or reasons for electing to use a mixed methods approach,
4. identify key features that distinguish six design types based on rationale or purpose (triangulation, enhancement/complementary, development, initiation, multilevel/expansion, evaluation/intervention, or process oriented),
5. weigh evidence about which of the rationales for using mixed methods is most prevalent in the literature,
6. illustrate the typology of purposes with examples from exemplary publications used in this book,
7. acknowledge complications associated with applying the typology of purposes to real-life examples from the literature,
8. explore situations where a mixed methods approach is unlikely to be the best choice, and
9. provide recommendations for crafting an effective mixed methods purpose statement.

ARGUMENTS FOR THE PREEMINENCE OF PURPOSE IN DISTINGUISHING MIXED METHODS STUDIES

Greene (2007) is one of the early adaptors of mixed methods who argues for the preeminence in using purposes and rationale to distinguish different types of mixed methods studies. She has been persuasive in her argument that it is purpose, not method or design, that is the first consideration in the appropriateness of using mixed methods. Making this point, she stated, "[Social] inquiry begins with a substantive intention or purpose and a substantive set of questions. Methodology is ever the servant of purpose, never the master" (2007, p. 91). Greene argued that all conversations about a research project, including between a student proposing a topic for a doctoral dissertation and his or her advisor, should begin with the purpose or rationale of the study. In Greene's view, any discussion of what methods are appropriate for the study should occur after the purpose of the study has been articulated clearly. I find Greene's arguments persuasive enough that I have deviated from other mixed methods textbooks by selecting articles to feature as exemplary by purpose or rationale rather than other features of the design.

All thinking about a classification system for the reasons for using mixed methods begins with a triangulation design that is undertaken with the goal of verifying or confirming results with multiple sources of data. This is the single most widely accepted reason for using multiple methods and/or multiple types of data. In the next sections, I will expand on the discussion about triangulation introduced in the first chapter and explain how academics interested in methodology have begun to see wider purposes for it. These wider purposes acknowledge that while confirmation of a theoretical perspective may be the principal goal of a study, as it was in the research about embarrassment, unexpected findings inevitably contribute to its further refinement.

AN OVERRIDING PURPOSE OF MIXING COMPATIBLE METHODS: TRIANGULATION

Mixed methods began to emerge as a distinct methodological movement in the late 1980s. One leading figure in mixed methods pinpoints its emergence immediately following the dampening down of the rhetoric that pitted qualitative and quantitative research in what came to be known as the *paradigm wars*. This researcher, Jennifer C. Greene, claimed in her 2007 book that growing consensus about the value-added of mixed methods emerged as a form of "rapprochement" between the warring sides. Greene argued that the pivotal shift in thinking occurred when qualitative and quantitative researchers found that they shared some common ground. That common ground was the centrality of validity to the quality of any kind of research. Validity is a measure of quality that transcends method (Onwuegbuzie & Johnson, 2006). In a general sense, **validity** *is a term used in both qualitative and quantitative research to refer to strategies that are used during data collection and analysis that confirm the credibility, confirmability, and justifiability of the findings and inferences drawn at the conclusion of a study.*

More specifically, according to Greene (2007), the rapprochement that lead to the growing acceptance of mixed methods as a distinct methodology involved not just validity in general but one particular type of validity that involves between- or across-method comparisons (Denzin, 1978). Common ground was found in a conviction shared by researchers from diverse methodological traditions that the triangulation of findings on a single construct from multiple sources enhances validity, particularly **convergent validity,** by providing evidence that the results are not biased or simply a by-product of the method used. In the case of mixed methods, this means *that the confidence or credibility of results is enhanced when two or more methods produce congruent or comparable data* (Jick, 1979). The emphasis on triangulation as a rationale for using multiple methods in order to advance both internal validity and external reliability is certainly evident in the research conducted by Keltner and his colleagues (introduced as a real-world example in the beginning of this chapter). Authors point to triangulation as a justification for using multiple methods even when, like Keltner, they do not situate their research as mixed methods.

This type of triangulation is different from what is called within method comparisons (Denzin, 1978) that is characteristic of some multimethod studies. The latter is a characteristic of multimethod studies and occurs when corroboration is sought from the results of one or more method from the same methodological tradition. Collecting data through both qualitative interviews and observations in the same study is an example of this. The limitation of this approach is that no steps have been taken to offset the bias embedded in any tradition. Denzin, generally credited with distinguishing different types of triangulation, observed somewhat caustically, "Observers delude themselves into believing that five different variations of the same method generate five distinct varieties of triangulated data. But the flaws that arise using one method remain" (1978, pp. 301–302). The use of multiple strategies from the same tradition (e.g., two qualitative methods or two quantitative methods) may magnify bias (Mathison, 1988) and is a limitation of a multimethod approach. The inability to serve the purpose of enhancing validity by offsetting biases inherent in any method is one reason that it is necessary to clearly distinguish multimethod and mixed methods research.

Mathison (1988) expanded the conversation about triangulation as a major rationale for using multiple methods and unwittingly picked up on an additional purpose of mixed methods research proposed by Rossman and Wilson (1985) in a publication that appeared at about the same time. Both of these authors put forward the argument that triangulation can serve more purposes than simply corroboration or congruent validity. Mathison proposed an alternative conceptualization of triangulation that embraces divergence by observing that results of analysis of different data sources or methods often produce inconsistent or contradictory findings. She observed,

> Practicing researchers and evaluators know that the image of data converging on a single proposition about a social phenomenon is a phantom image. More realistically, we end up with data that occasionally converge, but frequently are inconsistent and even contradictory. (1985, p. 17)

Mathison observed that inconsistent or contradictory evidence may not be solely attributable to biases in the methods but, instead, that different methods tap into different ways of knowing or different domains of knowledge. The challenge for any researcher is not to dismiss what appears to be inconsistent or contradictory results as simply an artifact of the method but to pursue them for what new insight that might be revealed about the phenomenon.

TYPOLOGIES FOR CATEGORIZING RESEARCH ARTICLES BY PURPOSE

In the mid- to late 1980s and through the 1990s, as mixed methods gradually transformed into a tradition with considerable credibility, a number of authors contributed to its legitimation by proposing typologies to categorize studies by the reason or rationale for using mixed methods (e.g., Bryman, 2006, 2007; Greene et al., 1989; Rossman & Wilson, 1985). Some of these presented purely conceptual models derived from the methodological literature, while others combined familiarity with that literature with what is actually recognizable in practice. In general, there is overlap among the categories of purposes because they were not derived empirically through a statistical procedure. As we have encountered before and will encounter again, what proponents of a methodology advocate and what actually occurs with any frequency in practice are not always one and the same thing.

Several cautionary notes are appropriate as we launch into a consideration of several typologies of purposes that have surfaced again and again in the methodological literature. The first is that the application of the typology requires interpretation and judgment. The second is that when applied to the literature, as compared to serving as a source of inspiration, the typologies are most useful when the detective work is to ferret out the purpose of a single study. Results from large studies where analysis spans many years are generally released in small increments and in the form of articles that cross-reference each other. This is certainly the case of the embarrassment example I referenced at the beginning of this chapter. It is nearly impossible to try to pinpoint a single purpose for such mammoth endeavors.

EVOLUTION OF TYPOLOGIES

Rossman and Wilson (1985) are credited with being the authors of one of the first typologies of purposes of mixed methods research. They identified three "analytic functions" or purposes for combining qualitative and quantitative research between method designs. These are corroboration, elaboration, and initiation. Corroboration, also known as triangulation, sets out to find agreement or convergence between results from different sources of data. Between-methods studies designed with the purpose of elaboration offer the possibility of expanding what is known about the same phenomenon through richness and detail. Most typically, these are studies where qualitative data are used to illustrate results from quantitative procedures. Studies falling under the label of **initiation** have the most complex design. *These set out to uncover paradox and contradiction and deliberately seek further exploration of areas where results do not converge.* As Rossman and Wilson state, "It can therefore initiate interpretations and conclusion, suggest areas for further analysis, or recast the entire research questions" (1985, p. 633). These studies are often intentionally designed to be provocative.

Greene et al. (1989) proposed an expanded typology of purposes or potential uses for mixed methods by directly building on Rossman and Wilson's work (1985). Greene (2007) maintained that this project was her first engagement with mixed methods. Greene et al. (1989) produced their framework by consulting the methodological literature and then applying their typology to identify the primary and secondary rationale of 56 mixed methods evaluation studies. When describing the typology, Greene (2007) used the expressions "purposes of mixed methods" and "purposes for mixing" interchangeably. Some of the categories in the Greene et al. framework also have some specific design features, but none represent a single type of design.

Greene et al.'s (1989) framework has been very widely used. It adds two additional categories of purposes to those identified by Rossman and Wilson (1985) and called the second category not *elaboration* but *complementarity*. The two additional categories are development design and extension. In studies with a **development design**, *the results of one method are used to inform the content or design of the other method. This label applies to two-phase instrument design studies, as well as to studies that combine both exploratory and confirmatory phases of analysis.* Both phases are studying the same set of constructs or phenomenon or a subset of them. Most evaluation studies fit the category of purposes Greene et al. called **expansion design**. These studies *are generally multistage, and the different stages address different research questions.*

Bryman (2006, 2007) advanced the conversation about categories of purposes or rationales for using mixed methods through a cross-disciplinary content analysis of 232 social science articles from five disciplines: sociology, psychology, management, geography, and media and cultural studies. His approach differed from that of Greene et al. (1989) in that the typology was derived empirically through an inductive approach to the analysis. In that sense, it could be said to more accurately capture the breadth of what was actually being used in practice than the typology generated by Greene and her colleagues. Bryman also explored the differences between stated reasons and actual execution by comparing the stated reasons for using mixed methods with the actual way that mixed methods were used or integrated. The fact that his database of articles was so large and that it spanned so many disciplines probably explains why Bryman's analysis generated a far more comprehensive list of (17) rationales, as compared to five generated by Greene and her colleagues. Authors of about one fourth of the articles failed to provide an explicit rationale for using mixed methods but did in fact report on ways the qualitative and quantitative strands were integrated in later sections of the articles.

Some of the differences between the five categories of purposes in Greene et al.'s (1989) typology and the more comprehensive list codes that emerged from Bryman's analysis (2006) reflect the diverse ways that mixed methods have been used in practice. Bryman's typology may be easier to apply in a content analysis because it is so comprehensive and because the language is both intuitive and concrete. This requires less interpretation on the part of the reader. Complementarity (undertaken for purposes of building a more comprehensive picture) and initiation (undertaken to pursue contradiction and paradox) are labels subject to considerably more interpretation than development (to develop an instrument or select a sample). On the other hand, the large number of categories offered by Bryman means it would require a much larger sample of articles to conduct a content analysis with credible results.

Bryman (2006) developed his typology through an inductive analytical process but did not follow through to collapse codes into categories in a way that is typical for a qualitative approach. Seven of the codes can readily be classified under the more comprehensive categories identified by Greene and her colleagues. For example, completeness and different research questions fall under the complementary category identified by Greene and her colleagues; diversity of views and unexpected results fit the intent of the initiation design; and explanation, instrument development, and sampling all fall under the development category.

Better characterized as representing models as compared to actual practice, Greene et al.'s (1989) categories do not prioritize any one type of purpose as being more credible than another. In capturing actual practice, Bryman's (2006) typology of purposes includes at least one type of study that is rarely considered a legitimate appropriation of the mixed methods label. He used the term *illustration* to describe the not-uncommon situation where studies with a strong quantitative bent use quotes from interviews to illustrate key points. This occurs when qualitative data, such as quotes from an interview, are used to illustrate a quantitative result without contributing the analytical framework. While widely used, the characterization of this as an appropriate use of the mixed methods label is subject to challenge.

There are inevitable differences between a typology generated to capture patterns of how mixed methods are actually being used in practice and a typology generated to provide a menu of models that might be effective in guiding or shaping practice. I have leaned toward the later in the typology I present in the next section.

AN EXPANDED TYPOLOGY OF PURPOSES

Table 2.1 elaborates on the typology offered by Greene et al. (1989) to categorize the different purposes for using mixed methods or for mixing. The table provides a list of some of the key terms that signal each purpose and lists typical examples. The signal words are helpful to keep in mind as you craft a purpose statement. All of the categories have design features associated with them, but it is the purpose or reason for using a mixed methods approach that is the principal way the categories are distinguished, not the design features. One reason for inclusion in the typology is that each type of study could feasibly be designed with either a qualitative or quantitative priority.

My typology or classification system is derived from the one developed by Greene and her colleagues. The differences involve three of the categories: development, initiation, and a new category I have called **evaluation/intervention design**, which *involves collecting qualitative and quantitative data to evaluate the effectiveness of an intervention, program, activity, class, or workshop*. In the typology presented in Table 2.1, the development design is expanded to explicitly include both instrument development and sample selection. The most important addition to the classification system of purposes is the addition of a separate category for process-oriented research called *evaluation/intervention*. There are several reasons for the decision to add evaluation/intervention as a separate category in the typology of mixed methods purposes when others have classified it as a subset of the **multilevel or expansion design**, which *describes studies where data are collected in more than two phases and from respondents at multiple levels of an organization or school (e.g., students, teachers, administrators)*. I opted to place these two types of studies together as a separate category in the classification system because this kind of mixed methods study is quite common in the health and education fields, and they share both a purpose and a number of design characteristics. This type of design has rarely been covered in detail in mixed methods textbooks (Song, Sandelowski, & Happ, 2010). There is

TABLE 2.1 ■ A Classification System of the Major Purposes for Conducting Mixed Methods Research Modified From Greene, Caracelli, and Graham (1989)				
Category Name and Range of Constructs Addressed		**Principal Purposes**	**Typical Examples**	**Signal Words**
Triangulation/Confirmatory (a single construct or phenomenon)		Enhance validity by using different kinds of data to measure the same phenomenon	Questionnaire with closed- and open-ended questions	Confirm, corroborate
Enhancement/Complementarity (different facets of the same complex phenomenon)		For wider and deeper understanding; to answer *what*, *how*, and/or *why* research questions; to generate and test a theory	Consolidation or merging of qualitative and quantitative data in one data set	Elaborate, illustrate, enhance, clarify, expand, deepen understanding
Development (same phenomenon or a subset of the same phenomenon)	Instrument development Sample selection	Develop an instrument; enhance participant selection; get information to customize an intervention to a setting	Qualitative focus group followed by development and pilot testing of an instrument	One phase informs or is directly linked to the other
Initiation (different facets of the same phenomenon)		Examine extreme or negative cases; test competing hypotheses or explore unexpected or contradictory findings	Test competing hypotheses	Discover, explain, paradox, or contradiction
Multilevel/Expansion (different but related constructs or phenomenon)		Study multilevel systems such as a school or medical system; nested designs	Develop case studies for cross-case comparison	Multilevel
Evaluation/Intervention/Process-Oriented* (different but related constructs)		Examine the effectiveness of an intervention; provide contextual understanding	Collect data from participants in order to design an intervention that suits the context	Improve recruitment; enhance effectiveness of an intervention

*This category was not identified in the Greene et al. (1989) typology.

a long history of the use of mixed methods in both the health and evaluation fields. Researchers weighing the benefits of using mixed methods may well have this kind of study in mind.

The underlying purpose for both evaluation and intervention studies is to determine whether a treatment, activity, or program influences an outcome. Creswell (2008) defined an *intervention research* as an experimental study designed to determine whether a treatment influences an outcome. Intervention studies and evaluation research are both process oriented and often involve collecting data to answer not only *what* questions about outcomes but also *how* and *why* questions about a medical or educational intervention that did or did not prove effective in the ways expected. Evaluation studies are highly context specific and unlikely to have a control group, while intervention studies often employ an experimental or quasi-experimental design.

One final feature of the classification system I have presented merits additional discussion. That is the decision to retain a separate category for what Rossman and Wilson (1985) were first to label as the **initiation design** which *involves exploring extreme or negative cases to test competing hypotheses or to explore unexpected or contradictory findings from earlier studies*. It is a design that has been underutilized but has tremendous potential. The rationale for this type of design aligns nicely with the overall Gestalt of mixed methods, which I described in Chapter 1, which is to use multiple methods or types of data to engage different points of view and types of knowledge. I have kept the category but defined it more broadly than others have by the explicit inclusion of studies that turn to mixed methods, not at the preliminary design phase, but at a phase after some data collection. This broadens the scope of the classification system and legitimizes studies that become mixed methods not out of design but out of necessity.

DESIGN FEATURES OF THE MAJOR CATEGORIES OF PURPOSE TYPES

Classification systems for categorizing different types of mixed methods studies have both a heuristic, instructional purpose and a research purpose. The instructional purpose is to serve as a model for designing a mixed methods research project or to confirm the appropriateness of a mixed methods label for a study that has been conceived already. The research purpose applies to crafting an effective purpose statement. It also relates to its usefulness for distinguishing the purpose of studies that already have been published.

Without losing sight of the purpose, some features of the design of a study, such as when the data were collected or if the same or different sample of respondents was employed, can ease the job of interpreting which purpose category can most aptly be applied to describe a study. The issue of the feasibility of the different designs in dissertation research is discussed more thoroughly in Chapter 9.

The following list provides some tips about distinguishing features of each of the purpose categories.

1. *Triangulation/Confirmatory.* Data are collected about the same construct in both the qualitative and quantitative strands, often at the same time and with the same sample. This design has often been used, as by Keltner, for hypothesis or theory testing. The classic example of this design is the single administration of a questionnaire with quantitative, forced-choice questions and open-ended questions that are analyzed qualitatively.

2. *Enhancement/Complementarity.* Data are collected about multiple constructs and are often sequential. It does not necessarily require the same sample in both the qualitative and quantitative phases. This design can be used, such as in grounded theory, when the purpose is to develop theory through an exploratory and confirmatory phase.

3. *Development.* Data collection and analysis occur sequentially. Data analysis from the first phase is linked to the second phase but is generally not revisited after this point of connection. The use of this design has been narrowly but explicitly construed for use in instrument development and to identify a sample for data collection in the second phase of a sequential or multiphase study.

4. *Initiation.* No specific design features are associated with studies with this purpose. Studies designed with this purpose in mind could be set up to test competing hypothesis or theoretical interpretations. Multiple constructs are likely to be involved, but nothing would prohibit both the qualitative and quantitative data from being collected at the same time.

5. *Multilevel/Expansion.* A signature of the design of this type of study is that data are often collected in more than two phases and from multiple constituent groups. This type of study often involves multiple constructs and research questions that range from *what* to *how* and *why*. This type of research often produces extended in-depth narratives or case studies, such as might be produced to describe an effective organization or leader.

6. *Evaluation/Intervention.* This type of study is directed to the goal of evaluating the effectiveness and outcomes of a medical or educational program, activity, or intervention. Evaluation studies often have a qualitative priority because of interest in participants' perceptions and to answer both outcome (e.g., what was learned) and process questions (e.g., what lead to improved outcomes).

Linking a description of a study to one of the purpose types in the classification system provides authors with a shorthand that readily communicates with other methodologists using mixed methods. The choice of the most appropriate label or of a primary and secondary label requires interpretation and is a matter of pinpointing the label that best matches the overriding purpose of the study. Some of the purpose categories, such as the development design, is narrowly defined and easy to identify because of the explicitness of its purpose. Others, most notably the enhancement/ **complementarity design** (which *seeks to gain a more holistic picture by exploring different aspects of the same phenomenon*), is so broadly defined as to seem an appropriate label for any study that generates and tests a theory or hypothesis.

PREVALENCE OF THE USE OF DIFFERENT TYPES OF PURPOSES

Quite a few authors have picked up on the Greene et al. (1989) typology and used it to try to discern trends in the use of mixed methods in applied fields and disciplines. Because of differences in how mixed methods are typically used in different disciplines, it is difficult to determine what category of purposes has been utilized most frequently. A few examples of how authors have employed the Green et al. (1989) typology are reviewed in this section.

To develop and test their typology of purposes, Greene et al. (1989) limited their review of mixed methods articles to the field of evaluation, where the use of a combination of qualitative and quantitative methods has a long tradition. Not surprisingly, given that data collected during evaluations often come from constituents at multiple levels of an organization, they found the multilevel/expansion design to be most prevalent, followed by the triangulation/confirmatory design. The initiation design, which invites diverse viewpoints or weighs competing explanations, was used by only 3% of the authors.

Bryman's (2006) conclusions about the patterns of usage of the categories of purposes may be more generalizable to a variety of settings because his analysis involved such a wide range of disciplines in the social sciences. Like Small (2011), who was reflecting on patterns in sociology, Bryman concluded that the enhancement/complementarity design was used most frequently across disciplines. Bryman identified five times more articles with purposes that coincided with the initiation design than did Greene and her colleagues.

Molina-Azorin's (2011) content analysis of articles appearing in five journals in business management presents yet another point of view on what types of rationales or reasons are provided for using mixed methods. In these fields, instrument development was the principal reason for using mixed methods in business management. While Greene and her colleagues categorized about 9% of the articles in evaluation under the development design and Bryman about 15%, Molina-Azorin pegged the majority of articles (67.7%) to this category. The enhancement/complementarity design was the second most frequent. No articles met the definition of the initiation category.

This brief review of just a few examples that illustrate how the Greene et al. (1989) typology has been used to confirm that many have found it useful while at the same time demonstrating that underlying disciplinary differences in the type of research that is typically conducted make it difficult to predict which type of rationale is used most frequently. Comparisons across studies are probably most readily made with categories (such as development) that are most concrete and specific. It is more difficult to synthesize results about categories that are far more broadly designed and subject to interpretation (most specifically, the complementarity design).

DESIGN FEATURES OF THE EXEMPLARY PUBLICATION (DURKSEN & KLASSEN, 2012)

The Durksen and Klassen (2012) article I am highlighting as exemplary in this chapter is an example of a fully integrated mixed methods study framed by an initiation design. This is the design that is often employed as further research is undertaken to understand unexpected or contradictory findings. Durksen and Klassen (2012) reported on a mixed methods study about how the motivation and engagement of preservice teachers developed over the course of nine weeks while they were completing what the authors characterized as a "high stakes final teaching practicum" (i.e., student teaching). The quantitative data revealed that over the time period studied, motivation and engagement followed a U-shaped pattern. There was a substantial dip in both motivation and engagement at the midpoint of the term but some (not all) students recovered during the final weeks. The authors turned to the qualitative data to understand what might distinguish the two groups of students.

Figure 2.2 summarizes key design features of the chapter exemplar.

The figure highlights key features of the chapter exemplar related to the design of the research, including the rationale/purpose, priority, timing of data collection, timing of data analysis, and mixing. It also identifies outcomes of the study, including the language the authors used to identify the value-added of a mixed methods approach and the inferences produced. It departs from traditional summaries by diagramming the meta-inference produced and by separating out the timing of the data collection and the data analysis phases.

The article has many of the hallmarks of a high-quality article reporting on the results of a mixed methods study. These include (1) a research design that is feasible or realistic for a dissertation, (2) methodological transparency about the reasons or purposes for using mixed methods, (3) intentional mixing of the qualitative and quantitative in many strands of the study, and (4) explicit articulation of the value-added of mixed methods. The study was longitudinal, which on initial impression would not seem like a good option for a dissertation. The clever strategy of using an online instrument to collect a small amount of data during each of the nine weeks makes the longitudinal time frame doable, even for a novice researcher undertaking a mixed methods dissertation.

Methodological transparency promotes replication by providing explicit detail about the steps taken to complete data collection and data analysis, as well as in specifying which results come from the qualitative analysis, which results come from the quantitative analysis, and which derive from mixing. Another feature that distinguishes the article is that the authors are eloquent about their reasons for conducting the research and describe it in ways that fit nicely within what Greene et al. (1989) called the initiation design. Durksen and Klassen (2012) explicitly describe their purpose as being about understanding the diversity of experiences. This fits well with the overall Gestalt of mixed methods and the goal of engaging different

FIGURE 2.2 ■ Exemplary Article About Preservice Teachers: Summary of Key Features of Durksen and Klassen (2012)			
Rationale/Purpose	Initiation		
Priority	Mixed		
Timing of Data Collection	Concurrent		
Timing of Data Analysis	Concurrent		
Mixing	Fully integrated: Yes		
	Design	✖	Two quantitative and two qualitative research questions
	Data collection	✖	Linked through extreme case sampling
	Data analysis	✖	Qualitative and quantitative data integrated in two case studies
	Inferences	✖	
Meta-inference	Fluctuations in motivation are related to personal qualities and job resources		
	Qualitative conclusion		Context and personal qualities influenced commitment and engagement.
	Quantitative conclusion		The pattern of commitment and engagement followed a U-shaped pattern.
Value-added	• Pursued contradictory data • Used qualitative data to explore differences between the two groups identified through analysis of the quantitative data • Captured complexity and how experiences varied by context		

viewpoints and ways of knowing that is also consistent with a feminist approach to mixed methods (Hesse-Biber, 2010b). Tying this function to the qualitative phase of the study, the authors observe,

> Our purpose of using qualitative analysis within the mixed methods approach was not to propose generalizable categories, but rather to show the variability in experiences during a practicum and to draw out commonalities in the experiences within each case. (Durksen & Klassen, 2012, p. 44)

Some features of the way this study was executed, including the sampling procedure, also mirror the initiation purpose. The authors used a form of extreme case sampling that is well worth replicating. They identified two different clusters of participants: one group whose engagement and commitment increased over the course of nine weeks and one group whose engagement and commitment decreased over the same time frame. They used the qualitative data to explore distinctions between members of the two groups. They concluded that the difference between members of the two groups lay in how they made meaning of the workload.

Mixing in the Chapter Exemplar

In addition to methodological transparency and its framing with an initiation rationale, the article is exceptional in another way: in the intentionality about mixing at every stage of the research process that is reflected in the labeling of the priority as *mixed*. By referring to it as an embedded mixed methods design, the authors not only framed the study as inherently about the integration of the qualitative and quantitative data but also continued with the same mindset through all of the subsequent stages of that analysis.

Table 2.2 elaborates on the template by demonstrating the ways that mixing occurred at each stage of the research process in the chapter exemplar.

The way that mixing occurred parallels the design features of an initiation rationale shown in Table 2.1. The purpose of the study was mirrored in the balance between two quantitative and two qualitative research questions about different facets of the same phenomenon. The two sources of data were integrated during analysis through case studies.

Value-Added of Mixed Methods in the Chapter Exemplar

The initiation purpose carried through to the way Durksen and Klassen (2012) described the value-added or the insight gained by combining qualitative and quantitative approaches. The interest in the range of experiences evident by the authors' self-identification with the initiation design and references to an interest in "complexity," "multiplicity," and "individual differences" was also evident in their reflexivity about the value-added of mixed methods. They supplied several explicit statements of the value-added of combining qualitative and quantitative approaches.

The value-added of a mixed methods approach is often unanticipated. It is not the same thing as its purpose. The term **value-added** *is an element of methodological*

TABLE 2.2 ■ Type of Mixing by Stage in the Exemplary Publication (Durksen & Klassen, 2012)	
Stage	**Type of Mixing**
Design	Qualitative and quantitative data answer different research questions.
Data collection	Qualitative data about types of experiences and quantitative data about engagement and motivation are collected concurrently.
Sampling	Extreme case sampling.
Analysis	Qualitative and quantitative data are integrated in two case studies.
Inference	Qualitative and quantitative results are juxtaposed with the literature.

transparency where the insight, inferences, or conclusions that are produced by the use of mixed methods are explicitly identified. It is something that, when it is acknowledged, is generally addressed in the discussion or conclusion of the paper. As with other parts of the article, Durksen and Klassen (2012) extended their pattern of methodological transparency by being explicit in what was gained by combining approaches. They noted,

> By focusing on (quantitative) patterns as well as pre-service teachers' (qualitative) explanations, we have attempted to capture the complexity inherent in understanding the teaching practicum, and the ways in which multiplicity of contexts influence[s] teaching experiences. Our inclusion of integrated quantitative and qualitative methods highlight[s] how context and individual differences interact to influence perceptions of motivation and emotions for individuals who may be going through the same experience, but whose cognitive processing of the experience results in notable differences in outcomes. (Durksen & Klassen, 2012, p. 44)

The fact that the Durksen and Klassen (2012) study is overtly framed with an interest in capturing differences in the experiences of preservice teachers engaged in their final practicum experience and that this framework is evident through every stage of analysis and reporting is completely consistent with the overriding purposes and Gestalt of mixed methods research to engage diverse perspectives, which is at the heart of one of the paradigms that undergirds mixed methods called *dialectical pluralism*. Paradigmatic issues are discussed in the next chapter.

SITUATIONS WHERE A MIXED METHODS APPROACH MAY NOT BE APPROPRIATE

This chapter has focused on the array of reasons that have been given for the selection of mixed methods as an appropriate approach for research. What has been left unaddressed is situations where mixed methods might not be an appropriate choice. The concerns I hear expressed most often are those of expediency rather than the more important issues of whether there is good match with the purpose of the study or the research questions.

Situations where a mixed methods approach is not likely to be the most appropriate methodological choice fall under three categories: nature of the problem, issues of expediency, and matters of expertise. Some of the reasons are related to the nature of the problem addressed by the research, but most are more about the context for conducting research. I address a number of these situations in the next section.

1. *When the research is very narrow in focus.* This is a situation where the nature of the research problem and the research approach are linked. Much scientific research has a very narrowly focused and highly specialized purpose that is

largely confirmatory. This might the case, for example, when the purpose is to collect quantitative indicators of health characteristics to determine the impact of a health intervention on a diet regime, but there is no intent to isolate other factors that might influence the outcomes or to understand how participants experienced the intervention.

2. *When the need is for a "quick and dirty" study.* Evaluators and consultants work in a world outside of academe when deadlines are tight and turnaround short. Sometimes a client or a policy maker needs data as input to decide on the best course of action and they need it quickly. Mixed methods are not likely to be nimble enough in this kind of situation.

3. *When the audience is such that only numbers will be credible.* I am fond of saying that a very practical reason for using mixed methods is that audiences like and remember stories but believe numbers. There are some audiences or stakeholders, however, that ultimately will only find results presented as numbers credible. It is important to be aware of the inclinations of the audience for your work and to be strategic about situations where the learning curve would be too steep to make the presentation of the results of a mixed method study feasible.

4. *Lack of expertise.* Mixed methods research projects tend to be more ambitious, are more likely to be multiphase and interdisciplinary, and are more likely to involve multiple researchers (Greene, 2007). Researchers working alone or with a small team face the challenge of having sufficient expertise in both qualitative and quantitative analytical procedures.

CONCLUSIONS

Considerably more space has been devoted in the methodological literature to offering models of different types of mixed methods designs than to typologies of purposes such as what I put forward in this chapter. Typologies based on design features and those based on categorizing purposes are both intended to offer novice researchers and those new to mixed methods the opportunity to examine models that might spur an idea for a new study or help to refine the design and sophistication of a study that has already been conceptualized. Both approaches offer a strategy for those who find themselves in the unexpected position of needing to turn to mixed methods to pursue contradictory or inconsistent findings. A principal advantage of focusing on purposes is that while the research design may well evolve over the course of a complex study as findings emerge, the overriding purpose for undertaking it is likely to remain constant.

As much as there is considerable value in emphasizing the importance of giving attention at the front end of a research project to clarifying the purpose or reason for undertaking research and what questions it is intended to address, it may oversimplify things to suggest this is entirely discrete from identifying the design elements of a study. Not everyone is capable of envisioning a study strictly in terms of its purpose.

It requires very linear thinking to envision a study strictly in terms of its purpose and to divorce any thoughts about the practicality of how the data will be collected and the other elements of the design until the purpose and research questions are solidly in place. Ideal or not, many studies start with an interest and, possibly, an opportunity and intermingle with practical concerns about the procedures that will be used to collect and analyze the data.

Recommendations for Practice

For readers who are in the midst of designing a study that can benefit by a mixed methods approach, several practical suggestions emerge from this discussion of typologies of purposes about shaping a purpose statement. The example of the article describing the results of research about students participating in a teaching practicum illustrates the advantages to the reader of being explicit about the reasons mixed methods were employed. Using the signal words associated with each type of purpose provides a shorthand that readily can be understood by others engaging in this type of research. It also communicates how a particular piece of research contributes to the wider body of knowledge.

Summary of Key Points

1. It is the purpose, not the design, that drives the decision to use mixed methods.

2. A value-added of mixed methods is an invitation to explore unexpected and/or contradictory results that emerge when two types of data or two or more analytical techniques are bought together.

3. Partly because of how broadly it is conceived, the complementarity design is used most frequently.

4. Intentionally setting up a study to pursue competing hypotheses or theoretical explanations is an underdeveloped way of framing the purposes of a mixed method study.

5. The reasons for using a mixed methods approach are often not stated explicitly.

6. Differences between the stated reason for using mixed methods and the actual execution are a testament to how even the most well-designed research project evolves over time as results emerge.

7. Situations where a mixed methods approach is not likely to be the most appropriate methodological choice fall under three categories: nature of the problem, issues of expediency, and matters of expertise.

Key Terms

- Complementarity design
- Convergent validity
- Development design
- Evaluation/intervention design
- Expansion design
- Initiation

- Initiation design
- Methodological transparency
- Multilevel/expansion design
- Validity
- Value-added

Supplemental Activities

1. Identify a sample of mixed methods articles on the same topic or from the same set of disciplinary journals. Read through the abstract and introduction to each article, focusing particularly on the area of the article describing the purpose of the research, and highlight sentences where the authors provide a reason for using mixed methods. Conduct your own inductive analysis of the reasons given for using mixed methods and see how the categories you generate compare to those of Greene et al. (1989) and Bryman (2006).

2. Follow the steps listed above and try to categorize each article using the typology of purposes proposed in this chapter. How useful is the typology in classifying purposes of the articles in your sample? What are the characteristics of articles that do not seem to fit in any of the categories?

3. Examine Keltner's (1995) article for the value-added of using multiple methods. What conclusions were discovered that would not have been possible with one method alone?

Recommended Reading

Durksen, T. L., & Klassen, R. M. (2012). Pre-service teachers' weekly commitment and engagement during a final training placement: A longitudinal mixed methods study. *Educational and Child Psychology, 29*(4), 32–46.

Greene, J. C., Caracelli, V. J., & Graham, W. F. (1989). Toward a conceptual framework for mixed-method evaluation designs. *Educational Evaluation and Policy Analysis, 11*(3), 255–274.

Sapolsky, R. M. (2013, July 27). The appeal of embarrassment. *Wall Street Journal.*

RECOGNIZING PARADIGMATIC ASSUMPTIONS

PRINCIPAL PURPOSES OF THE CHAPTER

1. To define what is meant by *paradigm*
2. To identify paradigms that embrace the value of mixing data collection and analytical strategies
3. To illustrate ways that a paradigm can influence the research process

It is almost obligatory to include a chapter about paradigms in a book about mixed methods. Paradigms reflect often-implicit assumptions about the nature of knowledge and how it is constructed. The centrality of paradigms in the dialogue about mixed methods may be a remnant of the so-called paradigm wars waged in the 1980s that pitted qualitative and quantitative research as polar opposite ways of answering scientific questions about the nature of organizations and the human condition. There is no doubt that there is a group of philosophically and practically oriented scholars—often described as *purists*—that hold deeply engrained views about qualitative and quantitative research: namely that they are different and incompatible approaches. The purist position is often driven by philosophical assumptions. The conviction is prevalent enough that the expression **incompatibility thesis** (*which argues that qualitative and quantitative research are different and incompatible approaches*) is applied to acknowledge this position.

At some level, the preoccupation with the philosophical assumptions that undergird a methodology seems at times both a matter of definitional differences and an argument fronted by methodologists rather than by practitioners. In real-world practice, evaluators, professionals in assessment, policy makers, and researchers design and execute mixed methods studies with little concern for its philosophical foundations. At the same time, notable voices in the field call for methodological transparency and argue that standards produced by the leading professional association in education

(American Educational Research Association, 2006) require authors to be "transparent in terms of clarifying the logic underpinning the inquiry" (Collins, Onwuegbuzie, & Johnson, 2012, p. 850). These authors put forward philosophical transparency as an important quality criterion in a holistic framework for judging the overall merits of a mixed methods publication. **Philosophical transparency** *is present when authors or presenters explicitly articulate the philosophical foundations of their work.*

Practice and the rhetoric generated by methodologists seem nowhere else more at odds than on the topic of the importance of being reflexive about how one's paradigm influences not only the selection of a topic but also the execution of a study. This chasm is evident in an ambitious analysis undertaken by Alise and Teddlie (2010) of articles published in the most prestigious journals in pure (e.g., sociology and psychology) and applied (e.g., nursing and education) disciplines. Their results make it clear that authors of scholarly publications rarely feel compelled to divulge their philosophical orientation. Only one of 600 articles contained language that explicitly acknowledged the author's philosophical paradigm. It remains to be seen if this omission is attributable to a lack of awareness of the philosophical foundations of some methodologies, a conviction that they are irrelevant to everyday practice, or to the sheer practicality of allowable space in the typical journal article.

PURPOSE, GOALS, AND CONTRIBUTION OF THE CHAPTER

This chapter is devoted to explaining how paradigms influence, but do not dictate, choices that are made about how to design and execute a research study, to distinguishing appropriate and inappropriate uses of the term, and to identifying research paradigms that intellectually embrace the contribution to knowledge achieved through the thoughtful intermingling of different research approaches. If we return to the arch metaphor that I first introduced in Chapter 1, a number of paradigms provide a sturdy threshold or foundation on which to build a mixed methods study.

Researchers who hope to impact practice and advance knowledge must be conversant with a variety of methods and a variety of paradigms (Greene, 2007). For settings where mixed methods are new or foreign, a working knowledge about alternatives for the paradigmatic grounding of a mixed methods project can provide a persuasive argument for its legitimacy and usefulness.

Goals of the Chapter

- Define research paradigms and distinguish them from mental models.
- Distinguish ontology, epistemology, and axiology.
- Identify ways that paradigms influence the way research is designed and conducted.
- Distinguish the main assumptions of the pragmatic, realist, dialectical, and transformative–emancipatory paradigms.

- Present arguments to support and refute the incompatibility thesis.
- Identify elements of one's own philosophical position about ontology, epistemology, and axiology.

First, we turn to the task of defining what is meant by the term *paradigm* and what is and is not an appropriate use of the term. My intent in this chapter is not to repeat or to try to summarize all that has been written about paradigms. My approach is different from my methodological colleagues in that I am not going to rehash the differences between qualitative and quantitative approaches, review all the paradigms that are embraced by educational researchers, or to give undue weight to the incompatibility thesis.

My approach is primarily a pragmatic one. Throughout the chapter, I use a publication that meets my standards to qualify as exemplary to illustrate the principal point of this chapter: that multiple, overlapping paradigms support the logic of combining methods and that these influence but do not dictate the choices of methods and approaches to data collection and analysis. Continuing in the same practical vein, I press readers to consider what their own paradigmatic position might be and to find an approach that is both persuasive and succinct to articulate it.

DEFINING WHAT IS MEANT BY A PARADIGM

Paradigms are human constructions. They are different from personal worldviews and what Greene (2007) calls *mental models*. **Paradigms** *are not original idiosyncratic constructions but a set of philosophical assumptions that are inherently coherent about the nature of reality and the researcher's role in constructing it that is agreed upon by a community of scholars.*

Guba and Lincoln (1994) are the authors most credited with bringing the discussion of paradigms to the forefront of the educational community. They identified four dimensions that distinguish paradigms and narrowed them to the discussion of assumptions about knowledge. They referred to the four dimensions as **ontology** (*reflects philosophical assumptions about the nature of truth and reality and whether it is external or constructed*), **epistemology** (*reflects philosophical assumptions about the relationship between the knower and reality and the participant and what constitutes credible or warranted conclusions or inferences*), methodology, and **axiology** (*reflects philosophical assumptions about the place of values in empirical research*).

These four dimensions of views of knowledge and its construction are defined in Table 3.1.

There is probably less diversity among social and behavioral scientists on the first dimension—ontology—than on the other three dimensions that define a paradigm. It is unlikely that someone would be doing this work who did not subscribe to the realist view that there is a concrete reality that we strive to know. Differences of opinion grow wider when it comes to the other dimensions of paradigms, such as the best methods to measure different aspects of reality, including those involving

TABLE 3.1 ■ Philosophical Issues That Define Paradigms	
Paradigm Dimension	**Definition**
Ontology	Views about the nature of reality (singular or multiple, knowable or never really knowable)
Epistemology	Views about the relationship between the knower and reality and the participant, what inferences are credible or warranted
Methodology	Strategies for generating and justifying empirical knowledge
Axiology	The role of values in social inquiry

human experience. A sizable group of educational researchers, including those in the pragmatist camp, believe that a commitment to values that promote democracy and equity is inherent to educational research.

DIFFERING VIEWPOINTS ABOUT THE RELEVANCE OF PARADIGMS

There are diverse views about the influence of paradigms on research. One perspective is that philosophical grounding drives research and that even while we may have given it little thought, our thinking is saturated by our philosophical assumptions. An emphasis on philosophical clarity or reflexivity as an indicator of quality is based on the assumption "that researchers' decisions about conducting mixed research are rooted in their choices of philosophical assumptions and stances" (Collins et al., 2012, p. 856). Others have taken a similar position when they have argued that questions, methods, and inferences are "a reflection of researchers' epistemological understanding of the work even if it is not articulated or made explicit" (Feilzer, 2010).

This rationale for the preeminence of philosophical transparency is at odds with the central, more pragmatic argument put forward in Chapter 2 that the reason or purpose of a study is what drives the choice of method. In the pragmatist's view, it is the need and the audience for the research that both limit and shape methodological choices.

Greene (2007) refers to **mental models** as another feature that contributes to the topics and methods we chose to pursue in our research. As compared to paradigms, these are *personal constructions that emerge from the experiences, beliefs, and values that come to pattern our lives*. These are inescapable lenses that shape not only our interests but also how we collect and make meaning of our data. The idea of a mental model or a personal worldview is helpful in its distinction from a paradigm, which is a well-developed statement of philosophical thought adopted by a whole community and often championed by one or more prominent thinkers and thought leaders.

KEY FEATURES OF PARADIGMATIC STANCES TO RESEARCH THAT ARE COMPATIBLE WITH MIXED METHODS

While views differ about whether the purpose or philosophical grounding is the key driver in steering the direction of research, there is little disagreement that it is important to be familiar with different paradigmatic positions that support mixed methods. Greene and Hall (2010, p. 124) took this position when they wrote, "At minimum, social inquirers today need to be mindful and intentional in learning about the plurality of frameworks for research and evaluation and then justifying the choices they make in particular inquiry contexts." Knowledge about paradigms is not merely about reflexivity; it is about finding the appropriate philosophical grounding and language to support the credibility of choosing a mixed methods approach. Explicit consideration of the paradigmatic grounding of an inquiry can provide a bridge to a wider body of literature and invite a wider audience for your work.

Although the position is not without its critics, the driving argument of this chapter is that most research methods are not intrinsically linked or determined by philosophical position or assumptions (Johnson, McGowan, & Turner, 2010; Maxwell & Mittapalli, 2010; Sheehan & Johnson, 2012). Because there is considerable overlap among them, an approach can be informed by more than one paradigm (Erzberger & Kelle, 2003; Greene, 2007). You will see this illustrated later in the chapter in the discussion about the exemplary article for this chapter, which is a study about preservice teachers in their final practicum.

Pragmatism

There is little question that **pragmatism** and its variants are most commonly associated with mixed methods. This matter-of-fact perspective *acknowledges diversity and complexity and sets aside debates about philosophy in favor of what works in a particular setting or for a particular set of research questions.* It is the paradigmatic perspective that is favored by researchers in both the qualitative and quantitative camps. Pragmatism can be seen as the umbrella for the other paradigms that will be reviewed in this section, including **dialectical pluralism** (*a paradigm that reflects what some consider to be the overarching logic of mixed methods: the deliberate engagement with different points of view and ways of achieving knowledge*) and **critical realism** (*a paradigm that views entities as existing independently of being perceived but are only being partially and imperfectly perceived. All knowledge is viewed as partial, incomplete, and uncertain*), which all share a common view about reality as being complex, characterized by diversity, and existing outside of the knower but not capable of being understood with full objectivity. Multiple paradigms are compatible not only with mixed methods research but also with qualitative and quantitative approaches.

One of the ways that pragmatism is a comfortable framework for a variety of approaches to educational research is its emphasis on flexibility of choice of methods to match the purposes of the inquiry and, sometimes, to the needs of the setting where the research is conducted. The pragmatist's perspective is that these, rather than philosophical assumptions, should drive operational choices about how to design and conduct research. Strauss and Corbin (1998), leading voices from the qualitative tradition who see a purpose for mixed methods, linked the dexterity in choosing methods to creativity when they observed, "Researchers in the human and social sciences are operational pragmatists. The more flexibly scientists work or are allowed to work, the more creative their research is apt to be" (p. 30).

Johnson and Onwuegbuzie (2004) provide a helpful table characterizing the assumptions of pragmatism. Table 3.2 reflects their thinking. It summarizes the philosophical assumptions of pragmatism, using the four different dimensions of philosophical thought introduced earlier in the chapter.

Pragmatists approach research with the purpose of producing something that will be both practical and useful.

Dialectical pluralism, critical realism, and the transformative–emancipatory paradigms share many features with pragmatism. They can be distinguished by what they position as central to the inquiry and their different types of involvement with issues of diversity. Both dialectical pluralism and critical realism place diversity of experiences and interpretations at the center of the inquiry, while critical realists are likely to be particularly interested in pursuing causal mechanisms that emerge through the interaction of individuals and settings. Those that affiliate with a transformative–emancipatory paradigm put questions about power differentials, social justice, and inequality at the center of their inquiry.

Further differences between the paradigms that are most often associated with mixed methods are pursued in the next section. The discussion begins with dialectical pluralism. Realist and critical realism and the transformative–emancipatory paradigms are also discussed as paradigms that are often used to frame mixed method investigations.

TABLE 3.2 ■ Philosophical Assumptions of Pragmatism	
Paradigm Dimension	**Influence on Research Process**
Ontology	Avoid theories about the nature of truth and reality and place the emphasis on what works; truth and knowledge are always uncertain, tentative, and changeable over time; challenge many traditional dualisms (e.g., objectivity–subjectivity); knowledge is context specific; emotions and opinions are every bit as real as the physical world
Epistemology	Quality is judged by usefulness, utility, or transferability.
Methodology	Relies on abductive reasoning that moves back and forth between both deductive and inductive analytical approaches (Morgan, 2007), methods are selected by what is appropriate for the setting
Axiology	Concern for linking research to practice, action focused

TABLE 3.3 ■ Philosophical Assumptions of Dialectical Pluralism	
Paradigm Dimension	**Influence on Research Process**
Ontology	Reality is constructed and multiple. Diversity is at the heart of both human and physical reality.
Epistemology	The researcher cannot stand entirely separate and independent of the participant.
Methodology	Pursue unexpected, contradictory, or dissonant results and what is missing. Explore negative cases and extreme cases; test competing hypotheses.
Axiology	Respect diverse viewpoints and ways of knowing.

Dialectical Pluralism

Dialectical pluralism is the paradigm that best fits the overall Gestalt of mixed methods as proposed by Greene (2007) and presented in Chapter 1. This is one case where a paradigm closely aligns with one of the principal rationales given for conducting research using a mixed methods approach as identified in the taxonomy of purposes developed by Greene, Caracelli, and Graham (1989)—that is, the initiation design.

Table 3.3 summarizes the philosophical assumptions of dialectical pluralism as put forward by Greene and Hall (2010), Johnson (2012), and Onwuegbuzie and Frels (2013). Unlike those who ascribe to pragmatism, practitioners of dialectical pluralism acknowledge the important role paradigm play in the choice of methods. Their view of reality (i.e., ontology) as inherently multiple and diverse lends itself to a mixed method approach.

The most important feature of this paradigmatic position is its de-emphasis on consensus and convergence and its emphasis on the knowledge and insight that can be gained by "thinking dialectically" and engaging multiple paradigms and mental models (Greene & Hall, 2010). This can be achieved through negative and extreme case sampling or the intentional pursuit of what at first appears to be contradictory, unexpected, or inconsistent findings. Although it declares no allegiance to it, the exemplary publication chosen for this chapter nicely mirrors the philosophical underpinnings of dialectical pluralism.

Realist and Critical Realist Paradigm

The philosophical assumptions of realism and critical realism share many features with pragmatism, including in its ontological and epistemological assumptions (Maxwell & Mittapalli, 2010). This is the paradigmatic framework that often undergirds evaluation research (Maxwell & Mittapalli, 2010).

Critical realists share the ontological view that there is a world that exists independent of our observation, while acknowledging that multiple different interpretations of it are not only possible, but likely. The philosophical assumptions of critical realism are summarized in Table 3.4.

TABLE 3.4 ■ Philosophical Assumptions of Critical Realism	
Paradigm Dimension	**Influence on Research Process**
Ontology	There is a real world that exists independently of our perceptions and our theories about them but it is not objectively knowable; all knowledge is partial and context dependent; emotions, beliefs, and values are part of reality; seeks to understand social processes through underlying causal structures
Epistemology	Our perception of the real world is inevitably a construction of it that is influenced by our own viewpoints and experiences; multiple valid interpretations of the same phenomenon are possible; differences in viewpoint is fundamental rather than superficial.
Methodology	Causality is not about controlling for extraneous variables but is embedded in processes; causality is inherently bound by context and thus local.
Axiology	Link to values is not overt.

Like the other paradigmatic positions reviewed in this chapter, the philosophical assumptions of critical realism are compatible with qualitative, quantitative, and mixed methods (Maxwell & Mittapalli, 2010). It shares with dialectical pluralism the conviction that "difference is [a] fundamental rather than superficial" element of reality (Maxwell & Mittapalli, 2010, p. 153). It also shares the conviction that a weakness in both qualitative and quantitative research is the tendency to emphasize convergence in results.

According to Maxwell and Mittapalli (2010), one distinguishing feature of this paradigmatic stance is the attention it awards to a definition of causality that is more expansive than that traditionally associated with qualitative research. Rather than the quantitative assumption that causality occurs from variance and the regularity of repeated associations, critical realists see causality as embedded in a particular context and social processes. Taking a realist approach to causality in both the qualitative and quantitative strands of a mixed method grounded theory study is one way that mixing can occur across methods.

Transformative–Emancipatory Paradigm

If you are driven to change or improve practice, whether it is in the classroom or outside of the classroom (as in nonprofit organizations or health-related settings), then it is very likely that the **transformative–emancipatory paradigm** (Mertens, 2007) is the paradigm that will most resonate with you. This paradigm is *distinguished by the overtness of its axiological commitment to address issues of social justice and its commitment to nonhierarchical methods.* Critical race theory is often associated with this paradigm. While it shares many features with the realist and pragmatic paradigms in terms of ontological assumptions and with the pragmatist's interest in action over philosophizing, the transformative–emancipatory paradigm is unique in its demand for philosophical transparency and the foregrounding of the axiological or value

TABLE 3.5 ■ Philosophical Assumptions of the Transformative Paradigm and the Implications for the Design of a Study	
Paradigm Dimension	**Influence on Research Process**
Ontology	Topics involve power, privilege, and inequity.
Epistemology	An interactive, nonhierarchical link with the participants is desirable; participants will judge the usefulness of research.
Methodology	Participants should help define the problem; methods must be molded to be suitable to the context; data are collected in an interactive way.
Axiology	The goal of research is to promote human rights and social justice at both the local and global level.

dimensions of the paradigm. The transformative–emancipatory paradigm can also be distinguished by the topics chosen for research. It places issues of power, privilege, and inequity at the center of all inquiry. Unlike the other paradigms I have reviewed, the transformative–emancipatory paradigm is sometimes also presented as a design because it is often equated with a single research method or approach—participatory action or interactive interview and observational research.

Table 3.5 uses the same format as I have used for the other paradigms to summarize the key philosophical assumptions of the transformative–emancipatory paradigm.

As pragmatism is driven by the practical needs of a setting, it could be said that the transformative–emancipatory paradigm is also driven by the needs of certain settings and participant groups. For example, research involving teachers or peer educators or about how to implement an educational or health intervention is rarely effective without grounding in the needs, preferences, and interests of the constituents in a particular setting.

It may be difficult to distinguish the key philosophical assumption of the different paradigms when they are left at such a context-free, abstract level, as is presented in the summaries. In the next section, I introduce an example from the mixed methods literature in teacher education to reiterate the point that paradigms are more malleable and less discrete than we are first led to expect. Multiple paradigms can be used as a framework to understand the philosophical underpinnings of this piece of research.

GROUNDED THEORY AND MIXED METHODS—EXEMPLARY PUBLICATION (GASSON & WATERS, 2013)

While I have not reviewed constructivism as one of the paradigms that is commonly associated with mixed methods because it is so closely tied to a qualitative perspective, the authors of the article by Gasson and Waters (2013) that I have selected to

FIGURE 3.1 ■	Exemplary Article About the Online Collaborative Behaviors: Summary of Key Features of Gasson and Waters (2013)		
Rationale/Purpose	Initiation		
Priority	Qualitative		
Timing of Data Collection	Multiphase		
Timing of Data Analysis	Quantitative → Qualitative → Qualitative/Quantitative		
Mixing	Fully integrated: No		
	Design	✖	Research question is qualitative
	Data collection	✖	Linked through extreme case sampling
	Data analysis	✖	Blended
	Inferences	✖	Blended
Meta-inference	Identified both visible and invisible learning strategies		
	Qualitative conclusion		Lurkers experienced vicarious learning
	Quantitative conclusion		Identified level of involvement and opinion leaders
Value-added	• Developed an innovative substantive theory of action in online learning communities • Disconfirmed some emerging theoretical propositions • Raised new analytical questions • Revealed inconsistencies in the data		

foreground as exemplary in this chapter provide philosophical transparency by making several references to the influence of their constructivist paradigm on the process they used to develop a grounded theory.

Figure 3.1 provides a template that summarizes the key design features of the Gasson and Waters (2013) article. Information about the rationale, priority, timing of data collection and analysis, meta inferences drawn, and value-added is highlighted in the template.

Traditionally associated with the family of qualitative approaches, advocates of grounded theory have signaled their openness to combining methods and types of data. In 1998, Strauss and Corbin, authors of a textbook about grounded theory, made this point when referring to qualitative and quantitative approaches: "We do not believe in the primacy of either mode of doing research" (p. 27). A leading authority in constructivist approaches to grounded theory, Kathy Charmaz, made a similar point when she commented in her 2014 textbook, "[An] emerging grounded theory can indicate needing more than one type of data and can incorporate more than one type of analysis" (p. 323).

The Gasson and Waters (2013) article appeared in a journal about information systems and involved analysis of data about the amount, timing, and types of interactions that occur between students in online classes. Research is beginning to emerge that involves analysis of every keystroke taken by students participating in the large online classes called Massive Open Online Courses (MOOCs), which can involve several thousand registrants. While this study did not involve a MOOC, it combined a quantitative analysis of patterns of responding to questions posted in an online discussion board with a qualitative approach to identify different patterns of engagement. In this part of the research project, the authors pursued the pattern of engagement of a group of students they called "lurkers." These were students who read other's posts but responded at a much lower rate than other students enrolled in the class. The research challenged the assumption that students characterized as "lurkers" inevitably learned less than those who played a more active role in the discussion.

While many researchers who conduct mixed methods research are inclined to refer to pragmatism as their paradigmatic base, we have already discussed that dialectical pluralism is the framework that is probably the most consistent with the initiation design. This rationale is evident in the way Gasson and Waters (2013) described the purposes of their study and how they executed the iterative stages of their analysis. They identified as one of their purposes "to challenge existing orthodoxy" (p. 98). Their approach to the initiation design shows originality because they chose to pursue what was not present or what was at first invisible. They referred to this as "lacunae" or gaps in the data, which turned out to be the group of nonparticipating students they called "lurkers." The correspondence of their intent with the initiation design is most evident in this statement:

> The identification of key categories by identifying lacunae in the data—which we have termed "complementary comparison"—diverges from the traditional GTM [grounded theory methodology] strategy of exploring themes suggested by commonalities across data samples. We inferred theoretical phenomenon and processes from inconsistencies in our visible engagement data that indicated *invisible* engagement with the learning community. Following these "vapor trails" in the visible data, we searched for additional data, which confirmed, refuted, or extended these inferences. If we had taken a triangulation approach to theoretical sampling, the vicarious learning that we uncovered would have been invisible to us. (p. 116)

In what they called "complementary comparison," they accomplished what others might refer to as *extreme case sampling*. Their analysis in this part of the project concentrated on the group of students that were the outliers in that their patterns of interaction departed from the norm. These were the students who made few ongoing connections over the course of the term with other students in the discussion board.

This article is noteworthy for its philosophical transparency. This type of methodological transparency is not apparent in other exemplars referred to throughout the text. This is discussed in more detail below. It shares several qualities with other articles designated as exemplary. These are, first, methodological transparency and, second, clarity about the reasons for using mixed methods and the value added by it. A scaled-down version of the research could be realistically replicated in a dissertation.

Because it was originally conceptualized by Glaser and Strauss in the mid-1960s with a more positivist stance that assumes an external reality and immutable laws, it is not uncommon for authors of articles utilizing a grounded theory approach to be reflexive about adopting a paradigm that departs from this. Gasson and Waters do this, for example, when they indicate their commitment to the constructivist–interpretivist ontological position that "there are no objective patterns to be discovered but there are generalizably useful patterns that are of interest to researchers" (2013, p. 115). They offer transparency as the reason for being explicit about their paradigm: "Our constructivist account of how data were collected, how they were analyzed, and how the resulting theory was derived is intended to make the difficulties and decisions of GTM analysis more transparent for other researchers (p. 115)."

Another form of methodological transparency is evident in multiple places in this article. These are in numerous statements that capture the value-added of mixed methods. This is what was gained by combining qualitative and quantitative data and approaches. Some of these statements reiterate the initiation design and the strategy of deliberately seeking evidence to disconfirm their emerging theories.

> By explicitly looking for negative occurrences (absences) of relationship that previous samples had suggested, we realized the need for new sources and ways of collecting and analyzing data in order to follow the vapor trails left by student learning strategies. (Gasson & Waters, 2013, p. 116)

Continuing to emphasize an intent that is consistent with the initiation design, they picked up on the critique mounted against traditional definitions of triangulation and the tendency to emphasize corroboration and confirmation, including in theory building, when they noted,

> We found that using confirmation techniques, such as the use of quantitative data to confirm our identification of thought-leaders, not only disconfirmed some of our emerging theoretical relationships, but also raised new analytical questions that allowed us to develop the theory more coherently. (pp. 115–116)

This statement reiterates the frequent observation that the contradictions and patterns of omission that occur when comparing qualitative and quantitative data are often the source of innovative insight.

I conclude the summary of the exemplary features of the article by Gasson and Waters by noting that it is innovative in its use of an overtly mixed methods approach with grounded theory methodology. While there has been growing discussion by methodologists about the fit between mixed methods and grounded theory as an exploratory technique to develop theory (e.g., Johnson et al., 2010), only a small number of authors have produced publications that are reflexive about the use of a grounded theory method with a mixed methods approach. There is tremendous opportunity for innovation and growth in the use of mixed methods with grounded theory.

PARADIGMATIC ASSUMPTIONS THAT ARE LIKELY TO BE INCOMPATIBLE WITH MIXED METHODS

Even within the body of literature about mixed methods, there are many different ways that the term *paradigm* is used. In this literature, most discussion about paradigms and arguments about the commensurability or incommensurability of mixing methods begin with detailing the differences between qualitative and quantitative approaches. For every author that takes the position that the terms *qualitative* and *quantitative* apply to methods or approaches, there is another that takes the position that these most appropriately should be labeled as paradigms. Brannen (1992), for example, affixes the label *paradigm* to qualitative and quantitative approaches because she sees them as employing a different analytical logic (inductive versus deductive). The term *inductive* is often used to describe qualitative research and *deductive* is often applied to quantitative research to describe ways of connecting theory to data (Morgan, 2007), but neither of these analytical processes are an expression of ontological or epistemological assumptions.

To be divergent or incompatible, two paradigms would have to articulate fundamentally different and incompatible views about the nature of reality (Howe, 1988). Those who refer to qualitative and quantitative approaches as paradigms are arguing, in essence, that they represent fundamentally different philosophies about the nature of reality and knowledge and how they are constructed. Johnson and Onwuegbuzie (2004), for example, call mixed methods "the third paradigm," following the qualitative and quantitative paradigms. Members of the group with this mindset are then likely to extend this position to the argument that mixing methods is also mixing paradigms (i.e., Sale, Lohfeld, & Brazil, 2002). This is quite a different position than the one taken by advocates of any of the paradigms I have described. Some advocates of this position believe it's possible to combine paradigms (e.g., Johnson & Onwuegbuzie, 2004), while others, finding little feasibility in the idea of mixing paradigms, are likely to support the incompatibility thesis that qualitative and quantitative approaches have an inherent logic that is incompatible.

Bergman (2008, 2010) is among those taking a more mainstream view, including those like myself who fly under the banner of pragmatism. His argument is that mixing methods is not the same thing as mixing paradigms because few methods are deeply embedded in a systematic philosophical framework. Arguing against the idea that qualitative and quantitative are research paradigms, Bergman observed,

> On closer inspection, however, it is difficult to sustain these differences because qualitative and quantitative techniques do not necessitate a particular view of

the nature of reality, privilege a specific research theme and how to research it, or determine the truth-value of data or the relationship between researchers and their research subjects. (Bergman, 2010, p. 173)

This reflects the position that methods and paradigms are two different creatures entirely and that mixing methods does not necessarily entail mixing paradigms. This argument is a fundamental cornerstone of the logic of adopting a mixed methods approach when the situation calls for it.

BEING REFLEXIVE ABOUT YOUR OWN PARADIGM

Although not all situations demand it, one of the arguments of this chapter is that it is important that educational researchers be prepared to articulate a coherent paradigm from which their work emanates. Not to do so is tantamount to dualistic thinking that there is only one "right paradigm" or that all researchers operate from the same post-positivist framework. This ignores the diversity and ever-changing nature of social and behavioral research.

As we found earlier in this chapter, a paradigm is a set of philosophical statements about ontology, epistemology, methodology, and axiology that is usually articulated by a few leading spokespeople and supported by a wider community. It is not an original or idiosyncratic construction. It is likely that most of us take a philosophical position that borrows from different paradigms and is not as coherent or articulated as fully as those put forward by philosophers who spend a lot of time thinking about such things.

Except in the context of prolonged discussion about philosophy, there is rarely time or room to be expansive about one's paradigm within the context of a journal article. As principally a pragmatist who is solidly in the realist camp, I share the emphasis on complexity and the opposition to dualism that dialectical pluralists advance. A statement I might use to accomplish philosophical transparency would look like this:

> Ontologically, I am committed to the belief that there is a reality external to the knower, but it is extremely complex, multifaceted, and pluralistic and it is never possible to be entirely objective about it. Epistemologically, it is my conviction that there are research settings where a trusting relationship with a participant is essential and there are others where a relationship with a participant strongly influences that type of information they are willing to share. Methodologically, I believe that purpose and audience delimits the choice of suitable methods and that all inferences and conclusions are interpretive. These are warranted not by supremacy of a particular design (e.g., experimental or quasi-experimental) or analytical strategy but by their link to data. In axiological terms, I am committed to research that informs policy and practice.

Even though the summary of my paradigmatic stance reflects views borrowed from more than one paradigm, the assumptions are not without logical coherence. This is why it is possible, as Greene (2007) has suggested, to mix some paradigms. The pragmatic strain and its emphasis on choosing methods that suit the needs of the setting and/or audience and the motivation to pursue research that informs policy and practice permeate the statement. The conviction that there is an external concrete reality situates me in the realist camp and reduces the ease of the fit with a pure constructivist stance that all reality is constructed by the human knower.

It is very likely that you, along with the majority of practicing researchers, have given very little thought to the philosophical assumptions that guide your researcher. I have offered my own statement not because I expect you to share my views but to illustrate what such statements might look like. The model I have presented could work in a dissertation or thesis, but it is likely that it would have to be condensed even further to meet the tight confines of a journal article.

In the list of supplemental activities for this chapter, I challenge you to draft a similar statement and to share it with a colleague who can critique it for logical consistency.

CONTROVERSIES ASSOCIATED WITH PARADIGMS

There is a single controversy that looms over the issue of paradigms. This relates to the incompatibility thesis and the charge that mixing methods is philosophically impossible because it mixes paradigms. The response to this charge is that methods are strategies to systematically gather and analyze data and not paradigms. While there are a few exceptions (such as ethnography and participatory action research), methods such as case study, observation, content analysis, interview research, questionnaires, and document analysis can be accomplished from the perspective of many different paradigms.

A second controversy that overrides mixed methods but has received much less attention in the methodological literature is the question about whether a shift from a predominantly qualitative research agenda or from a primarily quantitative approach necessarily mandates a shift in paradigm. A pragmatist would say no and that all three approaches readily can be undertaken under that umbrella. The grounded theory article described in an earlier section in this chapter makes it clear that a constructivist might also have little difficulty shifting between qualitative, quantitative, and mixed methods research as long as the assumption is carried forward that reality is something constructed by the participant or respondent. An opposition to simplistic thinking that is inherent in dualistic thinking and to an appreciation for the nuances involved in engaging multiple perspectives are features of paradigms most consistent with mixed methods.

CONCLUSION

To be effective (and probably employable!) as a researcher and credible as presenter or communicator of your work, it is necessary not only to be familiar with a variety of research methods but also to be sensitive to the different paradigmatic lenses collaborators or audience members may bring to the exchange. Methodological transparency is embraced as a quality tradition across all methods because meeting the expectation of empirical research requires that research be reported in a way that allows replication and verification. On the other hand, there is considerably less agreement on the necessity of philosophical transparency.

Methodological transparency requires language that reflects reflexivity about the philosophical domains that make up a paradigm. While it is often assumed to be the task of only those who are operating outside of the mainstream in terms of their choice of paradigm, there are situations where all can benefit by inserting a sentence or two about one's philosophical position in the purpose statement or introduction to a manuscript or presentation. Such statements can link your work to a related body of work that assumes the same paradigmatic stance. It can, most importantly, help to bolster the choice of a method or the reason for pursuing a topic, particularly when the setting is one where the method has not often been the method of choice. Finally, in the case of mixed methods, philosophical transparency can widen the audience for your work beyond the confines of those who share your disciplinary or topical interests.

Summary of Key Points

1. Paradigmatic views are theories about knowledge and how it is constructed that are shared by members of a community.

2. In addition to views about the nature of reality and knowledge, mental models (Greene, 2007) include personal beliefs, predispositions, and understandings of the social world. Rather than paradigms, these are what have the strongest influence on the research topics and aims that are of greatest interest to us.

3. Identifying yourself as having a preference for qualitative or quantitative methods is not tantamount to revealing the paradigm that is most compatible with your way of thinking.

4. Paradigms are incompatible when they are based on very different views about the nature of reality.

5. Only a few methods are intrinsically linked to a single paradigm.

6. Qualitative and quantitative research can be approached from the perspective of a variety of paradigmatic positions. They are methods for collecting and analyzing data and not paradigms in and of themselves.

7. There are four major strains of paradigmatic thought that provide the architecture to support the logic of mixing methods. These are the pragmatic paradigm, dialectical pluralism, critical realism, and the transformative–emancipatory paradigm.

8. It is possible to mix some paradigms because there is so much overlap in the philosophical assumptions of the paradigms that guide behavioral and social research.

Key Terms

- Axiology
- Critical realism
- Dialectical pluralism
- Epistemology
- Incompatibility thesis
- Mental models

- Ontology
- Paradigms
- Philosophical transparency
- Pragmatism
- Transformative–emancipatory paradigm

Supplemental Activities

1. Review the tables that have been presented to delineate the major philosophical positions for each of the paradigms reviewed in this chapter. Go through and circle the statements that match your views. Then use the model presented in the text to write a paragraph that has a sentence that reflects each of the domains of philosophical thought (i.e., ontology, epistemology, methodology, axiology).

Share your statement with a colleague and ask him or her to critique it to identify statements that are inherently inconsistent.

2. Use the blank table presented in Appendix D to identify which statement in each section most represents your point of view. Acknowledge statements where your opinion is not yet fully formed. Then construct a statement following the model presented in the chapter that you could use in situations that call for philosophical transparency.

3. Assume that there are skeptics in the audience for a presentation you are making on the results of a mixed methods study who are in the camp that mixed methods might better be called "mixed up" methods because they blur the lines between qualitative and quantitative approaches. In a couple of sentences, describe the defense you might mount in terms of paradigms for combining qualitative and quantitative approaches.

Recommended Reading

Gasson, S., & Waters, J. (2013). Using a grounded theory approach to study online collaborative behaviors. *European Journal of Information Systems, 22*, 95–118.

DISTINGUISHING MIXED METHODS DESIGNS

PRINCIPAL PURPOSE OF THE CHAPTER

To provide a classification system to distinguish basic types of mixed method research studies

Different strategies to present prototypes of ways to design a mixed method study is a topic that has received considerable attention in the literature in the field. Creswell, a leading spokesperson for mixed methods, acknowledged this when he observed, "No subject has been so widely discussed in the mixed methods literature as its designs and methods" (Creswell, 2011, p. 280). Attention is so great that it has led to the charge that practitioners of mixed methods are overly concerned with mechanics at the expense of concern for the logic of the inquiry or methodology (Hesse-Biber, 2010b).

Design *refers to a thoughtfully constructed link between the purposes of a research study and the strategies used to implement it.* Continuing with the metaphor of the arch, introduced in earlier chapters, an arch has to be well designed to remain standing, withstand the pressures of wind and weather, and provide a stable basis for the structures constructed above and around it.

There are multiple reasons why consideration of different potential designs for mixed methods studies has received so much attention in the literature. In the early days of the field in the mid-1980s, attention to design was probably a way to help researchers realize that some of their work already met the definition of mixed methods. The credibility of the field and the perception that it is rigorous was enhanced by demonstrating that a set of designs was being systematically used. Other reasons for the emphasis on the features of design include both quality and credibility. A strong design does not ensure a high-quality study, but it is unlikely that a study will yield valuable insights if it has not been thoughtfully conceptualized.

Every methodology has its own specialized dictionary of terminology that facilitates rapid communication among its practitioners. Adopting standard terminology to identify the type of mixed method design used, as in the purpose statement, is an important part of methodological transparency. It is an initial way to build credibility for the study and to demonstrate that the researcher is qualified to conduct it.

PURPOSES, GOALS, AND CONTRIBUTION OF THE CHAPTER

Many figures in the mixed methods community have tackled the task of reporting on typologies or classification systems that characterize the way that mixed method empirical studies have been designed. Because my principal goal is to arm the newcomer to mixed methods with the foundational tools needed to design and execute a mixed methods study, it is not my intent in this chapter to provide a comprehensive review of what has been written about mixed methods designs and the different strategies that have been used to classify them. I advance the same goal of avoiding complicating matters by introducing language that is already commonly used by mixed method practitioners. Keeping the newcomer to mixed methods in mind, I do not undertake the task of reviewing some of the more advanced longitudinal and multiphase designs for mixed methods studies that have begun to appear in the literature (e.g., Creswell, Plano Clark, Gutmann, & Hanson, 2011; Plano Clark et al., 2014).

The contribution of the chapter is to offer a straightforward way to identify key features of mixed methods designs that places equal emphasis on timing and priority. I keep the emphasis on mixed methods and do not review conventional qualitative designs (e.g., phenomenology, ethnography, grounded theory, case study) and quantitative standards such as experimental, quasi-experimental, and correlational research designs. I continue the use of a standard template to capture key features of a mixed methods publication that awards almost equal attention to design features and to the conclusions generated. It considers both features of the execution of the method but also foregrounds mixing by identifying the contribution of the qualitative and quantitative strands to the conclusions. Mixed methods researchers are expected to incorporate explicit language in the purpose statement for a study and to use widely adopted language to distinguish the timing and priority of the qualitative and quantitative strands.

The goals of the chapter are to

1. present a classification system that distinguishes different basic types of mixed method research studies,
2. identify priority as a key feature to distinguish mixed method empirical studies,
3. review a widely used notation system to represent the timing and priority of a mixed methods study,
4. offer reasons for the prevalence of a quantitative priority in many mixed method studies,

5. describe design features of an exemplary publication, and
6. review design features of equal priority mixed methods studies.

TIMING AND PRIORITY AS KEY FEATURES THAT DISTINGUISH MIXED METHODS DESIGNS

The design of a research study refers to key elements of how the phases of the research process (from identifying the purpose to conducting the analysis and drawing conclusions) are executed, as presented in a report, proposal, or article. Even with the wide array of new terms that are constantly being introduced, three terms are generally used to distinguish and sometimes compare mixed methods studies. The three dimensions frequently used to compare mixed methods studies are priority, timing, and mixing.

- **Priority** *has conventionally been defined to distinguish three types of studies: where the qualitative strand is given priority, where the quantitative strand is given priority, and where the qualitative and quantitative strands of a study are given equal priority.* A third option, *mixed priority*, is explored in detail in Chapter 6.
- **Timing** *generally refers to the timing of the collection of the qualitative and quantitative data. Qualitative and quantitative data are collected at the same time in a concurrent design. Sequential designs are those in which one phase of data collection leads to another. Multiphase designs have more than two, often iterative, phases of data collection.*
- *Mixing* refers to how mixing occurs and at which of four phases it occurs: (a) during the definition of the purpose and research questions, (b) during data collection, (c) during data analysis, and (d) while drawing conclusions or inferences.

As several authors have thoughtfully summarized (e.g., Creswell & Plano Clark, 2011; Nastasi, Hitchcock, & Brown, 2010; Teddlie & Tashakkori, 2009), numerous classification systems have been proposed to categorize prototypical ways that mixed methods studies have been designed. These include Greene, Caracelli, and Graham's 1989 intuitively logical classification system that contains five categories of purposes or rationale given for using mixed methods as well as other systems that concentrate on how and when mixing is achieved (e.g., Leech & Onwuegbuzie, 2009; Teddlie & Tashakkori, 2009). A prototype provides a model that can be used as a starting place to consider how to most effectively execute a study once the purpose has been established. A prototype is not a recipe that must be scrupulously followed. Just like the metaphor of arches, where there is a huge variety in appearances and the presence or absence of a keystone, there is an almost endless variety of creative permutations of each design type.

Design and purpose are two different things. Design refers to the methodological steps or strategies used to execute a study. Design and purpose are strongly linked, but this approach to cataloging designs is different from Greene et al.'s (1989) typology of purposes that I discussed at length in Chapter 2. I refer to them as design types, but these reflect the purpose of a study and the rationale the authors provide for using mixed methods rather than providing a concise way to capture how the phases of a study were executed. Purpose is established at the onset of a study and may evolve over the life of a project, but perhaps to a lesser extent than other features of the design.

A Classification System for Prototypical Mixed Methods Designs

A classification system provides a starting place for the early career researcher and others new to mixed methods to weigh a variety of standard options that are available for designing a mixed method study. Table 4.1 supplies a classification system that is a preliminary way to distinguish prototypical mixed methods designs based on timing of data collection and conventional definitions of priority. It provides a straightforward, not overly complicated way to review frequently used types of mixed methods designs while incorporating language that has already been widely adopted. Rather than to communicate a limited range of choices, the listing of multiple examples is meant to demonstrate the flexibility inherent in the designs.

TABLE 4.1 ■ Categorizing Types of Mixed Methods Designs by Timing and Priority		
Timing of Data Collection	**Timing of Data Analysis**	**Priority**
Concurrent	Concurrent/sequential	Quantitative
	Concurrent/sequential	Qualitative
	Concurrent/sequential	Equal
Sequential exploratory (qualitative first)	Concurrent/sequential	Quantitative
	Concurrent/sequential	Qualitative
	Concurrent/sequential	Equal
Sequential explanatory (quantitative first)	Concurrent/sequential	Quantitative
	Concurrent/sequential	Qualitative
	Concurrent/sequential	Equal
Iterative or multiphase	Multiphase	Quantitative
	Multiphase	Qualitative
	Multiphase	Equal

The possible number of combinations of these classic design types would expand even beyond those pictured if we added consideration of a new type of priority that I introduce in Chapter 6.

Contributions of the classification system. While Table 4.1 owes much to Creswell and Plano Clark's (2011) widely adopted typology of designs, it departs from theirs in the way that priority is conceptualized. A major conceptual difference is that it does not make the assumption that the choice of timing (i.e., concurrent, sequential, or multiphase) dictates priority. The combinations listed demonstrate that explanatory studies are not restricted to a quantitative priority, nor are exploratory studies inevitably guided by a qualitative priority. Priority is not necessarily assumed to be equivalent in concurrent studies. In this way, the classification system I have proposed places greater emphasis on priority and what might be called the analytical logic of the inquiry than on timing.

The absence of mixing in identifying design types. The classification system presented in Table 4.1 does not use mixing to distinguish design types. While I see mixing as a defining feature of mixed methods research and the quality of the results that can be produced, there are several reasons why I share the view that mixing is not a design element because it is not determined or set at the onset of a project. Timing and priority do not predetermine when and how mixing might occur. It is my argument that the full potential of mixing is better classified as an analytical than a mechanical design feature. I also argue that while the intent to integrate the qualitative and quantitative strands should be present during the design phase, the full potential for mixing cannot be planned but emerges as the analysis unfolds. In the exemplar for this chapter and for the last chapter, for example, it was the discovery of a perplexing or intriguing finding that spurred the authors to add what proved to be a very substantial qualitative phase that contributed to theory construction. This is a key reason why many studies that are not initially conceived this way evolve to become mixed methods.

Summary About Design Types

The classification system I propose identifies a wide range of variations of mixed methods designs based on two of the standard ways the design of mixed methods studies have been conceptualized: timing and priority. The classification system invites innovation by suggesting that all mixed methods studies have the potential to be conceptualized with either a qualitative, quantitative, or equivalent priority. It is only a starting place. There are many variations within these designs and many creative ways to extend them.

Mixed methods studies also vary by the type of mixing they employ and at how many stages of the research process mixing is employed. Because opportunities for mixing cannot be fully anticipated at the onset of a project, pinpointing when and how it will occur during the design phase could actually inhibit creative redirections that often occur as the result of unanticipated findings.

In the typology presented in Table 4.1, priority is one of two factors considered in distinguishing the different types of mixed methods designs. Priority is one of the most debated features of mixed methods designs. This topic is pursued in greater depth in the section that follows.

PRIORITY AS A KEY FEATURE OF MIXED METHOD DESIGNS

Whether a study reported in a journal article has a quantitative, qualitative, or equal priority is one of the features that is frequently used to distinguish the overall design of a mixed methods study. Although there is no single way to distinguish it, priority reflects if the qualitative and quantitative strands of a study are given equal priority or if either the qualitative or the quantitative strands receive more emphasis. Like using a common set of labels to identify the different ways that data can be collected and analyzed in a mixed methods study, establishing priority provides a handy way to compare the use of mixed methods both within and across academic disciplines and topic areas. Somewhat surprisingly, no one has mounted the argument that one type of priority is more strongly associated than another with the overall quality of a mixed methods research report.

Several arguments can be put forward for why priority is an important element of the design of a mixed methods study. One of the principal arguments is that rather than trying to encapsulate the steps taken to execute a study, explicit references to priority provide a direct link to the philosophical assumptions of a methodology. This is sometimes referred to as the **logic of inquiry**, *the overriding methodological or philosophical emphasis.*

Priority has been considered an integral part of distinguishing the type of design, even though it is likely that priority can never by comprehensively evaluated until a study is complete. This is because the direction and execution of a research project shifts over time as unexpected challenges and obstacles reshape every study over its life course. This is the reason why Teddlie and Tashakkori (2009) exclude priority as an element of the typology of designs they utilize. I include it in the template I present in a later section of this chapter (summarizing key features of the exemplary publications) because priority, similar to other terms that refer to the design of study, is routinely part of the shorthand used by savvy researchers to communicate key features of a study and because it simplifies the task of comparing studies by providing a common unit of analysis.

A NOTATION SYSTEM THAT INCORPORATES PRIORITY AND TIMING

Priority is central to the notation system to distinguish mixed methods research design first developed by Morse (1991, 2003). In the now widely adopted notation system, capitalization of either QUAL or QUAN signals priority. Capitalization of both

TABLE 4.2 ■ The Morse (2003) Notation System		
Priority	**Implementation**	**Notation for Design**
Equivalent	Sequential	QUAL → QUANT
Equivalent	Concurrent	QUANT + QUAL
Qualitative dominant	Sequential	QUAL → quant
Quantitative dominant	Concurrent	qual + QUANT

signals equal priority. An arrow signals a sequential timing of data collection, while a plus sign is a textual device used to indicate studies where qualitative and quantitative data are collected concurrently. Table 4.2 provides some examples of what the Morse notation looks like and what it communicates.

Contemporary practice may be outstepping the notation system that was originally conceived principally in terms of two-strand mixed method designs. The growing presence of publications describing projects executed in multiple phases is probably attributable to the shift in academe to team-based research supported by external funding.

Authors of the rapidly emerging body of content analyses analyzing the use of mixed methods in a variety of academic fields almost uniformly report that a stronger emphasis has been placed on the quantitative than the qualitative strand of mixed methods study. The prevalence of the quantitative priority across studies is evident in Table 4.3. This table summarizes the results from a selection of studies that have been done in a variety of academic fields to characterize this design feature of studies using mixed methods.

Although each of the authors of the content analyses listed in Table 4.3 probably used a different strategy to determine it, each concluded that the majority of publications in the body of literature they analyzed displayed a quantitative priority. Across the eight studies, 63.8% of the articles were classified as having a quantitative priority; 14.2% a qualitative priority; and 22% an equal priority. These data reinforce the idea that a qualitative priority mixed method study is not very common.

EXPLAINING THE PREVALENCE OF A QUANTITATIVE PRIORITY

The prevalence of a quantitative priority in mixed methods studies is most pronounced in health-related fields where experimental designs and randomized clinical trials are viewed as the gold standard for research. This generally translates to a strong quantitative logic of inquiry and a decidedly secondary, and sometimes ornamental role, for qualitative research (Howe, 2004). The exemplar discussed below is a rare exception to that. Table 4.3 provides evidence that the dominance of the quantitative component

TABLE 4.3 ■ Reporting of Priority Rates across Content Analyses in Different Academic Fields					
Author, Year	**Field(s)**	**Priority**			**Number of Articles**
		Quantitative	**Qualitative**	**Equal**	
Gambrel & Butler, 2013	Marriage and family therapists	17	12	3	32
Hanson, Plano Clark, Creswell, & Creswell, 2005	Counseling psychology	11	7	4	22
López-Fernandez & Molina-Azorin, 2011	Interdisciplinary education	8	7	7	22
Molina-Azorin, 2011	Management	116	7	29	252
O'Cathain, Murphy, & Nicholl, 2007b	Health services	26	5	17	48
Palinkas, Aarons, Horwitz, Chamberlain, Hurlburt, & Landsverk, 2011	Health intervention research	19	2	1	22
Plano Clark, Huddleston-Casas, Churchill, Green, & Garrett, 2008	Family sciences	8	4	7	19
Stentz, Plano Clark, & Matkin, 2012	Leadership	7	3	5	15
TOTAL		**212**	**47**	**73**	**332**
		63.8%	**14.2%**	**22.0%**	

is less pronounced in behavioral science fields, particularly in family sciences and counseling psychology, where studies with a qualitative priority are more evident.

Evidence of the priority being awarded to the quantitative strand of mixed methods studies has led to suspicion from some leading qualitative researchers that mixed methods devalues qualitative research and is a disguise for yet another example of a quantitative or positivist mindset that marginalizes qualitative research (Giddings, 2006). This charge may be one explanation for the prevalence of the concern for the compatibility of using qualitative and quantitative approaches in the same study.

The counterpoint to this argument has been offered by a number of qualitative researchers who have demonstrated how a quantitative component can extend a study with a strong qualitative logic in meaningful ways (Hesse-Biber, 2010b; Mason, 2006). Mason (2006), for example, mounts a persuasive argument that "a qualitatively driven approach to mixing methods offers enormous potential for generating new ways of understanding the complexities and contexts of social experiences" (p. 10).

It is not difficult to generate a list of reasons why the quantitative strand of a mixed methods study has generally been given more weight than the qualitative strand. Reasons for the overemphasis on the quantitative dimension of a mixed methods study range from the practical or strategic to more methodologically grounded ones. Practical reasons for the dominance of the quantitative strand include the following:

1. Although funders, including the National Institute of Health, encourage getting the patients' perspective through qualitative data collection strategies, it is the quantitative data about outcomes that are given priority because they provide evidence about whether a treatment has been effective.
2. There are a limited number of venues available in journals for articles with a strong qualitative priority.
3. In some fields where the quantitative logic of inquiry has been dominant for a long time, such as marketing and the health sciences, mixed methods has, in more recent times, been utilized as a way to add legitimacy to qualitative research.

Methodological explanations for the dominance of the quantitative strand include the following:

1. Many of the classic reasons for using mixed methods may inadvertently prioritize quantitative procedures. This includes the development and triangulation designs. A study shaped with a development purpose is the design used almost exclusively in some disciplines, such as management, where the principal reason for using mixed methods is to collect qualitative data through interviews or focus groups in order to design a survey instrument.
2. Mixed methods studies have long been a feature of the research emerging from health science fields, such as nursing. Particularly when funded, their studies tend to use variations of an experimental design. When a qualitative component is present, it tends to play a secondary role.
3. As multiple content analyses have revealed, there are few studies that meet the purposes specified for the initiation design. This design purpose is grounded in qualitative logic that places priority on the dialectical engagement of contradiction and diverse views.
4. Mixed method studies with a transformative purpose (Mertens, 2007) are also well suited to a qualitative logic but still relatively difficult to locate in mainstream mixed methods journals.
5. It is very common to find articles where qualitative data in the form of quotes is used to accessorize conclusions that are derived from the analysis of the quantitative data or where qualitative data are immediately transformed into quantitative data for analysis. Teddlie and Tashakkori (2009) designate this a *conversion design*. In these kinds of studies, a qualitative explanatory logic is decidedly absent.

MIXED METHODS STUDIES WITH UNEQUAL PRIORITY

Placing priority at the center of how designs of mixed methods are categorized is an inclusive approach. It legitimizes studies where a second approach takes an auxiliary or backseat role. This is the case even when that role might be considered to be not only secondary but also minor in terms of its contribution to the explanatory power of the research. At the same time, identifying priority as an important element of design makes a point of distinguishing between studies where one strand is subordinate to other studies and where the qualitative and quantitative strands have equal priority. Although not a common occurrence, this is the case for the exemplars using grounded theory in both this and Chapter 10.

A very secondary role for one of the strands. The embedded design is among the six prototypes for mixed methods designs presented by Creswell and Plano Clark (2011). They apply this label to studies with an experimental design and a secondary qualitative strand. This design is distinguished as one that always has unequal priority because the role of the qualitative strand is so secondary. This is the methodology used in randomized control studies in the health fields, where patients are randomly assigned to a control or treatment group. Unlike the exemplar of a randomized control trial featured in this chapter, the role of the qualitative is often a decidedly secondary role in that it serves no analytical purpose and is not used to answer any research questions. This is the case, for example, in an evaluation or intervention study where the qualitative phase is used to collect information from participants in order to determine how to best tailor an intervention to fit their interests and needs. Although this phase is likely to contribute to the effectiveness of the design and, potentially, to the evidence accumulated of positive outcomes, it generally does not contribute to the inferences or conclusions drawn from the analysis.

In the classification system of prototypical designs that are present in this chapter, a mixed methods study with embedded design is most likely to fit the multiphase design and may have any of three priorities.

MIXED METHODS STUDIES WITH A QUALITATIVE PRIORITY

Other leading voices about methodological topics, particularly those with a penchant for considering the philosophical issues, take exception to labeling studies with an experimental design and small qualitative strand as mixed methods. Giddings (2006), for example, pithily castigated such studies as "positivism in drag." Howe (2004), ever the writer of eloquent and thoughtful pieces about methodology, took a similarly critical view of applying the label of mixed methods to studies with an experimental design. He argued, "Mixed-method experimentalism, although incorporating an auxiliary role for qualitative methods, fails to understand the deeper epistemological roots of qualitative methods" (p. 42).

Howe (2004) considers it inappropriate to label any experimental study as mixed methods because they are thoroughly saturated with a methodological mindset that is quantitative. His principal argument is that elevation of experimental design as the gold standard at the top of the hierarchy of research methods necessarily delegates qualitative methods to a secondary superfluous status. He maintains that studies of this type have an explanatory logic that is necessarily overshadowed by the quantitative bias embedded in the methodology.

Rather than objecting to mixed methods or denying the possibility that a mixed methods study could have a qualitative priority, Howe (2004) joins a group of authors that have demonstrated that mixed methods can extend the explanatory logic of interpretivist, constructivist, and transformative qualitative priority. Like Mason (2006) and Hesse-Biber (2010b), it is not his argument that it is inherently illogical to combine qualitative and quantitative methods. He argues for the possibility of what he called "mixed methods interpretivism." In Howe's interpretivist paradigm, this includes a value commitment to democracy and inclusiveness, recognizing the diversity of views of participants rather than emphasizing homogeneity, acknowledging the role of context and culture, and a view of causality that is not about prediction and control (Howe, 2004).

The inductive logic of the analytical procedures and philosophical assumptions about how the micro-, individual-level perspectives can help to explain change in wider, macro-level contexts (Mason, 2006), locate a methodology such as grounded theory so squarely in the qualitative camp that it might seem impossible to incorporate it with an approach such as random controlled trials, so roundly criticized for possessing an inescapably quantitative logic of explanation. Yet, this is exactly what the exemplary publications that used grounded theory in a mixed methods study associated with both this and Chapter 3 set out to achieve. Catallo and her colleagues (2013) sidestepped the usual subsidiary status claimed for the qualitative strand in a randomized controlled trial and declared equal priority for both strands of their study. Similar to the Gasson and Waters (2013) article reporting on research about preservice teachers, Catallo illustrates that it is possible to use analytical strategies that combine qualitative and quantitative data for purposes of developing theory. This is a more substantive role for both strands of a study than to simply use the quantitative or qualitative strand for triangulation purposes or to use the quantitative data to extend generalizability or transferability principally for sample selection.

DESIGN FEATURES OF THE EXEMPLARY PUBLICATION

The Catallo et al. (2013) article about intimate partner violence is the first example of a featured study that comes from the nursing and health field where there has been a long history of the use of mixed methods. Similar to other articles identified as exemplary, one of its principal qualities is its methodological transparency. This is because of the use of explicit and appropriate language to frame the study's purpose, rationale, reasons and strategies for accomplishing mixing, and specificity about using mixed methods.

The Catallo et al. (2013) article is also characterized by what Creswell (1998) called *rigor,* achieved through **methodological consistency** that *occurs when rigor is demonstrated by adherence to the philosophical and methodological assumptions of a method.* With its use of a randomized controlled trial, where the article differs from others selected up to this point is that the design is more ambitious than one would expect for the lifespan of the typical dissertation.

Figure 4.1 uses the standard template that was introduced in Chapter 2 to summarize key features of the research described by Catallo et al. (2013). The template used to summarize all the exemplary publications featured in this textbook affirms the valuable role figures play in providing a shorthand to summarize the key features of a mixed method study. Whenever possible, the language that appears in the template mirrors the wording used by the publication authors.

The template is distinguished from strategies used by others to visually highlight key design features in that it does not stop at the purpose statement. It awards equal attention to both design features and attributes of the conclusions. The template provides methodological transparency by (a) distinguishing the timing of the qualitative and quantitative strands in both the data collection and data analysis stages, (b) clearly delineating what type of mixing, if any, occurred at each of the stages of the research process, and (c) when a meta-inference was presented, distinguishing how results from the quantitative strand and findings from the qualitative strand contributed to it. A meta-inference links, compares, or contrasts inferences generated from the qualitative and quantitative strands.

One of the contributions of the template provided to summarize design features of exemplary mixed methods studies is that it rejects the idea that there is a narrowly prescribed set of designs that are typically used in mixed methods studies. By considering multiple elements of design and execution of a study, the template is intended to provide evidence of the diversity that exists in the ways mixed methods research has been executed in practice. The template offers a way to compare key design features of different articles, with design broadly defined to reflect not just purpose but all phases of the research process.

Describing Key Features of the Chapter Exemplar

The purpose, priority, types of mixing, and construction of a meta-inference shown in Figure 4.1 are discussed in further detail in the next few sections.

Purpose—Complementarity. Catallo et al. (2013) pointed to the inclusion of a qualitative phase in their randomized control trial as being a product of opportunity. They described their approach as pragmatic and said it motivated them to take advantage of a unique opportunity to extend their research. According to them, their pragmatic approach "enabled the identification of unique research opportunities that would otherwise have been missed" (p. 9). An equal priority is a good match with the complementarity design.

Catallo et al.'s (2013) incorporation of grounded theory in their design gave equal weight to the qualitative and quantitative analysis that involved different dimensions of the phenomenon. The authors used classic language to signal a complementarity rationale for their study. A complementarity rationale occurs when the reasons

FIGURE 4.1 ■ Exemplary Article About the Disclosure of Intimate Partner Violence: Summary of Key Features of Catallo, Jack, Ciliska, and MacMillan (2013)			
Rationale/Purpose	Complementarity		
Priority	Equal		
Timing of Data Collection	Separate and sequential		
Timing of Data Analysis	Quantitative ➔ Qualitative ➔ Qualitative/Quantitative		
Mixing	Fully integrated: Yes		
	Design	✖	Qualitative and quantitative research addressed linked but separate phenomenon
	Data collection	✖	Linked at sampling
	Data analysis	✖	Blended
	Inferences	✖	Blended
Meta-inference	Women who experienced the most violence were the least likely to disclose because of fear of judgment from health care providers.		
	Quantitative conclusion: Women who experienced the most violence were the least likely to disclose.		
	Qualitative conclusion: Reluctance to disclose was associated with fear of stigmatization.		
Value-added	• Collected data from various perspectives • Produced a more thorough understanding of a complex phenomenon • Proposed a strategy for adjusting the grounded theory sampling strategy • Offset selection bias by identifying participants for the qualitative phase from the random sample		

for using mixed methods are to accumulate a more comprehensive view of the phenomenon. Catallo et al. explained their reason for opting for a mixed methods approach using this language:

> A mixed methods study was identified as the most ideal method for this study, as it could *provide a more comprehensive analysis* of the quantitative data . . . a qualitative component could expand on these results *to better understand* abused women's decision making regarding disclosure of violence. [emphasis added] (Catallo et al., 2013, p. 3)

Priority Equal. Even in the best studies, statements that explicitly acknowledge priority are uncommon. Catallo and her colleagues once again demonstrated methodological transparency by using clear language to identify the priority of the qualitative and quantitative phase in their study. Priority was identified in a sentence that highlighted the contribution of the research to the field. In this case, nursing research used a design that gave equal weight to the qualitative and quantitative strands. The authors observed, "A unique contribution to nursing research is this study's use of grounded theory in an equally weighted approach alongside the RCT [randomized controlled trials] to improve the depth and richness of results when examining a complex intervention" (p. 4). Their claim of equal priority is supported by the fact their principal conclusion was only achieved by blending the qualitative and quantitative data into a meta-inference.

Mixing: A Fully Integrated Design. Catallo and her colleagues continued with reflexivity through the discussion and conclusion sections of their article. They eased the interpretive demands left to the reader by using clear language to dissect when and how mixing occurred. They offered textual signals by using a heading in the results section and providing several paragraphs of texts that clearly labeled how and when the qualitative and quantitative were integrated. A clearly labeled section in the discussion section of the article about where and how integration occurred and what was learned from it was an extremely helpful summarizing feature of the layout of this publication that I encourage others to adopt.

In the section of the article devoted to integration, Catallo and her colleagues described two forms of mixing, which they called *connecting* or *embedding*. **Connecting** (or **linking**) *is a type of mixing that involves the integration of the qualitative and quantitative strands at the sampling stage by using quantitative data to select participants in the qualitative phase or, more rarely, by using qualitative data to identify the sample for the quantitative phases.* In this case, quantitative data about the type and intensity of the violence experienced were the criteria used to select the sample of participants to interview.

Catallo et al. used the term **embedding** to refer to *a type of mixing that occurs during data analysis that strategically brings qualitative and quantitative data together for analysis.* In their case, it meant that they used quantitatively derived variables—type and intensity of abuse—to test emerging theories and to see if they distinguished the characteristics of women who were and were not likely to disclose intimate violence to a health care provider.

Meta-inference. A final feature of this article worthy of note is that it is the first time I have introduced an exemplary article that reflects equal priority awarded to results from the analysis of both the qualitative and quantitative data in the form of a meta-inference. I have referred to this type of inference as being similar to the keystone that, once dropped into a well-designed arch, stabilizes and balances it and makes it possible to shoulder additional weight by distributing it equally across the materials used to construct the arms or wings. In the academic world, this superstructure translates to a study with findings that are robust enough and original enough to generate a long line of new studies built from its conclusions.

After completing the grounded theory phase of her study, Catallo and her colleagues used their quantitative (survey) data to sort their interview data in terms of the amount and type of violence. As basic as this mixing strategy is at the analytical stage, sorting led to the principal but counterintuitive conclusion that women reporting the highest levels of partner violence were the least likely to feel comfortable disclosing it to a health care provider. The qualitative data helped the researchers identify that the reason for this reluctance was apprehension about being stigmatized.

The use of mixed methods to execute studies using a grounded theory is discussed in greater detail in the chapter about analysis. The grounded theory methodology offers exciting possibilities to generate, extend, or confirm existing the explanatory power of theory. The grounded theory mixed methods study featured as an exemplar in this and Chapter 3 demonstrates that it is possible to use quantitative data and analysis in ways that extend, but not necessarily compromise, the qualitative logic of analysis that is at the heart of grounded theory.

STRATEGIES TO ESTABLISH PRIORITY

Despite the widespread acceptance of priority as a way to distinguish the design of mixed methods study, there is no generally accepted way to assess it. Authors of content analyses reporting on the priority placed on the qualitative or quantitative strands of a mixed methods studies, such as those listed in Table 4.3, rarely provide an explanation of the procedures they used to establish priority.

Creswell and Plano Clark (2007) listed four very general signals of priority: (a) wording of the title or abstract, (b) the primary aim established in the purpose statement, (c) reflexivity about paradigm or guiding worldview, or (d) the amount of space devoted in the results, discussion, and conclusions section of a research article or more in-depth analysis of the qualitative themes or statistical analysis. Probably because authors are so rarely reflexive about their paradigms, little attention has been paid in the literature about the connection between priority and worldview or paradigm.

EQUAL PRIORITY MIXED METHODS STUDIES

As shown in Table 4.3, across a variety of fields, about 22% percent of empirical mixed methods articles were assessed to have equal priority. Labeling the priority of a study is more challenging when, unlike the chapter's exemplar, the authors are not forthright about declaring their conviction that they managed to maintain an equal priority in the execution of the study. Success at executing a study with equal priority could be signaled by any one of the following textual clues:

1. *Design phase.* The presence of both quantitative and qualitative (i.e., *how* and *why*) research questions.
2. *Data collection and analysis phase.* The use of a method, such as case study or observation, that is compatible with a variety of paradigmatic approaches and, consequently, compatible with both qualitative and quantitative applications.

3. *Expertise.* Evidence that the authors have both qualitative and quantitative expertise.
4. *Inference phase.* In the portion of an article labeled *discussion* and/or *conclusions*, textual strategies demonstrate the mixing of the qualitative and quantitative strands. In the exemplary publication in this chapter, for example, the authors included a section with a heading that referred to the integration of the two. Separate sections with associated headings that distinguish qualitative and quantitative results normally signal a failure to integrate and, often, the absence of a meta-inference.

In Chapter 6, we pursue the possibility of a fourth type of priority that has not yet surfaced in the literature. This is a priority that could be awarded to studies where mixing is so tightly and iteratively interwoven throughout the logic and execution of a mixed method study as to constitute its own strand.

CONCLUSIONS

Incorporating the standard names of prototypical designs in a purpose statement or title in a research article is a component of methodological transparency. It is required for submission to journals that specialize in mixed methods, such as *The Journal of Mixed Methods Research.* Labeling a study with a standard design name provides a shorthand for communicating a macro-level perspective about how a study was executed.

The typology presented in this chapter with prototypical designs differs from that proposed by Creswell and Plano Clark (2011) in that it gives as much weight to priority as timing in distinguishing ways to design a mixed methods study. There are so many possible permutations of designs, especially those that emerge from unexpected opportunities during the course of conducting a research project, that it is not realistic to imagine that any typology can capture all possible permutations of the way a mixed methods study can be designed.

There are number of other strategies that have been used to distinguish mixed methods designs. In their foundational text, Teddlie and Tashakkori (2009), for example, propose a typology of five basic designs based on when mixing occurs. This typology is reviewed in Chapter 5. Others have taken the position that designs should be distinguished by how qualitative and quantitative data are integrated during the analysis stage. This approach to classifying the design of mixed methods studies is discussed in Chapter 6.

Prototypes of designs are probably most helpful during the planning phase when a study is being conceptualized. They can spark consideration of different alternatives about how a study might be executed. Situating the design of a study within the literature is a particularly critical aspect of a research proposal, where a study is judged by its design rather than its outcomes. A certain amount of credibility is gained by demonstrating knowledge of the literature and methodological consistency.

No one has mounted the argument that modeling a study after one of the prototypes necessarily produces a high-quality research study or that one type of design is superior to the other. The link between transparency about preplanned design features and quality is probably strongest in that it provides an incentive to give thoughtful attention to the design of a study. A thoughtfully designed and executed study that produces warranted and original conclusions is the type of study that is most likely to be cited by colleagues, replicated by others, and used to build future studies.

The overall quality of a research report is judged both by its inferences and conclusions and the process used to reach them (Greene, 2007). The template I use to summarize key design features of exemplary articles is unusual in that it places as much emphasis on the conclusions and inferences of a study as to how it was executed. This is consistent with its principal use in summarizing key features of the publications that appear in peer-reviewed journals rather than in encapsulating the design of a proposal to conduct a study that has not been executed.

The template used to summarize each of the articles featured as exemplary is designed to capture the link between conclusions or inferences drawn from the qualitative and quantitative strands of a study and the meta-inferences that link them. This reflects the conviction that the principal argument for the value-added of mixed methods is not the way it is designed or the stated rationale for using mixed methods but in its potential to produce original insight through meta-inferences. The presence of a meta-inference that puts forward a causal explanation (i.e., reluctance to disclose for fear of judgment from the health care provider) that is warranted by the analysis is a key feature of the overall quality of the Catallo et al. (2013) article about intimate partner violence that I used as the exemplar in this chapter.

Summary of Key Points

1. Mixed methods designs are most frequently distinguished by timing and priority.

2. There are many possible innovative variations of the basic prototypes of mixed method designs.

3. Timing is more readily distinguished than priority, but priority is more important because it is the key to evaluating the overall logic of the inquiry.

4. The timing of data collection and analysis (i.e., concurrent, sequential, or multiphase) does not determine priority.

5. An effective way to determine priority is through a judgment about the overriding logic of inquiry.

6. One design type does not necessarily produce a higher-quality study than another.

7. There is no generally accepted way to judge priority when it is not explicitly stated in an article.

Key Terms

- Connecting or linking
- Design
- Embedding
- Logic of inquiry
- Methodological consistency
- Priority
- Timing

Supplemental Activities

1. Imagine a study comparing the types of verbal interactions a parent has with preschool children over the course of the day using electronic toys (such as a baby laptop or talking farm) and traditional storybooks, such as pursued by Sosa (2016). Propose research questions that might be suitable for a mixed methods study seeking data about the frequency and length of parent–child interactions with the toy and that considers the quality or complexity of those exchanges.

2. Take the blank template provided in Appendix D and summarize the key features of the mixed methods grounded theory study by Gasson and Waters (2013) about interaction in online classes featured as the exemplary publication in Chapter 3.

Recommended Reading

Catallo, C., Jack, S. M., Ciliska, D., & MacMillan, H. (2013). Mixing a grounded theory approach with a randomized controlled trial to intimate partner violence: What challenges arise from mixed methods research? *Nursing Research and Practice*, 1–12. DOI: 10.1155/2013/798213

EXECUTING FULLY INTEGRATED MIXED METHODS RESEARCH

PART TWO

5

STRATEGIES FOR
MIXING PRIOR TO ANALYSIS

PRINCIPAL PURPOSES OF THE CHAPTER

1. To describe and illustrate a variety of strategies for mixing during early phases of a research project, including through the wording of research questions, sampling procedures, and coding during data collection

2. To provide an exemplar that illustrates how mixing can be achieved at each stage or phase of a research project

EXAMPLE FROM THE POPULAR MEDIA: THE BLUE ZONES

There is no question of more universal fascination than the pursuit of lifestyle factors associated with a long life. This was the question an international team of demographers and gerontologists first undertook as a scholarly research project in 2004; it later blossomed into a project supported by the National Geographic Society and, in 2010, a mass market popular book by Dan Buettner that became a New York Times *best-seller,* The Blue Zones: Lessons for Living Longer from People Who've Lived the Longest. *The original interdisciplinary group of coauthors from Belgium, France, Italy, and the United States identified what they thought was a unique Blue Zone populated by centenarians on the island of Sardinia off the coast of Italy. This is an isolated geographical community where people live to the age of 100 at 10 times the average population.*

Interest in the project exploded in unexpected ways when a self-proclaimed explorer, Dan Buettner, teamed up with the National Geographic Society to further explore the idea of Blue Zones. Four additional Blue Zones were identified in Okinawa, Japan; Loma Linda, California;

Nicoya Peninsula in Costa Rica; and the island of Ikaria off of Greece. These researchers drew blue circles on a map and referred to the areas as Blue Zones.

Mixing of different kinds of data and analytical strategies occurred at multiple stages in this project. In its earliest stage, mixing was used for purposes of sampling. Quantitative indicators made it possible to identify geographical areas with a high concentration of centenarians who had reached or exceeded the age of 100. Mixing of data and methods occurred as the focus temporarily narrowed to confirm members of the sample by triangulating information through analysis of birth, baptismal, and military records and newspaper accounts. Attention returned to the community as teams of researchers in each location constructed case studies that combined observation in the field, individual interviews about lifestyle and eating habits, and the study of the naturalistic and geographic features of the location, including its vegetation.

Mixing occurred across the case studies of each community and considered the characteristics of the participants, the community, and the naturalistic features of the five locales. A form of meta-inference was constructed to explain the unusual concentration of long-living individuals in these communities. Centenarians in these isolated communities shared a number of qualities, including a plant-based diet, daily exercise, a strong relationship to a social community, moderate alcohol consumption, and a sense of purpose and meaning.

While it would be impossibly ambitious for a newcomer to social science research to imagine a project that could become a media sensation, such as the above account about research on the Blue Zones, features of the design of the project are replicable in producing case studies in educational settings. The use of a set of quantitative indicators, for example, to pick a sample of participants, communities, or organizations is a classic example of mixing at sampling that will be explored in more detail in this chapter. In an educational setting, this type of mixing could facilitate the comparison of high-performing individuals, classrooms, or schools.

There are many different ways to integrate qualitative and quantitative approaches throughout the different stages of the research process. During interviews, mixed methods experts have talked about mixing in many contexts (Johnson, Onwuegbuzie, & Turner, 2007). The definitions of mixed methods supplied by experts have made references to mixing methods, methodologies, rationales, or types of research. Mixing also can occur by integrating types of data and worldviews. Leading figures are united in the position that mixing must be an explicit and intentional feature of a single study to fit snugly under the label of mixed methods.

Mixing is the design feature that distinguishes a mixed method from a multimethod study. Multimethod studies often use multiple sources of data to answer different research questions, but the sources of data are kept quite separate. Teddlie and Tashakkori (2009) use the expression, "quasi-mixed methods" to refer to situations where two types of data are collected but they are not linked or integrated in a meaningful way. A research project supported by external funding might, for example, be conceived as mixed methods but actually be executed in a parallel way. In this context, one researcher may be responsible for the qualitative aspects of a study and a second takes the lead on the quantitative phases of the study. The two may publish in different journals and never really engage the two strands in meaningful ways. A telltale sign of this kind of parallel study is when the conclusions are described in such a way that it suggests that the principal results are derived exclusively from one strand. In this case, the second strand could be removed and the research is still viable (Bazeley & Kemp, 2012).

Mixing as the key mechanism for the value-added of mixed methods research and its potential to produce creative and coherent explanations and conclusions. This has been referred to as **significance enhancement** (Collins, Onwuegbuzie, & Sutton, 2006), which *increases the comprehensiveness, cohesiveness, robustness, and theoretical power of inferences and conclusions.* Creswell and Plano Clark (2007) summarized the value-added argument when they maintained, "The central premise [of mixed methods research] is that the use of quantitative and qualitative approaches, in combination, provides a better understanding of research problems than either approach alone" (p. 5). Maxwell and Mittapalli (2010) also linked the value-added of mixed methods research directly to increased explanatory power. They argued that the use of qualitative and quantitative approaches together makes it possible to "to draw conclusions that would not be possible with either method alone" (p. 148).

Several authors of methodological articles about mixed methods have taken the position that the more mixing that occurs, the better. "The most dynamic and innovative of the mixed methods designs are mixed across stages" (Teddlie & Tashakkori, 2009, p. 46). This is a key signature of a fully integrated mixed method design. Bazeley and Kemp (2012) agreed with the proposition that more mixing produces stronger results. They tied it directly to explanatory power when they observed, "The greater the degree of integration, the more likely it is that the combination will create an impression that is quite different from, and richer than, the separate components" (p. 59). Integration at multiple stages of the research process is the hallmark of high-quality fully integrated mixed methods studies.

Yin (2006) also promoted this argument by advancing the point of the value-added of mixing across all stages of a research study. Overlooking steps associated with presenting and writing up findings, he distinguished the following five generic stages or phases in the research process: (a) research questions, (b) unit of analysis, (c) sampling, (d) instrumentation and data collection, and (e) analytic strategies. As he put it, "The claim is that, the more that a single study integrates across these five procedures, the more that mixed methods, as opposed to multiple studies, is taking place" (p. 42). This "more is better" argument is one that I take up in the chapters that follow.

PURPOSES, GOALS, AND CONTRIBUTION OF THE CHAPTER

This chapter is structured to launch a detailed discussion of strategies for mixing that spans three chapters. It explores different strategies for mixing during the first phases of the research process prior to analysis. These include (a) how research questions can reflect the intention to mix the qualitative and quantitative strands, analytical procedures, or data; (b) mixing during sampling; and (c) mixing during the process of data collection. The most detailed attention is given to the topic of mixed method sampling because of its prominence in conclusions that can be drawn about the generalizability or transferability of the findings. The two chapters that follow this one are devoted to a discussion of innovative ways to accomplish mixing during analysis, including through data transformation (the topic of Chapter 7).

The goals for this chapter, as always, are practical in that they are oriented to help the novice researcher design and evaluate a mixed methods study. Goals for the chapter include the following:

1. to describe and illustrate a variety of strategies for mixing during early phases of a research project, including through the wording of research questions, sampling procedures, and coding during data collection, and
2. to provide an exemplar that illustrates how mixing can be achieved at each stage or phase of a research project.

There are a number of ways that the approach I take in this chapter differs from that taken by leading figures in the mixed method community. First, as surprising at it may seem, although it is not uncommon for a mixed methods textbook to devote one chapter to mixing, no one has yet to separate it out in order to provide a detailed discussion of mixing during the design phase, mixing during analysis, and mixing through data transformation. Second, I depart from a number of my colleagues who offer typologies of mixing that emphasize the link between types of mixing and design features, such as timing (e.g., Collins, Onwuegbuzie, & Jiao, 2007; Onwuegbuzie & Collins, 2007; Onwuegbuzie, Slate, Leech, & Collins, 2007; Teddlie & Yu, 2007). Instead, I join Mason (2006) to highlight explanatory power as the key quality that makes mixing so instrumental to the value-added of mixed methods. Third, I offer the idea that wording of research questions is a way to communicate the priority of mixed methods study. Fourth, I introduce the idea that meaningful mixing can occur during the process of collecting qualitative data.

Organization of the Chapter

The remainder of the chapter is organized into two major parts. In the first section, different strategies for accomplishing mixing through the construction of well-crafted research questions are identified. This is followed by a discussion of mixing during sampling and data collection.

DESIGN PHASE MIXING: MIXED METHOD PURPOSE STATEMENTS AND RESEARCH QUESTIONS

Even as the number of mixed methods research publications appearing in journals continues to grow at a pace that is nothing short of astonishing, it remains a challenge to find examples of mixed method publications with research questions that include references to how mixing will occur. My purpose in this section is to explore different strategies for writing research questions for a mixed methods study and to illustrate these with the exemplars used in this textbook. As compared to a purpose statement that specifies the overriding aim of a study and its focus, research questions are more narrowly defined and identify the way that data will be collected and analyzed for the constructs being studied. Research questions are much more likely than a purpose statement to be revised or replaced over the life of a research project.

It would be difficult to surpass the masterful job Creswell and Plano Clark (2007, 2011) have done to distinguish the characteristics of qualitative, quantitative, and mixed methods research questions. They provide useful scripts for how these might vary between exploratory, explanatory, and mixed method research designs. Others have taken a similar approach (e.g., Onwuegbuzie & Leech, 2006). My emphasis differs from these authors in that I award less attention to a prescriptive set of mixed methods designs. My emphasis is on the link between research questions and the potential for mixing the qualitative and quantitative strands of a study in ways that enhance explanatory power. The wording of research questions communicates priority and also has implications for the way the qualitative and quantitative results are organized and presented in a research publication.

A logical parallel between research questions and what is presented in the results and discussion sections of a research publication is one indicator of quality of a research publication. Consistency between research questions, the way the analysis is executed, and how it is presented in the results and discussion section of a report is a measure of validity that supports the author's credentials to accomplish the research and the credibility that accrues from the way the results are explained. Newman, Ridenour, Newman, and DeMarco (2003) underscore this point with the following observation:

> Researchers strengthen validity (e.g., legitimacy, trustworthiness, applicability) when they can show the consistency among the research purposes, the questions, and the methods they use. Strong consistency grounds the credibility of the research findings and helps to ensure that audiences have confidence in the findings and the implications of research studies. (p. 167)

As Bryman (2006) discovered in the process of completing a content analysis of mixed methods articles, a surprising number of authors of research publications fail to update an initial set of research questions to mirror what was ultimately reported.

In practice, projects take such unpredictable turns that it is not uncommon that research questions get repurposed as the shift is made to writing up findings. To underscore this point to those new to research, some authors distinguish a separate step before finalizing the analysis and drawing conclusions as one that allows the research questions to be reevaluated (i.e., Collins, Onwuegbuzie, & Sutton, 2006). Unexpected opportunities for integrating the qualitative and quantitative strands often arise as researchers fail to find support for an initial hypothesis or find that data are erratic enough to generate a wealth of alternative explanations. Authors will face questions about the credibility and quality of their results if research questions, analysis, and results do not align in a logical and coherent manner.

Wording Research Questions to Reflect Priority

There is a reason why it is not uncommon for new researchers to spend many hours writing and fine-tuning the wording of their purpose statement and research questions. Wittingly or unwittingly, the words used in a purpose statement and research question communicate compatibility with either a quantitative, qualitative, or mixed research approach. In mixed methods, this is a feature of design referred to as priority. Would-be authors who have chosen a mixed methods approach for its fit to their research interests and paradigm should strive to be intentional about using wording that mirrors that intent.

Questions phrased to test the relationships between a predefined set of variables—the effect, impact, or relationship between one variable and another—or to test for statistically significant differences communicate a quantitative mindset or priority. This type of priority seems evident in the wording of one of the two research questions posed in the exemplary article discussed in greater detail later in this chapter. Signaled by the word *influence* and the explicit linking of two constructs, one of the research questions is clearly a quantitative one: "What is the influence of HIV-related conversations and subsequent requests for HIV testing?" (Young & Jaganath, 2013, p. 162). As we will see in the next section of the chapter, this quantitatively oriented research question is balanced by a qualitatively oriented one.

Open-ended language and words such as explore or investigate and words that reflect an interest in the perceptions and experiences of participants are associated with qualitative approaches. The words why or how in a research question often signal a qualitative approach. Reviewed as an exemplar in the previous chapter, the purpose posed by Catallo, Jack, Ciliska, and MacMillan (2013) initially signals a qualitative mindset: How do women decide to disclose intimate partner violence in urban emergency department settings?

Open-ended, nondirectional language that is methodologically neutral is most compatible with communicating the logic associated with mixed methods in research questions and purpose statements (Onwuegbuzie & Leech, 2006). For example, the purpose statement from the exemplar in Chapter 2 is very consistent with the logic associated with mixed methods. The careful blending of qualitative and quantitative concerns in a single sentence clearly communicates a balance between the qualitative and quantitative approaches. Durksen and Klassen (2012) framed their purpose and research questions in ways to address both the *what* and *why* of the phenomenon that was of interest to them:

> The current study examines how pre-service teachers' commitment and engagement develop during high-stakes final teaching practicum, with attention paid to broad patterns (quantitative analysis), and the particular reasons and experiences associated with increasing and decreasing patterns (qualitative case study analysis). (p. 35)

Explicit identification of the quantitative and qualitative phases of the analysis further distinguished this purpose statement. The merger of the qualitative and quantitative elements of the study into a single sentence is one of three approaches to writing mixed methods research questions described in the next section.

Three Approaches to Writing Mixed Method Research Questions

The authors of the chapter exemplars used several different approaches to wording research questions in ways that effectively expressed the intent to integrate qualitatively and quantitatively derived data or analytical procedures. These reflect mixing at the design phase. Three approaches to wording research questions that reflect mixing include (a) a blended approach, (b) separate but linked research questions, and (c) separate mixing questions.

Table 5.1 provides examples from the chapter exemplars that illustrate three different approaches to wording research questions that reflect mixing.

I have reworded some of the questions for purposes of clarity. Sentences placed in quotes reflect wording that was used in the original source. More detail about the three approaches to writing research questions follows.

Blended into a single statement. One strategy for crafting research questions that are suitable to mixed methods is to link the qualitatively derived and quantitatively derived analysis in a single sentence (Plano Clark & Badiee, 2010). As we just saw, the exemplar from Chapter 2 by Durksen and Klassen (2012) used this strategy in their study about how preservice teachers experience their culminating field experience (see Table 5.1). With the insertion of an explicit reference to qualitative and quantitative variables, this example has the added advantage of methodological transparency. The research questions and purpose statement are merged in a way that explicitly identifies quantitatively (i.e., levels of commitment and engagement) and qualitatively derived

TABLE 5.1 ■ Three Strategies for Posing Research Questions With Examples	
Example of Strategy # 1: Blended Into a Single Sentence	
Durksen & Klassen, 2012 (Chapter 2)	"The current study examines how pre-service teachers' commitment and engagement develop during high-stakes final teaching practicum, with attention paid to broad patterns (quantitative analysis), and the particular reasons and experiences associated with increasing and decreasing patterns (qualitative case study analysis)." (p. 35)
Example of Strategy # 2: Separate But Linked Research Questions	
Elliott et al., 2014 (Chapter 6)	1. "To what extent is perceived neighborhood belonging associated with well-being in three separate cohorts of older adults?" (p. 45) 2. "How do older adults conceptualize and talk about neighborhood belonging in the context of a semi-structured, biographical interview?" (p. 45)
Example of Strategy # 3: Explicitly Labeled Mixing Question	
Creamer & Ghoston, 2012 (Chapter 6)	1. (QUAL) "What values, skills, and outcomes are identified in mission statements in colleges/schools of engineering . . .?" (p. 3) 2. (MIXED) Do the values endorsed in mission statements differ between institutions with lower- and higher-than-average enrollment of women?

constructs (i.e., resources and levels of support through interaction with peers and colleagues). The blended format has the advantage of implying that mixing will occur across the qualitatively and quantitatively derived analytical constructs.

Separate but linked research questions. A second, probably more prevalent strategy, is to pose two separate but interlinked qualitative and quantitative research questions that are not explicitly labeled as such. This is the approach taken by the authors of an exemplar that we do not encounter until the next chapter. In an article about the relationship between a sense of neighborhood belonging and mental and physical well-being, Elliott, Gale, Parsons, Kuh, and The HALCyon Study (2014) posed an initial research question that required quantitative analysis and then a second, qualitatively oriented question that addressed the *how* and *why* of the same central phenomenon. The two questions are linked because both are approaches to evaluating neighborhood belonging. Research questions that address separate, nonoverlapping constructs are much less conducive to the potential for meaningful mixing.

An explicitly labeled mixing question. A third way to craft a well-written set of research questions that effectively communicate the intent to mix the qualitative and quantitative strands is still uncommon in practice. This is when an analytical strategy for mixing is identified in a separate, explicitly labeled research question. Creamer and Ghoston (2013) used this approach in a mixed method content analysis of mission statements of colleges of engineering. Their mixing question could be worded in this manner: Are there significant differences among the (qualitatively derived) values, skills, and outcomes endorsed in the mission statements of colleges/schools of engineering by different measures of the proportional or numerical enrollment of women (quantitatively derived)?

Explicitly labeling research questions to indicate the analysis that will be qualitatively derived, quantitatively produced, and accomplished through mixing provides the kind of methodological transparency that is highly valued in frameworks to evaluate the quality of mixed methods reports and is an expectation for publication in methodologically oriented journals, such as the *Journal for Mixed Methods Research* and the *International Journal of Multiple Research Approaches.*

The nature of the sample and the unit of analysis are two aspects of a research study that are commonly identified in a purpose statement. The unit of analysis can be at the individual level (e.g., students, clients, patients, teachers), at the program or activity level, at the organizational level (e.g., schools, nonprofit or for-profit organizations), or at the community or neighborhood level. Ways that mixing can be accomplished through sampling is the topic of the next section of the chapter.

MIXING DURING SAMPLING

After the purpose statement and research questions for a study have been finalized, it is time for the researcher to turn his or her attention to considering how to maximize what can be gained from strategically executing a sampling strategy. This holds true whether the research is shaped by a qualitative, quantitative, or mixed methods logic.

There are pronounced differences between quantitative and qualitative approaches to sampling. Probability (associated with quantitative research) and purposeful sampling (associated with qualitative research) are driven by fundamentally different assumptions about sampling. Probability sampling is characterized by a large sample size. It is designed to capture breadth and prioritizes the value of a randomly selected sample (Teddlie & Yu, 2007). A sample size of at least 50 units is recommended for probability sample in order to establish representativeness (Teddlie & Tashakkori, 2009).

The sampling plan is important because it determines the types of statistical procedures, if any, that are appropriate and the generalizations or conclusions that can be drawn from a study (Collins et al., 2007). On the other hand, purposeful sampling is guided by expert judgment rather than concerns for random selection. It is designed to pursue depth and complexity (Teddlie & Yu, 2007). A purposeful sample is typically smaller than 30 cases (Teddlie & Tashakkori, 2009). A researcher risks his or her credibility by overlooking the requirement for a relatively large sample size to conduct statistical analysis, including correlational or causal comparative research (Collins et al., 2007; Onwuegbuzie & Collins, 2007).

Using more than one sampling strategy is a defining characteristic of mixed methods research (Teddlie & Yu, 2007): "The researcher's ability to creatively combine these techniques [i.e., probability and purpose] in answering a study's questions is one of the defining characteristics of [mixed methods] research" (p. 85). The expectation for multiple strategies for sampling fits the complexity of much social science research: "Many of the research topics under study in the social sciences are quite complex and require a combination of sampling techniques to adequately explore the phenomenon of interest" (Kemper, Stringfield, & Teddlie, 2003, p. 283). Others see it as instrumental to the ability to generalize conclusions to other settings and to construct warranted meta-inferences (Onwuegbuzie & Collins, 2007).

There are multiple ways to design sampling procedures to optimize the potential for meaningful mixing. Three are addressed here: (a) combining probability and purposeful sampling strategies, (b) using a concurrent or a sequential approach to identify a sample, and (c) using either a nested or identical sample of participants. All of these can distinguish mixed methods studies from those that use multiple data collection methods but in ways that are more accurately described as parallel studies.

Combining Probability and Purposeful Sampling

There are pronounced differences between qualitative and quantitative approaches to sampling. Mixed method sampling procedures are unique to mixed methods (Teddlie & Yu, 2007). **Mixed method sampling procedures** *use various approaches to combine a traditional quantitative (i.e., probability) approach to sampling with a* *qualitative (i.e., purposeful) approach.* The authors of the exemplar discussed later in this chapter used this type of mixed method sampling procedure first by identifying a purposeful sample of men with high-risk sexual behaviors and then by incorporating a quantitative, probabilistic approach by randomly assigning the participants to a control and experimental group.

The principal value-added of combining probabilistic and purposeful sampling in a mixed methods study is that it more readily supports the claim that results are generalizable to other settings and populations. This is not just something to dutifully acknowledge in a sentence in the limitations sections of a research report. As the Blue Zones example illustrates, a carefully designed sampling procedure that includes 50 or more participants can lay the groundwork to justify the claim that results have significance that extend well beyond a single setting or group of participants.

Combining one or more probability and purposeful sampling techniques is not the only way to achieve mixed methods sampling. Mixed methods sampling can also be conceived in terms of two different design features: first, the timing of the data collection and sampling and second, the relationship between the members of the sample used in the qualitative and quantitative strands. The timing of the data collection is less directly related to overall quality than the presence of a link between the samples used in the qualitative and quantitative strands. Each of these strategies is explained more fully in the next section.

Timing as a Way to Distinguish Mixed Method Sampling Approaches

Both concurrent and sequential approaches to participant selection are amenable to the purpose of enhancing quality by optimizing opportunities for mixing in creative ways.

Concurrent mixed methods sampling. **Concurrent mixed methods sampling** *utilizes a single sample of participants where qualitative and quantitative data are collected simultaneously but not necessarily at a single point in time.* This was the case, for example, in the exemplar that is discussed in greater detail later in the chapter about the effectiveness of using social media to promote an increase in interest in HIV prevention by Young and Jaganath (2013). These authors traced the link between changes in attitude and behavior change by collecting qualitative and quantitative data simultaneously from the same group of participants over a 12-week period.

Sequential mixed method sampling. Mixed method studies that use analytical procedures in the first phase to identify a set of qualitative and/or quantitative indicators to select participants for the second phase are not unusual. **Sequential mixed method sampling** *occurs when a subsequent sampling strategy is directly linked to the results of analytical procedures in an earlier strand or study.* This is a case where mixing is achieved through sampling across two or more stages. Because the results of analytical procedures from an earlier phase are linked to subsequent analysis, it is a type of mixing that is achieved through sampling. Its utility extends to multiphase studies as well.

The Blue Zones example had multiple design features that supported the integration of qualitative and quantitative data and analytical procedures, including through sampling. It illustrated the use of sequential mixed methods sampling in a multiphase study. In the initial phase, demographers used what might be called *critical case sampling* to assemble a set of global indicators associated with a single island community off the coast of Italy with an exceptionally high concentration of long-lived individuals. Mixing occurred because those indicators were further explored more qualitatively in a subsequent, more dominant phase of the study. This occurred when a team of researchers visited the site to conduct interviews and to study geological and geographic features and traditional plants and herbs in order to narrow down a battery of contextual and individual qualities associated with longevity. These strategies generated a conceptual explanation that subsequently could be tested in other settings.

Using Identical or Nested Samples

Unlike the issue of timing, whether the sample in a mixed method study is entirely distinct, overlapping, or identical has direct implications for whether it facilitates or obstructs mixing. Unless it is utilized strictly for the purpose of triangulation, two entirely different samples for the qualitative and qualitative strands of a mixed methods study can signal distinct or parallel studies rather than one that is mixed methods (Yin, 2006). Using an identical sample of participants for both the qualitative and quantitative strands of a study is an inherently mixed methods sampling procedure (Bazeley, 2006). Nested or overlapping samples also generate opportunities for mixing.

In a set of interlinked publications that appeared first in 2006 and subsequently in 2007, Collins et al. (2007) confirmed that authors reporting on mixed methods studies used identical samples most frequently. The first study involved a quantitative analysis of 42 mixed methods studies in counseling psychology; the second study added a strategy for evaluating quality and analyzed 121 mixed methods articles from nine fields in the social and health studies. In both studies, identical sampling was most prevalent, followed by nested sampling (where one group of participants or respondents is a subset of a larger group).

The results were not as consistent for the timing of the sampling procedures in the two content analyses reported by Collins and her colleagues in 2006 and 2007. Sequential or multiphase approaches to the timing of sample collection were found most frequently in the analysis of research publications in counseling psychology, while the concurrent approach to mixed methods sampling was found more frequently in the follow-up study using a larger sample of articles from fields in social and health sciences, which often employ clinical trials and control and treatment groups.

Collins and her colleagues did not filter the publications they analyzed for any measure of quality. Table 5.2 extends the research by Collins and her colleagues (2006, 2007) by identifying the sampling strategies used in the chapter exemplars.

TABLE 5.2 ■ Sampling Strategies in a Selection of Fully Integrated Mixed Methods Exemplars				
Exemplar	Topic	Timing of Data Collection	Timing of Data Analysis	Sample Type
Catallo et al. (2013)	Intimate partner violence	Sequential	Iterative	Nested
Cooper (2014)	Classroom teaching practices	Sequential	Sequential	Nested (multisite, multilevel)
Creamer & Ghoston (2012)	Learning outcomes identified in mission statements	Concurrent	Sequential	Identical
Durksen & Klassen (2012)	Preservice teachers' commitment & engagement	Concurrent	Concurrent	Identical
Gasson & Waters (2013)	Online collaborative behaviors	Sequential	Sequential	Identical
Elliott et al. (2014)	Elderly and a sense of community	Sequential	Iterative	Nested
Jang et al. (2008)	Leadership practices in successful elementary schools	Concurrent	Iterative	Nested (multisite, multilevel)
McMahon (2007)	College athletes' perceptions of rape myths	Sequential	Sequential	Nested
Young & Jaganath (2013)	HIV education through Facebook	Concurrent	Sequential	Identical

The articles listed in this table differ from those analyzed by Collins and her colleagues because each underwent multiple stages of filtering in order to be distinguished in this textbook as exemplary.

Information in Table 5.2 supports the argument that there is some link between quality and the nature of the sample but counters the claim that mixing is unlikely to occur when data are collected concurrently. As with the studies by Collins et al. in 2006 and 2007, all the exemplary publications used an identical or nested approach to sampling. As with the earlier studies by Collins et al. in 2006 and 2007, however, the results about what type of timing of sample collection distinguishes exemplary articles are not clear-cut. The number of authors using a two-step process to collect a sample is equal to the number of authors that had a concurrent sampling strategy, where all the data were collected simultaneously. This counters

Yin's (2006) concern that concurrent sampling can jeopardize mixing. This fits my argument that though design features, such as timing and priority, are helpful to categorize and describe articles in a succinct way using terminology that is familiar to others using mixed methods, they do not in and of themselves necessarily give us any consistent clues to the overall quality of the research or reporting.

There are many creative alternatives to advance opportunities for mixing through sampling. Because it is inextricably linked to the assertions that can be made about the transferability of the findings to other settings, after establishing the purpose of the study and the questions to be pursued, it may well be the single most important design decision a researcher makes.

We transition now to consider key methodological features of the chapter exemplar reporting on a study to test the efficacy of using social media to promote education about sexually transmitted disease among a population of high-risk men. Despite its remarkable brevity, the study serves as a good model for ways to present key features that signal fully integrated mixed methods study. The intent to integrate the qualitative and quantitative strands is reflected in the (a) purpose statement and research questions, (b) sampling procedures, (c) analytical procedures, and (d) inferences drawn.

EXEMPLARY ARTICLE: A MIXED METHOD STUDY USING SOCIAL MEDIA (YOUNG & JAGANATH, 2013)

Researchers from many walks of life are motivated to test and discover whether an intervention promotes changes in attitude or behavior. This is exactly what led Young and Jaganath (2013) to explore the feasibility of using a private page on social media to employ peer leaders to introduce conversations about HIV prevention among a high-risk population of men. Although it lacks some of the qualities of a mixed methods publication (i.e., methodological transparency), one of the reasons I elected to identify this article as an exemplar is because it is highly translatable (i.e., replicable) to other contexts. Posts on social media or in blogs can readily serve as a source of both qualitative and quantitative ways to assess change in attitudes and behavior over time, as in response to mindfulness training or during the recovery process from an illness or addiction.

Figure 5.1 uses the standard template we have employed before to summarize key design features of the Young and Jaganath (2013) study.

A second reason this article is of particular interest to this chapter is because of the variety of ways that mixing is incorporated in this study. This includes in the purpose statement, through sampling procedures, during data collection and prior to analysis, during analysis, and in the construction of conclusions. These are explored in the section that follows.

FIGURE 5.1 ■	Exemplary Article About Online Social Networking for HIV Education and Prevention: Summary of Key Features of Young and Jaganath (2013)		
Rationale/Purpose	Complementarity		
Priority	Equal		
Timing of Data Collection	Concurrent		
Timing of Data Analysis	Sequential		
Mixing	Fully integrated: Yes		
	Design	✖	One qualitative; one quantitative research question
	Data collection	✖	Identical samples for the qualitative and quantitative strands
	Data analysis	✖	Longitudinal component with time stamp by qualitative themes
	Inferences	✖	
Meta-inference	Prevention-related conversations increased over time and were related to the request for a HIV-testing kit.		
	Qualitative conclusion		Five HIV-related themes were noted.
	Quantitative conclusion		Prevention-related themes increased over time.
Value-added	"Results demonstrate the utility and acceptability of using social networking technologies for HIV prevention, especially minority populations" (p. 166).		

FIVE TYPES OF MIXING IN THE CHAPTER EXEMPLAR

Mixing in the purpose statement and research questions. Young and Jaganath (2013) posed two separate research questions that are interlinked because both refer to conversations that took place on a private social media site. The qualitative question asked about the nature of topics raised in the online discussion and how they varied by time. The second question involved quantitative analysis and involved mixing. It sought to determine whether any of the qualitatively derived topics had a significant impact on the desired outcome of the intervention, which was a request for HIV testing. This is the second approach to writing mixed methods research questions described earlier in the chapter.

Mixing through sampling procedures. The sampling procedure used in the exemplar warrants the mixed method sampling label because it uses both quantitative (i.e., probabilistic) and qualitative (i.e., purposeful) approaches. A purposeful sample of high-risk men was recruited (qualitative strategy) and then randomly assigned to an intervention or no-treatment group (quantitative strategy). The data were collected at the same time from all participants in the treatment group (i.e., concurrently).

Mixing during data collection. Creating blended variables to be used in subsequent analytical procedures is a type of mixing (Bazeley, 2009). Young and Jaganath (2013) employed this strategy and introduced a longitudinal component to their study by linking a time/day stamp with the textual data they extracted from the social media site and then coded to identify topics of the conversational exchanges. This strengthened the explanatory power of the study because they were able to document changes over time in attitudes about HIV prevention among a high-risk population by linking postings to the time/day stamp in social media. In this case, mixing occurred by creating a new variable that linked the one quantitative variable (i.e., time stamp) with the conversational topics.

This type of coding procedure has been referred to as *text-in-context coding* (Sandelowski, Voils, Leeman, & Crandell, 2012). **Text-in-context coding** *is a form of mixing that occurs during the process of qualitative coding of textual or visual data. It is a systematic procedure to flesh out variation in the way a variable or theme is manifested.* It has been described as a "new method for extracting findings" (Sandelowski et al., 2012, p. 1428). Sandelowski and her colleagues (2012) experimented with its use in the context of a systematic or empirical review of the literature in order to quantify the strength of evidence provided to support outcomes of an intervention. Castro, Kellison, Boyd, and Kopak (2010) referred to a similar process as dimensionalizing data because of its ability to demonstrate variations in the strength of a construct. In research involving field notes from observations in classroom, for example, this type of coding procedure could create an opportunity to produce a new variable that links strength of evidence of a theme to a physical object in the environment.

Approaches to text-in-context coding range from highly descriptive or literal coding that links qualitative and quantitative variables using language explicitly used in the original text to other approaches that involve more interpretation. Descriptive coding is quite literal when it links a qualitatively derived code, category, or theme with an external measure, such as date and time or location. For example, in an article cited by more than 6,000 people, Eisenhardt (1989) described what could be called a very literal or descriptive approach to text-in-context coding by proposing that when used to report findings, words such as *some*, *a few*, *many*, or *most* can be converted to a number equivalent for purposes of further analysis.

Interpretive text-in-context coding makes specific links between the text that is being analyzed and the interpretation the researcher draws from it (Stenvoll & Svensson, 2011). This approach could be applied to create a theoretical code in a grounded theory study by linking an attitude or outcome to a stage in a temporal process. Judgment is required in the type of text-in-context coding that assigns a value to how weakly or strongly a particular passage supports a theme that emerged during the process of qualitative coding. Castro et al. (2010) provide a practical suggestion that a researcher could use the following ordinal scale to evaluate the degree of emphasis given to a theme or attitude: 0 = no mention, 1 = implicit mention, 2 = explicit but brief mention, and 3 = explicit and emphasized. A similar approach could be taken to quantify degrees of achievement of an outcome, such as the development of civic engagement, self-authorship, or a higher-order math skill. One of the advantages of this approach is that it adds to construct validity (the parallels between that measure and the actual construct) by forcing the researcher to find a way to recognize how often a theme is missing from individual reports. This kind of measurement technique makes it easier to compile convincing evidence to refute a hypothesis (Eisenhardt, 1989).

Mixing during analysis. After quantifying the frequency of the qualitative conversational themes, Young and Jaganath (2013) used a form of multiple regression to identify which conversational themes significantly predicted the dependent variable. These results provided statistical support for the principal conclusion of the study: "HIV prevention-related conversations are associated with HIV-related behaviors such as HIV testing" (Young & Jaganath, 2013, p. 166).

Constructing conclusions through mixing. As defined in Chapter 1, a meta-inference combines results from the qualitative and quantitative strands of a research study in ways that can range from a descriptive statement that simply compares the qualitative and quantitative findings to a more interpretive statement that offers a conceptual explanation for how the two are linked. The meta-inference produced by Young and Jaganath (2013) is less speculative than other types of inferences because it is a conclusion that arose directly from the analytical procedure that linked the qualitatively derived conversational themes (the increase in frequency of discussion about HIV prevention) to a behavioral measure (i.e., a. request for HIV testing). Although this type of wording is lacking in the exemplar, a meta-inference is made more transparent, and consequently credible, by explicit acknowledgment about which conclusions derived from the qualitative analysis and which came from the quantitative analysis.

Methodological Transparency in the Exemplar

The most innovative, forward-looking uses of mixed method approaches do not always incorporate references that suggest familiarity with the methodological literature. As admirable as the Young and Jaganath (2013) article is for its innovative use of social media in ways that could be highly useful to others interested in researching changes in behavior or attitude, it shares this weakness in reporting. For example, the phrase mixed methods appears in the title but does not appear elsewhere in the article. No references to foundational texts or articles about mixed methods appear in the reference list. It is the only exemplar that I have used so far that is not transparent about either the rationale for using mixed method or the value-added, expected or not, of doing so.

As a relatively new methodology that is still evolving, the demand for methodological transparency is especially great in mixed methods research. As noted in an earlier chapter, this is a form of reflexivity that promotes replication by providing explicit details about procedural steps in data collection and analysis. In mixed methods, this also generally includes language that acknowledges the reasons for using mixed methods and the value added by its use.

Methodological transparency appears at the top of any list of criteria to evaluate the quality of a mixed method article. Language that explicitly links an interpretive conclusion to an analytical procedure or source of data adds to the credibility of research. It is a way to document that the conclusions are warranted. The failure to include language that links a conclusion to a source of data is probably one reason why many authors of content analysis of mixed method literature have been forced to conclude that a sizable number of articles flying under the mixed methods banner fail to include any significant form of mixing.

CONCLUSION

This chapter has introduced the idea of the integration of qualitative and quantitative aspects of a study as a defining characteristic of mixed method research. It points to ways that the intent to mix can be built into the earliest phases of a research project through the wording of the purpose statement and research questions, by using multiple sampling strategies, and by creating blended variables during the initial process of qualitative coding.

The example of the ambitious, interdisciplinary initiative to identify the characteristics of communities or Blue Zones across the world with unusually large populations of people living past the century mark illustrates that a priority to mixing diverse sources of data can be embedded in the way a project is conceptualized and a research team assembled. It also illustrates the way that quantitative indicators identified in the first phase of a sequential study can be productively used to select a qualitative sample to qualitatively explore through in-depth case studies for purposes of explanation rather than simply triangulation. Further discussion of mixed method approaches to case study research appears in the next chapter, where we move on to consider a variety of ways that mixing can be accomplished during analysis.

Summary of Key Points

1. Mixing is the design feature that distinguishes a mixed method from a multimethod study.

2. The principal value-added of mixing is its potential to strengthen explanatory power.

3. The value-added of mixed methods is enhanced when mixing occurs at multiple stages of the research process.

4. The greatest potential to enhance explanatory power through mixing is to employ a recursive or iterative approach to analysis, have interlinked qualitative and quantitative research questions, and to have both qualitative and quantitative data for a nested or identical sample of participants or respondents.

5. Well-conceptualized research questions communicate preliminary ideas about how mixing will be accomplished.

6. Opportunities for mixing can never be fully anticipated at the onset.

7. Open-ended, nondirectional language that is largely method neutral is the most compatible with communicating the logic associated with mixed methods.

8. The wording of research questions is one indicator of qualitative, quantitative, or mixed priority.

9. Most mixed methods studies use more than one sampling procedure.

10. A sampling design that is unique to mixed methods is one that combines the feature of a traditional quantitative (i.e., probability) approach to sampling with those of a qualitative (i.e., purposeful) approach.

11. Timing and type are two features that distinguish mixed method sampling.

12. Using either an identical or nested sample of participants is an inherently mixed methods sampling procedure.

13. Statements that explicitly identify the value-added from integrating qualitative and quantitative approaches and that link conclusions to the source of data that supports them are a form of methodological transparency that is unique to mixed methods.

Key Terms

- Concurrent mixed methods sampling
- Mixed method sampling procedures
- Sequential mixed method sampling
- Significance enhancement
- Text-in-context coding

Supplemental Activities

1. The approach taken by the exemplar in this chapter (i.e., Young & Jaganath, 2013) could be used to evaluate social media posts for an increase in knowledge about many topics, such as nutrition, mindfulness, or some aspect of interest in or knowledge about math or science. Identify an attitude that interests you that you think is linked in positive ways to an outcome or behavior, such as the association between mindfulness and management of eating. Using the Young and Jaganath article as a model, write one qualitative research question, one quantitative research question, and one research question that requires mixing. Then rewrite these into two questions that involve mixing qualitatively and quantitatively derived data.

2. Do a digital library search using the search terms *mixed methods research AND* [*the current year*]. Eliminate the articles with a methodological purpose and pull out those that explicitly state research questions. Of those, study the research questions to see if any explicitly address the topic of mixing.

Recommended Reading

Young, S. D., & Jaganath, D. (2013). Online social networking for HIV education and prevention: A mixed-methods analysis. *Sexually Transmitted Diseases, 40*(2), 162–167.

MIXED METHOD ANALYTICAL PROCEDURES

PRINCIPAL PURPOSES OF THE CHAPTER

1. To introduce several different mixed method analytical procedures
2. To use three exemplars to illustrate how mixed method analytical procedures can be used

Like Chapter 5, this chapter maintains a focus on elements of the design and execution of a mixed methods study that strengthen its potential to produce a coherent conceptual explanation that could not be generated by any one method in isolation. Its purpose is to introduce a variety of strategies that can be used effectively to execute a mixed methods analysis. Mixed methods analytical procedures consolidate or link qualitative and quantitative data or sources for purposes of analysis. An integrative mixed methods analysis can be achieved by using an analytical strategy that incorporates more than one source or form of data (Bazeley, 2012) or by mixing qualitative and quantitative analytical strategies (Small, 2011). A mixed methods analysis is most frequently accomplished by using a combination of qualitative and quantitative analytical procedures.

Mixing during analysis is the most challenging aspects of executing a mixed methods study (Yin, 2006). Although in terms of the potential to enhance explanatory power it is probably the single most important place in the research process for mixing to occur (Greene, 2007), there is a convincing body of evidence that mixing during analysis is hardly common (Caracelli & Greene, 1993; O'Cathain, Murphy, & Nicholl, 2007a). In one of the first studies of its kind, Greene, Caracelli, and Graham (1989) launched a long line of researchers to eventually conclude that there was a low level of mixing in published articles of the qualitative and quantitative strands, particularly during analysis. Authors of nearly half of the 57 articles Greene et al. reviewed kept the analysis and interpretation of the two data sets separate. When any type of mixing was present, it was most likely to occur during the interpretation phases. Less than 5% actually mixed during analysis. Although levels are likely to have increased somewhat in more recent times, authors of countless content analyses conducted using articles from a variety of disciplines have reached similar conclusions about the rarity of examples of articles reporting on the results of mixing during analysis.

The emphasis in this chapter is on the subset of mixed method analytical procedures that are unique to mixed methods. Above all, I frame the discussion in ways to challenge the idea that mixed methods are merely a loose cobbling together of a strand that uses a qualitative approach with a strand that uses a quantitative approach and that the purpose is always primarily for confirmation or triangulation. The multimethod label is most appropriate for studies where the qualitative and quantitative strands are not interwoven and where one strand makes virtually no substantive contribution to the conclusions. In the highest-caliber mixed methods studies, the qualitative and quantitative strands are often so cleverly and iteratively interwoven that it becomes an exercise in semantics to disentangle the two.

RETURNING TO THE METAPHOR OF THE ARCHITECTURAL ARCH

In the previous chapters, I have periodically revisited the architectural arch as a metaphor that is useful to understanding key points about mixed methods and mixed methods methodology. I use the keystone as a metaphor for a meta-inference, which is the endpoint of the analysis in a research study. Figure 6.1 shows that even as a keystone serves a vital practical purpose, it also can be aesthetically pleasing.

FIGURE 6.1　■　Keystone

© iStock/Rudi Tapper

FIGURE 6.2 ■ Illustration of a Keystone

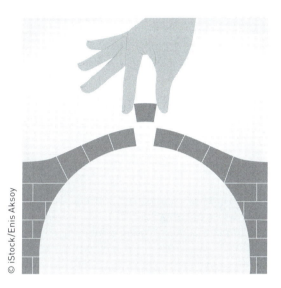

© iStock/Enis Aksoy

In an arch, a keystone is the wedged shape block that is slotted into place at the final step of construction. Its purpose is simultaneously decorative and highly functional. The entire structure relies on the power of the keystone to hold the structure in place. Once the keystone is in place, the temporary supporting structure can be removed. Figure 6.2 is an illustration that demonstrates the important last step in erecting an arch so that it can stand.

The ability of the keystone to hold the structure together stems from the fact that even without mortar, the pressure from the arch tightly bonds the smaller wedges together by pushing them together rather than apart. This is similar to an equal or mixed priority study whose explanatory power is derived from inferences emerging from tightly interlocked qualitative and quantitative strands.

The keystone as a metaphor for a meta-inference extends to divergent findings. One of the biggest methodological differences between qualitative and quantitative approaches is in their perspective about divergent data and findings. Whereas outliers and extreme cases are often removed in the later stages of analysis in quantitative approaches, these are more likely to be pursued for their explanatory power in qualitative and mixed method approaches. There are parallels between this and the final act of the artisan building an arch. There is no doubt that even the most talented artisan found it necessary to smooth down the edges of the keystone (i.e., meta-inference) to ensure the snug fit necessary to drop it in place and withdraw the supporting structure. In a similar way, incongruities in data and between sites often propel a researcher to explore the weaknesses of his or her explanatory model.

Even though it can be argued that an arch has some fluidity as the forces that distribute the weight and that allow the arch to stand are continually interlinked, the process of refining meta-inferences in mixed methods research is much more fluid and the endpoint less fully visualized at the onset than is necessarily in the design of an architectural structure. Unlike the task of an engineer designing an arch or bridge, no formula or set of calculations can help a researcher fully anticipate their final conclusions. An algebraic mindset is unlikely to produce conclusions that will spark both replication and new lines of research.

PURPOSE, GOALS, AND CONTRIBUTION OF THE CHAPTER

The purpose of this chapter is to illustrate different ways to use mixed method analytical procedures. Mixing during analysis is not simply a matter of borrowing analytical procedures from other methods and combining them. I take a different tact than most authors of textbooks about mixed methods in that I am not approaching the topic of mixed methods analysis by naming and then distinguishing types of concurrent and sequential mixed methods designs and then linking them to a specific analytical strategy. My reason for deviating from the more conventional approach is that I want to emphasize that there is not a limited number of ways that mixing during the analysis can be accomplished. It is one of my principal methodological assumptions that it is counterproductive to the idea of a mixed methods way of thinking to fix the design of a study early in the research process and in such a way that bars the option to pursue alternative explanations and inconsistencies in the data in unexpected and creative ways.

Rather than follow the pattern I have used in previous chapters (using a single exemplar to illustrate key points), in this chapter, I refer to three exemplars to illustrate ways that mixed method analytical procedures have been used. While previously my selection criteria have been restricted to articles that are realistic for a researcher working alone to replicate, this is not the case for the exemplars highlighted in this chapter. I acknowledge that the implicit risk in selecting such complex studies is that it could reinforce the misperception that a mixed method study is an impossibly ambitious undertaking for graduate student research.

This chapter has two fundamental purposes: (a) to introduce several different mixed method analytical procedures and (b) to use three exemplars to illustrate how mixed method analytical procedures can be used. Goals of this first chapter about ways to integrate qualitative and quantitative data sources or analytical procedures (mixing) are to

1. illustrate how data consolidation, blending, converting, extreme case sampling, and cross-case comparison have been used to facilitate mixing during analysis;
2. provide examples to illustrate interpretive transparency;
3. provide examples of meta-inferences;

4. trace design features that facilitate reaching a conclusion that can accurately be characterized as a meta-inference; and
5. summarize ways that strategies to promote the development of meaningful meta-inferences can be embedded in the design of a mixed method study.

In this chapter, I introduce some ideas that are new to the methodological literature about mixed methods. One of these is about the element of the design of a mixed method study referred to as *priority*. This is an aspect of design that I first considered in Chapter 5. Priority refers to which type of analytical strategy or causal logic is awarded the most attention in a research report. Creswell and Plano Clark (2007, 2011) have framed priority as being inherently linked to timing of the data collection. As they position it, an explanatory study is a two-phase study where a qualitative phase follows a quantitative phase where the dominant logic is established. This would be the case, for example, when an explanatory model developed through quantitative procedures is illustrated in a narrative profile or case study. Similarly, Creswell and Plano Clark (2007, 2011) apply the same logic to the design they call exploratory. In this case, the qualitative phase has priority and occurs first. In their view, equal priority studies are distinguished by simultaneous collection of qualitative and quantitative data.

In this chapter, I pursue the idea of a fourth type of priority. As compared to an equivalent priority that gives equal attention to the qualitative and quantitative strands of a study but may keep the strands distinct, **mixed priority mixed method studies** *award the most attention to results that are produced through mixed methods analytical procedures*. A telltale signature of a mixed priority study is that the discussion of the results and conclusions of a study are highly intertwined. Rather than being reported separately, textual and numeric evidence is interwoven in both the text and the visualizations in this type of study.

The interpretive act of drawing conclusions is the final phase of the research process. A contribution of this chapter is that it includes an extended discussion of meta-inferences. It provides examples to illustrate what a meta-inference looks like and traces features of the design of studies that facilitate reaching a conclusion that can be accurately characterized as a meta-inference. At this point in time, a well-developed integrative inference is more of an idealized endpoint for a mixed methods study than one that is widely evident in practice.

MIXED METHOD ANALYTICAL STRATEGIES

A number of textbook authors have pointed to the similarity in the set of basic analytical procedures that are shared by all social and behavioral research. Greene (2007) argues, for example, that regardless of the research method, all researchers seek to accomplish three basic tasks during data analysis. She identifies these as (a) reducing and organizing data into a manageable and meaningful form; (b) making comparisons, assessing relationships, and identifying patterns and trends by considering both similarities and differences in the data; and (c) supporting or validating conclusions or inferences (Greene, 2007, pp. 144–145). Miles and Huberman (1994), authors familiar to qualitative researchers, identify the same basic steps but add creating data visualizations or graphic display as a distinct step. Figures and tables are often critical to reporting results from an analysis that consolidates qualitative and quantitative data.

There is no single set of prescribed procedures for mixing methods during the analysis. **Mixed methods analytical procedures** *set out to identify, compare, and consolidate thematically similar results by using more than one source or form of data.* Table 6.1 lists five different types of procedures that can be used to mix qualitative and quantitative data and analytical strategies: blending, converting, extreme case sampling, cross-case comparison, and meta-inferences. This is not an exhaustive list. There are many other creative ways in which mixed method analytical procedures can be accomplished.

All but the last procedure listed in Table 6.1 (meta-inferences) are executed by consolidating qualitative and quantitative data for purposes of further analysis. **Blending** *is a strategy for data consolidation where a variable, category, or theme generated from one type of analysis is tested using another type of data or where a variable, category, or factor is created by combining qualitative and quantitative data.* Ways this can be accomplished are illustrated in Figure 6.3.

Blending generally involves data transformation or conversion. **Converting** *is a strategy for data consolidation where qualitative data are converted to quantitative data or quantitative data are converted to qualitative data so they can be analyzed together.*

TABLE 6.1 ■ Types of Mixed Methods Analytical Procedures	
Type	**Definition**
Blending	A variable, category, or theme generated from one type of analysis (e.g., qualitative or quantitative) is tested using another type of data
	A variable, category, or factor is created by combining qualitative and quantitative data
Converting	A strategy for data consolidation where qualitative data are converted to quantitative data or quantitative data to qualitative data so that they can be analyzed together
Extreme case sampling	A type of purposeful (rather than representative) sampling and involves selecting cases because they are at the extremes of a sampling distribution (i.e., outliers)
Cross-case comparison	A mixed method analytical strategy that consolidates qualitative and quantitative data by constructing holistic, internally coherent profiles that are used to test or expand upon qualitatively or quantitatively derived themes for the purposes of comparison
Meta-inferences	Inferences that link, compare, contrast, or modify inferences generated by the qualitative and quantitative strands

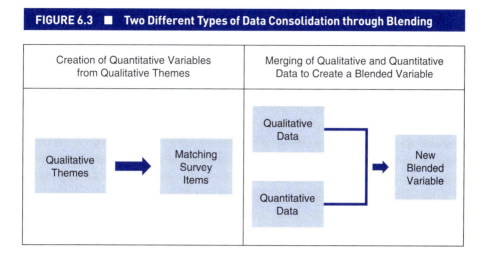

FIGURE 6.3 ■ Two Different Types of Data Consolidation through Blending

Critical or extreme case sampling and cross-case comparisons are also executed for purposes of further analysis. Examples of how these mixed method analytical procedures have been used are explored in the next section.

EXAMPLES OF THE USE OF MIXED METHOD ANALYTICAL STRATEGIES

In this section, I use three exemplars of fully integrated mixed methods studies to illustrate how mixed methods analytical techniques have been employed. All of these can be considered to fit the definition of a mixed priority study because their explanatory power rests in a meta-inference that links separate inferences drawn from the quantitative and qualitative analysis. One (i.e., Creamer & Ghoston, 2012) approached analysis in a conventional, two-step, sequential way. The other two (i.e., Elliott, Gale, Parsons, Kuh, & The HALCyon Study, 2014; Jang, McDougall, Pollon, Herbert, & Russell, 2008) are multiphase. Each approached the analysis in three iteratively linked stages. Qualitative and quantitative data were first analyzed concurrently. Mixing occurred in the third phase through consolidation or blending.

Each of these articles describe fully integrated studies where mixing occurred throughout each of the major stages of the research process. For purposes of this discussion, I narrow the focus to aspects of the articles dealing with mixed methods analytical strategies. Later in the chapter, we consider the process each used to reach a meta-inference. The templates appear in Appendix D because the discussion only involves the analytical procedures.

The three exemplars share a purpose for using mixed methods to develop a more comprehensive understanding of a phenomenon but address these with very different populations. The first exemplar is a readily replicable study by Creamer and Ghoston

(2012) that explores the values and outcomes emphasized in mission statements from colleges of engineering and questions whether these differed significantly between institutions that were more and less diverse. The second article by Elliott et al. (2014) describes a study about the relationship between positive attitudes about engagement in neighborhood activities and mental well-being among the elderly, while the third by Jang et al. (2008) pursues questions about how schools with high populations of impoverished students managed to promote increases in student achievement.

Two of the three (i.e., Elliott et al., 2014; Jang et al., 2008) articles describe the results of ambitious large-scale research-based projects that utilized relatively advanced mixed methods analytical procedures. Both of these articles are unusual in that the use of multiple integrated analytical procedures made it necessary to be highly reflexive about the process and produced a methods section with admirable detail. Jang et al. (2008) followed mixed methods conventions by including a figure showing the steps in the analytical process. Both studies illustrated how the mixing strategies listed in Table 6.1 can be used individually and in tandem but are not perfect models for graduate students and novice researchers because of their ambitious scope.

Table 6.2 is used to summarize the mixed method analytical strategies used in the three exemplars featured in this chapter.

The studies differ by how many mixed method analytical procedures were used. The first exemplar by Creamer and Ghoston (2012) used a single mixed method analytical procedure. Jang et al. (2008) described four different mixed method analytical procedures and Elliott et al. (2014) used two.

Example 1: Illustrating Data Transformation: Creamer and Ghoston (2012)

In its exploration of the types of values and outcomes endorsed in mission statements of a stratified sample of colleges of engineering, Creamer and Ghoston's (2012) article falls within the body of literature about gender and science, engineering, and technology (SET) in the higher-education setting. Like the two other articles reviewed in this section, it is explicitly framed as a mixed methods study. It differs in that the analytical procedures are less complex and occurred sequentially in two phases rather than iteratively across three phases.

TABLE 6.2 ■ Summary of the Types of Mixed Method Analytical Procedures Used in Three Exemplars		
Mission Statements (Creamer & Ghoston, 2012)	**School Improvement (Jang et al., 2008)**	**Neighborhood Cohesion (Elliott et al., 2014)**
1. Data transformation	1. Data transformation	1. Blending
	2. Blending	2. Extreme case sampling
	3. Extreme case sampling	
	4. Cross-case comparison	

Data transformation. Creamer and Ghoston (2012) used a single mixed method analytical strategy. Data transformation enabled the use of statistical procedures to compare the types of values and outcomes endorsed by institutions characterized by different levels of diversity in the undergraduate population.

Data transformation or conversion occurs most frequently when qualitative data, often in the form of frequency counts, is transformed into quantitative data for purposes of enabling statistical analysis. This is a mixed method analytical strategy referred to in the literature as **quantitizing**, *where measures on quantitative instruments are summarized in narrative form for purposes of further analysis and cross-case comparison* (Sandelowski, 2001; Sandelowski, Voils, & Knafl, 2009). This made it possible to test the significance of the association between a measure of institutional diversity (i.e., proportion and number of undergraduate women enrolled in engineering degree programs) and a range of types of values endorsed in mission statements.

In the example described next, Jang et al. (2008) used four mixed methods analytical strategies, including both **qualitizing** and **quantitizing**, *which is when qualitative data is transformed into a quantitative format, often through frequency counts* (Sandelowski, 2001; Sandelowski et al., 2009). *Qualitizing is a mixed methods analytical strategy where measures on quantitative instruments are summarized in narrative form for the purposes of further analysis and cross-case comparison.*

Example 2: Illustrating Four Mixed Methods Analytical Strategies: Jang, McDougall, Pollon, Herbert, and Russell (2008)

The Jang et al. (2008) study addresses complex policy issues within the body of literature about school effectiveness or improvement. Their aim was to identify leadership practices that distinguished schools that had been successful in improving student performance within challenging, economically disadvantaged neighborhoods with large immigrant populations. Results from the analysis of a questionnaire completed by principals and teachers suggested few differences between schools, while a qualitative approach using cross-case comparisons revealed that leaders had to navigate unique circumstances in every setting. Differences between schools and how each had to adapt to unique circumstances in their settings did not emerge as a key conclusion until the final, cross-case analysis was conducted.

The Jang et al. (2008) study is unusual in its complexity and because it employed four different mixed methods analytical strategies during the course of the analysis. It illustrates that mixing can occur during analysis even when a study begins with a concurrent design. They described their approach to analysis as both emergent and highly iterative. They emphasized the iterative nature of their experience when they observed, "The nature of the integration was iterative, moving back and forth between the qualitative and quantitative strands of data and allowing for the recognition of emergent themes and insights" (p. 241).

Data transformation. In addition to other mixed method analytical procedures, Jang et al. (2008) used data transformation. Data transformation occurred relatively early in the process when survey data were transformed into detailed, narrative descriptions of nine underlying factors, such as parental involvement, distributed leadership, and community involvement (i.e., qualitizing). This was done to provide a direct way to compare qualitative interview data with survey data by blending.

Blending. This is a type of data consolidation where a variable or category is created that combines qualitative and quantitative data. The key to the ability to use blending as a mixed method analytical technique is that qualitative and quantitative data are available on overlapping constructs.

Jang et al. (2008) distinguished their study by using an analytical strategy that allowed them to consolidate their qualitatively derived themes with quantitative data from the survey to create eight blended or consolidated variables. They used these words to describe this process:

> In our use of the data consolidation analytical strategy, the results from the qualitative and quantitative data were jointly reviewed and merged into a new set of thematic variables for further analysis. We quantified the new set of thematic variables by matching them with the survey items and used the new variables to examine the interrelationships across the themes and individual schools. (p. 242)

The new quantitative variables facilitated comparisons across schools and revealed that the themes were addressed differently in each school setting.

Extreme case sampling. Also known as negative case sampling and deviant case sampling, **extreme case sampling** *is a type of purposeful (rather than representative) sampling and involves selecting cases because they are at the extremes of a sampling distribution (i.e., outliers)* (Teddlie & Tashakkori, 2009). Extreme cases have the potential to introduce new variables in a study that may explain differences between cases and what may initially appear to be inconsistencies between the qualitative and quantitative data.

Jang and her colleagues used the blended variables in a sampling strategy to identify schools for a cross-case analysis. They used a form of critical or extreme case sampling by selecting schools that showed statistically significant differences in the means on several central thematic factor scores.

Cross-case comparison. **Cross-case comparison** *is a mixed method analytical strategy that consolidates qualitative and quantitative data by constructing holistic, internally coherent profiles that are used to test or expand upon qualitatively or quantitatively derived themes for the purposes of comparison.* It is instrumental in identifying inconsistencies and consistencies across cases and for generating explanations for why these might occur.

The authors described the value-added of this type of mixed method analytical strategy this way: "Comparative case analyses highlighted and contrasted strategies and processes that schools employed to mitigate challenging circumstances" (p. 244). The findings from this stage highlighted variability across sites. The cross-case comparison produced the principal conclusion of the study: Some overlapping characteristics across the schools were reflected by themes, such as parental involvement, as well as unique features associated with elements of the context and the nature of the student body and professional staff. Jang et al. (2008) commented on the valued-added of this approach by observing, "Without mixing different data sources, we would not have gained this enriched understanding of the unique characteristics of school improvement in schools facing challenging circumstances" (p. 241).

Example 3: Illustrating Two Mixed Methods Analytical Strategies: Elliott, Gale, Parsons, Kuh, and The HALCyon Study (2014)

The authors of this 2014 article took advantage of an existing longitudinal data set of quantitative scores on survey instruments and biographical interviews with three cohorts of now-elderly men and women living in southeast England to pursue questions about the relationship between healthy aging and neighborhood cohesion. The authors used two mixed methods analytical procedures and a three-phase approach to analysis to determine if scores on a scale of neighborhood cohesion were significantly related to scores on a measure of mental well-being and, if this was stronger for older cohorts, to investigate a number of explanations for the relationship that emerged from the qualitative analysis. The use of blending and the analysis of qualitative data from a nested sample of extreme cases made it possible to isolate social support, social participation, and mobility as instrumental to understanding why perceptions of a positive neighborhood environment, despite more limited personal mobility, were slightly more positive for older adults.

Extreme case sampling. As is appropriate for a mixed method study, Elliott and her colleagues used a two-phase sampling strategy. Both could be described as variations of purposeful rather than representative sampling. Quantitative data were available for more than 10,000 participants in three cohorts. Qualitative data were also available for a nested sample of 230 participants, who were selected because they had high scores at the extremes of the distribution of quantitative measure of neighborhood cohesion. Qualitative analysis of transcripts of this group of participants made it possible to identify a set of variables that contributed to understanding why and under what circumstances positive attitudes about neighbors influenced well-being.

Blending. Like Jang et al. (2008), Elliott et al. (2014) advanced their analysis by creating a quantitative way to test the influence of the factors identified during the analysis of qualitative data. Overlap between the types of questions posed in both the qualitative biographical interviews and on the survey instruments created an unusual opportunity to identify, cluster, and eventually sum related items on the survey into a set of consolidated variables that matched the qualitative themes. Relating to mobility, social support, and social participation, these variables subsequently proved to play a significant role in predicting differences between cohorts.

Two of the three exemplars reviewed in this chapter (i.e., Creamer & Ghoston, 2012; Elliott et al., 2014; Jang et al., 2008) demonstrate how mixing can occur at multiple points in the design and execution of a mixed methods study. They possess an additional quality that adds to their distinction as exemplary. These authors accomplished an additional level of mixing by constructing meta-inferences that provided a connection between the qualitative and quantitative components of their studies. This type of mixing that occurs at the last stage of the research process is the topic of the next section.

MIXING BY CONSTRUCTING INFERENCES AND META-INFERENCES

Regardless of the method employed, every researcher that reaches the point of writing up the results of a research study finds him or herself in the position of moving beyond a descriptive stance to adopt the more overtly interpretive mindset that is required to construct conclusions and generate inferences. Inferences are generalizations or abstractions constructed by a researcher that go beyond the results, participants, context, and (sometimes) theory (Ercikan & Roth, 2006; Miller, 2003). Although it is common for people to attach the label *objective* to quantitative research and *subjective* to qualitative research, all researchers reach a point in the research process where it is necessary to interpret the significance or contribution of a set of findings, situate these findings with the larger body of previous research, and explore the implications for policy and practice (Creamer & Tendhar, 2015; Creamer, Edwards, & Musaeus, 2016). The interpretive act requires the ability to move beyond a simple description of results to conceptualizing conclusions at a more abstract level.

There are several reasons why it is problematic that the most common form of mixing is at the stage of generating inferences and that, most often, this is the only place that mixing occurs. This would be akin to designing an arch without constructing a durable structure to link the two sides. Linking the qualitative and quantitative findings during the process of constructing conclusions opens the researcher to questions about the credibility of his or her findings and whether the results are warranted or supported by the data or analytical procedures.

While constructing inferences at the conclusion of the analytical process is a step that is instrumental to achieving high-quality research, the potential to link conclusions from the qualitative and quantitative strands of a study is an analytical strategy that is unique to mixed methods. A meta-inference is a conclusion generated by integrating inferences from the qualitative and quantitative strands of a mixed methods study (Tashakkori & Teddlie, 2008). As compared to a descriptive conclusion, a meta-inference is produced by linking conclusions from qualitative and quantitative data, sources, or analytical strategies in an explanatory way. Like the keystone metaphor that was presented earlier, a meta-inference is not supported by one type of data or a single strand of a study but is a statement that explains important links between the two. It is rarely a conclusion that could have been predicted from the literature. This type of inference is greater than the sum of its parts because it articulates an understanding of a phenomenon that is not contained in its separate parts (Bazeley & Kemp, 2012).

Although acknowledged not to be part of most mixed methods reports, leading methodologists in mixed methods have taken a decisive position about the centrality of meta-inference to any framework to evaluate the quality of a mixed methods publication. Teddlie and Tashakkori (2009) made this point unequivocally when they observed, "The quality of the entire research project depends on the degree to which integration, blending, or linking of QUAL and QUAN inferences is achieved" (p. 292). In a similar vein, Greene and Hall (2010) elevated the centrality of meta-inferences to any judgment about the overall quality of a mixed method publication when they observed, "The actual mixing of consequence lies in the construction or composition of inferences, drawn from purposeful integrations of different threads of data patterns" (p. 125).

The strength of a meta-inference lies in its interpretive efficacy (Teddlie & Tashakkori, 2009) or interpretive validity (Maxwell, 1992). **Interpretive efficacy** *refers to the degree to which inferences in each strand of a mixed methods study are effectively integrated into a conceptually coherent and substantively meaningful meta-inference.* These types of statements can be further warranted by references to the literature (Creamer et al., 2016).

Examples of Meta-Inferences

Despite the priority that has been awarded in the methodological literature to meta-inferences as an analytical conclusion that is instrumental to the value-added of mixed methods research, it is no easy task to locate examples that demonstrate what they look like or the process that is used to produce them. The two chapter exemplars already described in some detail in this chapter that used multiple method analytical procedures followed through with this action to integrate inferences from the qualitative and quantitative strands into a theoretically and conceptually consistent explanatory framework. The portion of the discussion section from each article that integrates the qualitative and quantitative conclusions is reproduced in Table 6.3.

TABLE 6.3 ■ Examples From Exemplars of Conclusions Reflecting a Meta-Inference	
Elliott et al. (2014) Mixed Methods Study of the Link Between Participation in Neighborhood Activities and Healthy Aging	**Jang et al. (2008) Study of Effective Schools**
"The *quantitative* findings suggest that neighborhood cohesion is more strongly associated with well-being at older ages. Analysis of the *qualitative* interviews provided some clues as to the possible underlying mechanisms. First, those in the older age groups were more likely to talk about the importance of membership in social groups, second, there was more mobility or anticipated mobility in the younger groups." (p. 50) [emphasis added]	"The final synthesis . . . was drawn from findings from both approaches collectively. For example, these schools demonstrate concerted efforts to (a) build distributed leadership . . .; (b) support professional learning . . .; (c) create a welcoming school culture; and (d) foster students' academic development. . . . These schools also demonstrate different levels of sensitivity to issues related to the relationship between school and community, parental involvement, and students' non-cognitive development. Because these challenging circumstances involve families and community, it is important for these schools to develop unique, yet successful, school improvement strategies to address these challenges in order to sustain school success." (p. 242)

Differences in the design of the two studies meant that different approaches were taken to meta-inferences. The process of reconciling conclusions was minimized in the Elliott et al. (2014) study about healthy aging because the quantitative and qualitative data answered different research questions. The quantitative data demonstrated the link between healthy aging and a sense of affiliation with neighbors while the qualitative data provided clues as to its benefits. On the other hand, in their study of school effectiveness in challenging settings that had a qualitative priority, Jang et al. (2012) had to grapple much more seriously and in greater detail with differences between settings and the strategies employed by leaders in the different settings.

A second feature that distinguishes these authors' use of advanced mixed method analytical procedures is not only the presence of a summative, explanatory meta-inference, but the explicitness of the language that is used to accomplish this. They accomplish what might be called *interpretive transparency*. **Interpretive transparency** *is a type of reflexivity that enhances the credibility of a study by explicitly linking the source of data to a conclusion or inference.*

This type of transparency has a double value. It aids the reader by not only clearly labeling a conclusion but also, in mixed methods, by making clear the conclusion derived from both qualitative and quantitative sources. Jang et al. (2008), for example, signal their meta-inference with the words "the final synthesis in this study." Elliott et al. (2014) take this type of methodological transparency one step further by explicitly linking the source of data to the inference or conclusion reached. They specify, for example, that the quantitative data documented a significant link between the variables they studied, while the qualitative data suggested the other factors, such as mobility and participation in neighborhood-based social activities, and explain why the variables are linked.

Both of these authors organize their discussion/conclusions in ways that provide sustained attention to the interplay between qualitative and quantitative findings and those that are derived from mixing the two. Paragraph to paragraph, they move back and forth between what was learned from the different sources and analytical procedures. This differs in very important ways from a presentation format that divides the discussion of the qualitative and quantitative findings in two separate sections.

A manuscript that disaggregates the discussion of the qualitative and quantitative results into separate sections with distinct headings can signal that little thought has been devoted to integrating the qualitative and quantitative results in a meaningful way. This often signals that a study lacks mixing and is therefore more accurately described as a multimethod study. A much more detailed discussion of strategies for effectively writing up mixed methods studies appears in Chapter 9.

Embedding Design Strategies That Promote Meaningful Meta-Inferences

The three exemplars featured in this chapter demonstrate that different features of the design and execution of a mixed methods study can be particularly conducive to the construction of an innovative meta-inference. Derived from the exemplars, the following list identifies some of the strategies that facilitate mixing during analysis:

1. Establish a rationale for using mixed methods that places more emphasis on explanation than confirmation.
2. Develop interlinked research questions that address the *what* and *why* or *how* of the phenomena.
3. Collect both qualitative and quantitative data about the same constructs.
4. Establish a sampling plan that involves an identical or nested sample.
5. Create composite or blended variables of qualitative and quantitative data about the same construct.
6. Use extreme or negative cases to explore alternative explanations.

CONCLUSIONS

It has only been possible to touch on a few of the many creative ways that mixed methods analytical procedures can be used in a research project. Two of the exemplars discussed at length in the chapter are unusual in that they used a mixed method analytical strategy with tremendous explanatory potential that I have referred to as *blending*. Elliott et al. (2014) created blended variables by compiling questionnaire items that reflected constructs that emerged during the qualitative analysis. Jang et al. (2008) created a new set of thematic variables by consolidating qualitative themes and survey items in an original way. Blended variables can provide evidence to support the strength of the relationship between two qualitatively derived variables, to explore differences between groups or organizations, or to demonstrate their contribution to understanding a predictor variable.

The desired endpoint of the analytic process in mixed methods research is the production of a meta-inference that identifies conclusions from the qualitative and quantitative analysis in a methodologically transparent way and that offers an explanation for why or how the two are linked. Similar to the keystone in an architectural arch that serves both decorative and functional purposes, this is an endpoint that brings together the qualitative and quantitative strands. A meta-inference is the principal conclusion of a study. It is the part of a publication most likely to merit marking by a yellow highlighter!

The more tightly the qualitative and quantitative strands of a study are interlinked during the planning and execution of a research project, the more appropriate (and meaningful) it is to associate it with a mixed method label. Meaningful mixing at any point of the research process (but particularly during analysis) is central to a contemporary understanding of mixed methods. The multimethod label is the most appropriate choice for studies that have taken advantage of multiple sources of data or analytical techniques but executed the analysis in such a way as to produce two or more distinct conclusions that are only related in the most tangential or implicit way.

Summary of Key Points

My goal in this chapter was to introduce a number of analytical strategies that could not be employed in studies that are driven by an exclusive qualitative or quantitative logic. The key points that emerge from the discussion presented in this chapter are as follows:

1. Not all mixed methods studies use analytical strategies to integrate qualitative and quantitative data or during analysis.

2. Mixing during analysis can be accomplished without using any analytical procedures that are unique to mixed methods.

3. The potential to link conclusions from qualitative and quantitative strands of a study in a meta-inference is an analytical strategy that is unique to mixed methods.

4. The overall quality of a mixed methods research report rests on the development of a coherent explanation that links inferences that are qualitatively and quantitatively derived.

5. Interpretive transparency makes the principal conclusions of a study and their sources explicit.

6. Separating out the discussion of the results of qualitative and quantitative analyses into different sections without a section about mixing is antithetical to the idea of fully integrated mixed methods.

This chapter has focused on mixing during analysis. I have avoided any language that implies that analyses necessarily unfold in a predictable, linear, step-by-step way. Unexpected twists and turns occur as the results from different analytical procedures emerge. Sandelowski, Voils, Leeman, and Crandell (2012) observed, "Within acceptable limits, methods are reinvented every time they are used to accommodate the real world of practice. Methodological innovation is arguably the norm in conducting research" (p. 320). The creative application of methods, including insightful ways to depict the results derived at through analysis, is a prerequisite for original insight.

The next chapter is the third of three chapters devoted to the topic of how mixing can be accomplished in a mixed methods study. Chapter 5 looked at how mixing can be accomplished during sampling and data collection. This chapter introduced a number of mixed method analytical strategies that are unique to mixed methods. The focus narrows in the third and final chapter on mixing. This is where we undertake the task of understanding the different ways that a mixed method analysis can be accomplished through data transformation. Many, but not all, mixed methods analytical procedures require data transformation.

Key Terms

- Blending

- Converting

- Cross-case comparison

- Extreme or negative case sampling

- Interpretive efficacy

- Interpretive transparency

- Mixed methods analytical procedures

- Mixed priority mixed method studies

- Qualitizing

- Quantitizing

Supplemental Activities

1. Look at the discussion and conclusion sections of the exemplars featured in earlier chapters of this textbook to see if you can locate other examples of authors who provide statements that reflect a meta-inference to integrate conclusions drawn from the qualitative and quantitative data or analytical procedures. Look particularly at the Durksen and Klassen's (2012) longitudinal study about the experiences of preservice teachers during student teaching.

2. Researchers have begun to test the effectiveness of using small robots to help autistic children develop more effective social and interactive skills. Draft research questions for a mixed methods observational study with videotapes showing a child alone in a room with a robot. These questions should address the amount of interaction between the child and the robot and create categories for the types of interactions between the child and the robot. See related articles (Salisbury, 2013; Wang, 2013).

Recommended Readings

Creamer, E. G., & Ghoston, M. (2012). Using a mixed methods content analysis to analyze mission statements from colleges of engineering. *Journal of Mixed Methods Research*, *7*(2), 110–120.

Elliott, J., Gale, C. R., Parsons, S., Kuh, D., & The HALCyon Study. (2014). Neighborhood cohesion and mental well-being among older adults: A mixed methods approach. *Social Science & Medicine*, *107*, 44–51.

Jang, E., McDougall, D. E., Pollon, D., Herbert, M., & Russell, P. (2008). Integrative data analytic strategies in research in school success in challenging circumstances. *Journal of Mixed Methods Research*, *2*(3), 221–247.

DATA TRANSFORMATION AND OTHER STRATEGIES FOR MIXING DURING ANALYSIS

PRINCIPAL PURPOSES OF THE CHAPTER

1. To introduce different ways that data transformation can be used as a mixed method analytical approach
2. To explore mixed method approaches to case study

Whether they acknowledge it or not, all researchers advance their analysis by using numbers (Onwuegbuzie, 2003). Implicitly or explicitly, both qualitative and quantitative researchers analyze and report their findings by counting. This can be seen in tables that foreground the results of statistical analysis as well as language employed by researchers that implicitly use numbers to describe findings. Words such as *few, many, most, several, typical, prevalent,* and *rare* can readily be translated to numbers. They reflect a type of verbal counting where numbers are implied without actually being explicitly stated (Sandelowski, 2001, p. 236). Without numbers, results of an empirical study can appear anecdotal and unscientific.

Numbers serve both rhetorical and analytical purposes in mixed methods research. They serve a rhetorical purpose because they are associated with scientific precision and rigor. Maxwell (2010) observed, "Numbers can be used rhetorically to make a report appear more precise, rigorous, and scientific without playing any real role in the logic of the study and thus misrepresenting the actual basis of the conclusions" (p. 480). Numbers also play a role in generating meaning and testing interpretations and conclusions. Sandelowski (2003) put forward this argument this way:

Anytime qualitative researchers place raw data into categories or discover themes to which they attach codes, they are drawing from the numbered nature of the phenomenon for analysis. Numbers are a powerful way to generate meaning from qualitative data; to document, verify, and test interpretations or conclusions, and to represent target events or experiences. (p. 341)

Although it is sometime an illusion, numbers and tables are part of the way that scientific rigor is communicated (McGill, 1990).

The single most compelling argument put forward for the value-added of a mixed methods approach is the potential to expand explanatory power and enhance significance (Maxwell & Mittapalli, 2010). We have linked this rationale for mixed methods research by returning on a number of occasions to the metaphor of the keystone at the apex of an architectural arch. Much as the findings from the qualitative and quantitative phases in a study can be woven together in a way that produces a coherent and practically meaningful meta-inference, a keystone serves to provide durability and stability to a structure that essentially frames air by bonding the two sides of an arch together. Mixed method analytical procedures do most of the intellectual work of generating meta-inferences.

Many, but not all, mixed method analytical procedures rely on data transformation. **Data transformation** *is the conversion of qualitative data into quantitative data or quantitative data into qualitative data for the purposes of analysis* (Greene, 2007). Most often, this takes the form of converting qualitative data to numbers for descriptive and, subsequently, analytical purposes. Data transformation is a frequent fixture of mixed methods research, but not all mixed methods research includes data transformation.

Data transformation may well be ubiquitous to mixed methods research, but that does not mean that it does not generate its own set of lively debate and controversy. Researchers operating largely from either a qualitative or quantitative perspective each put forward different paradigmatic views about data transformation. Harry Wolcott (1994), a name well-known to ethnographers, simply describes data transformation as what a researcher actually does with data once it is collected (1994). Sandelowski captured the gulf in argumentation when she observed, "In quantitative research, the appeal to numbers gives studies their rhetorical power. . . . By contrast, in qualitative research, numbers are looked on with some suspicion as overly simplifying the complex" (2003, p. 339). While qualitative researchers may object to quantifying as being too simplistic and stripping data of its context, quantitative researchers are likely to focus their ire on the potential abuse of using statistical procedures with a small qualitative sample that is neither randomly selected nor representative of a wider population. With its ready potential to count words or to identify the most frequently used words in a passage, the rise of the use of qualitative software has probably contributed to uneasiness about the potential misuses of counting with qualitative data.

PURPOSE, GOALS, AND CONTRIBUTION OF THE CHAPTER

This is the third and final chapter about mixed methods analytical strategies. My main purpose in this chapter is to introduce different ways that data transformation can be used as a mixed method analytical approach.

The principal goals of the chapter are to

1. acknowledge controversies related to data transformation, particularly to converting qualitative data to numbers;
2. distinguish between quantifying and quantitizing of qualitative data;
3. describe ways that quantitizing of qualitative data can be used to document relationships, demonstrate change over time, and identify clusters of individuals;
4. explore strategies for qualitizing quantitative data, including by developing case narratives or profiles;
5. provide exemplars of published reports using a mixed methods approach with case study research; and
6. sensitize readers to the importance of recognizing conventions regarding appropriate sample size for using quantified data in statistical procedures.

Contributions of the Chapter

Except at the most perfunctory level, there has been limited discussion of the ways that data transformation can be used to advance the sophistication and effectiveness of mixed method analytical procedures. The principal contribution of this chapter is that it provides a far more detailed discussion of data transformation than has been consolidated heretofore in a single location. In addition, although others have provided examples of how both qualitative and quantitative data have been transformed for purposes of analysis (e.g., Bazeley, 2009; Teddlie & Tashakkori, 2009), no one has foregrounded tables from exemplary mixed methods publications as a way to provide a detailed commentary on different approaches to using data transformation as a mixed methods analytical strategy.

A second contribution of the chapter is the addition to the methodological literature of a preliminary discussion of the use of mixed methods approaches to case study research. Given that it is explicitly framed as a method that incorporates data from multiple sources, it is surprising that so little has been published that explores the compatibility of a mixed methods approach with case study research.

In the section of the chapter about quantifying, I defy convention somewhat by putting forward as an exemplar a study by Mazzola, Walker, Schockley, and Spector (2011) that achieves its principal insight by integrating two qualitatively derived variables. Small (2011), among others, supports this strategy as an example of mixed method data analysis, while the convention still is to argue that this does not truly embody mixed methods because qualitative and quantitative data are not combined. The more expansive view of the definition of mixed methods research is intended to invite continued experimentation in its uses.

Organization of the Chapter

Attention in this chapter is almost equally divided by the two main approaches to data transformation: converting qualitative data into quantitative data (quantifying or quantitizing) and converting quantitative data to case studies, profiles, themes, or clusters (qualitizing) as were first introduced in the preceding chapter (Chapter 6). I illustrate the two approaches to data transformation with four examples and one exemplar that I explore more fully with the use of the template that has become a standard across the chapter. Because data transformation is the only aspect of the article discussed, I do not provide the standard template for the four examples. We turn our attention, first, to the strategies for converting qualitative data.

QUANTIFYING AND QUANTITIZING QUALITATIVE DATA

Quantitizing, the process of assigning numerical values to textual data for purposes of further analysis is a staple of mixed method research (Sandelowski, Voils, & Knafl, 2009). It is generally accomplished by attaching codes to passages and, subsequently, attaching numerical values to the codes either through a deductive process (i.e., hypothesis generated from the literature) or inductively through an emergent approach. The inclusion of quantitized data does not necessarily mean that the research is mixed methods (Maxwell, 2010).

Similar to the analytical procedures in other methods, the purpose of quantitizing is to aggregate or compare data in order to discern patterns of regularities and irregularities and to convert qualitative data to a form that is amenable for statistical manipulation (Sandelowski et al., 2009). Procedures to transform qualitative data into numbers or scores can be done with purpose of (a) merging or consolidating the data for further analysis; (b) confirmation; (c) typology development; (d) facilitating comparison or showing relationships; (e) exploring, predicting, or explaining; or (f) aiding in detecting a temporal or time-based sequence (Bazeley, 2009).

Quantifying

Possibly as a counteroffensive to the widespread but mistaken assumption that any research that quantifies qualitative data is mixed methods, some mixed method scholars have moved to underscore a distinction between quantifying and quantitizing data (e.g., Teddlie & Tashakkori, 2009). In this context, *quantifying* data refers to the process of reporting on the prevalence of qualitative code, themes, or categories either by reporting on total occurrences or total number and percentage of participants mentioning it. Quantifying is simply counting, while quantitizing involves mixing because it is done with the purpose of combining qualitative and quantitative data for further analysis. Sandelowski made this point forcibly when she wrote,

> Without further analysis, a simple frequency count of topics raised by participants in response to an open-ended question or of the number and percent of respondents offering a reply that falls in a qualitative category can hardly be considered an example of mixing qualitative and quantitative research. (2003, p. 323)

Attending to Sample Size

Other than the most straightforward types of quantifying that involve the reporting of simple frequency counts, the process of quantitizing raises a myriad of complex issues related to sample size that challenge conventional practices in qualitative research. The intent to quantitize textual data for the purpose of using mixed method analytical procedures generally requires a sample size that is much larger than the 20 or fewer participants that are characteristic of most qualitative research (Castro, Kellison, Boyd, & Kopak, 2010). Castro et al. advise that, depending on the type of statistical procedures planned, a sample of between 20 and 40 respondents is necessary to conduct an integrated mixed methods analysis. While this number may seem impossibly ambitious for a qualitative study that involves nonmechanistic ways of coding, it is well below the 64 participants recommended by Onwuegbuzie and Leech (2004) as the sample size for causal and comparative designs. Because the number of respondents not addressing a category may further skew the data, Castro et al. further caution against using thematic categories in statistical analyses that contain less than 20% of the responses. The demand for a comparatively large sample size in the qualitative portion of a mixed method study is a quality that is more characteristic of team-based than individually powered research. It may be one reason for why the range of different types of mixed method analytical procedures that are used in practice seems relatively narrow.

EXAMPLES OF QUANTIFYING AND QUANTITIZING QUALITATIVE DATA

Research is often about combining an innovative topic area with a tried-and-true design to achieve replication of results across diverse settings. The ability to replicate the results using the same procedures is a gold standard for all types of research. In this section, I present four real-world examples to illustrate a range of ways that transforming qualitative data through quantitizing has been used as an analytical procedure in high-quality mixed method research publications. I reproduce or extract data from tables appearing in each of these publications in order to demonstrate a range of ways that quantitizing can be used to produce meta-inferences or conclusions that derive from both qualitative and quantitative data. Presenting data in visual form is important not only to advancing the analysis but also to communicating results and conclusions with an audience in a succinct way. By orienting my discussion around examples of figures and tables that reflect quantization, I underscore how important visualization is to social science research, not only to advance the analysis but also as a rhetorical device to communicate with the reader (McGill, 1990). Tables add to credibility by demonstrating the link between data and conclusions. Their sequencing shows steps in the development of a conclusion. The topic of visualizations and graphics is one I take up again in Chapter 9.

Table 7.1 summarizes the type of mixing and purpose of mixing in analysis in four mixed methods articles I use as examples in this section. The examples should help others to envision different ways that it is possible to accomplish mixing using data transformation when the sample size allows.

The figures and tables I have selected to include in this section use straightforward approaches to accomplish mixing during data analysis through data transformation in ways that have contributed to innovative insight. Each found a practical, meaningful way to link qualitative themes with a quantitative score or index on a related construct. They challenge the idea that the qualitative component of a study necessarily plays a subservient role in a mixed methods study involving large quantitative databases. Only one of the examples (Odom et al., 2006) features a graphic that is likely to require qualitative software such as NVIVO or AtlasTi to produce. As important as this software is to large qualitative projects, this approach is consistent with my intent throughout the book to introduce basic strategies for conducting mixed methods research. For this reason, I avoid discussion of the small number of articles that are out there that use very advanced quantitative techniques to incorporate both qualitative and quantitative data.

The overriding feature that is most noteworthy about the examples is that each was able to garner a sample of participants that is considerably larger than the 20–40 that Castro et al. (2010) and others (e.g., Small, 2011) have said is characteristic for most research with a qualitative component. With the exception of Young and Jaganath (2013), it is also worth noting that all of the projects are relatively ambitious in that they are either part of a long-term research project or, similar to Odom et al. (2006), conducted with the benefit of external funding. It is very likely that this has something to do with their ability to secure unusually large samples.

TABLE 7.1 ■ Examples of Tables and Figures Reflecting Different Purposes for Quantitizing			
Analytical Procedure	**Purpose of the Table or Figure**	**Source of Example**	**Qualitative Sample Size**
Mixing qualitative variables	Document relationships	Mazzola et al., 2011	199
Mixing qualitative and quantitative variables	Document relationships	Castro et al., 2010	52
	Demonstrate a temporal change	Young & Jaganath, 2013	57
	Identify clusters of individuals	Odom et al., 2006	80

Design features, such as timing of the data collection, are not included in the table because they are varied. One author (i.e., Mazzola et al., 2011) used a concurrent design for data collection, while the others used either a sequential or multiphase design. Only the article by Young and Jaganath (2013) reported on results of a study that had a longitudinal design.

Example 1 From Mazzola, Walker, Schockley, & Spector (2011): Quantifying Two Qualitatively Derived Variables for Purposes of Demonstrating a Relationship

In an article appearing in the *Journal of Mixed Methods Research*, Mazzola and his colleagues (2011) set out to identify sources of stress among graduate students and to determine what kind of link there was between the different sources of stress and physical and psychological symptoms. They used a classic concurrent mixed model design by simultaneously collecting qualitative and quantitative data through an online survey. The qualitative portion of the instrument included open-ended questions that were treated as critical incidents. The critical incident technique is generally classified as a qualitative procedure. It is a "qualitative interview procedure which facilitates the investigation of significant occurrences (events, incidents, processes, or issues) identified by the respondent, the way these are managed, and the outcomes in terms of perceived effects" (Chell, 1998, p. 56). Each critical incident was coded by multiple researchers for the type of stress, level of stress, and associated psychological symptoms. The respondent's level of stress was evaluated from 1 (for very little stress) to 5 (for a high level of stress). This created many opportunities for mixing during analysis. It also lends itself to intensity scale coding. This is a type of text-in-context coding that was explored in Chapter 5.

Although Mazzola et al. (2011) also present tables reporting on the results of statistical analysis, two of their tables illustrate how quantitized data can be used to provide evidence of a connection between two or more variables without using statistical procedures. Table 7.2 reproduces Table 3 from the Mazzola et al. (2011) article. It summarizes the frequency and percentage of the 177 participants in the categories of stressors and psychological strains identified in the critical incidents.

This table is a classic example of quantifying. It quantifies qualitatively derived results without transforming them. Qualitative and quantitative data are not mixed in this table, but it served as the basis for a type of mixing in a subsequent table.

Table 7.3, duplicated below, illustrates how quantifying qualitative data can be used to support an argument for a relationship between variables. In this case, mixing is achieved by juxtaposing two qualitatively derived variables that emerge from an inductive coding of critical incidents. The table only shows partial results from 177 participants. Data are only shown for the top four most frequently reported sources of stress for graduate students (work overload, interpersonal conflict, constraints, and evaluation/recognition issues).

This table from Mazzola et al. (2011) serves the purpose of supporting a relationship between stressors and psychological strains and suggests that different symptoms are linked to different strains that were later tested with statistical procedures. For example, frustration was the most common type of strain associated with practices

TABLE 7.2 ■ Quantifying Qualitatively Derived Categories of Stressors and Strains	
	Frequency, n (%)
Stressors	
Work overload	53 (29.9)
Interpersonal conflict	40 (22.6)
Constraints	29 (16.4)
Evaluations/recognition	25 (14.1)
Conditions of employment	8 (4.5)
Time and effort wasted	6 (3.4)
Role conflicts	6 (3.4)
Role ambiguity	6 (3.4)
Lack of control/autonomy	1 (0.6)
Other	3 (1.7)
No event reported	30 (n.a.)
Psychological strains	
Frustration	75 (42.4)
Anger	60 (33.9)
Anxiety/worry	48 (27.1)
Sadness/depression	35 (19.8)
Annoyance	30 (16.9)
Overwhelmed	25 (14.1)
Disappointed	14 (7.9)
Acceptance	11 (6.2)
Scared	9 (5.1)
Withdrawn	3 (1.7)
Other	45 (25.4)

Note: Percentages for both stressors and strains are calculated out of 177, the total number of participants who reported a stressful event. n.a. stands for "not applicable" as the frequency of stressors was computed out of those who reported an event, and those who reported "No events" were not part of that group.

Source: Mazzola, J. J., Walker, E. J., Schockley, K. M., & Spector, P. E. (2011). Examining stress in graduate assistants: Combining qualitative and quantitative survey methods. *Journal of Mixed Methods Research*, 5(3), 198–211. doi: 10.1177/1558689811402086.

that interfere with the ability to perform (what they called *constraints*), while anger was more commonly identified as the strain associated with interpersonal conflict.

The authors acknowledge issues related to insufficient sample size that explain why only partial data is reported in the table. They observed that the small number of

TABLE 7.3 ■ Quantifying Qualitative Data to Explore the Relationship Between Variables					
Stressor	**Psychological Strain**				
	Anger	**Frustration**	**Anxiety**	**Annoyance**	**Overwhelmed**
Work overload	10 (18.9)	8 (15.1)	21 (39.6)	6 (11.3)	14 (24.5)
Interpersonal conflict	20 (50.0)	18 (45.0)	2 (5.0)	10 (25.0)	2 (5.0)
Constraints	2 (6.9)	21 (72.4)	9 (31.0)	6 (20.7)	4 (13.8)
Evaluations/ recognition	7 (28.0)	9 (36.0)	10 (40.0)	2 (8.0)	2 (8.0)

Note: Figures in parentheses are percentages. Table excerpted from Mazzola, Walker, Schocklcy, & Spector (2011).

Source: Mazzola, J. J., Walker, E. J., Schockley, K. M., & Spector, P. E. (2011). Examining stress in graduate assistants: Combining qualitative and quantitative survey methods. *Journal of Mixed Methods Research, 5*(3), 198–211. doi: 10.1177/1558689811402086.

respondents in a number of the cells in the table duplicated above complicated their ability to make comparisons and to substantiate the link between the type of stressor and associated psychological strain. In a subsequent table, they achieved mixing by using quantitative scores from standardized instruments to compare the differences in the stress scales by type of stressor (not duplicated here). Even with a relatively large original qualitative sample, they only had enough respondents to compare mean differences on the stress scales derived from other quantitative instruments on the top three most frequently reported types of stress.

Example 2 From Castro, Kellison, Boyd, & Kopak (2010): Demonstrating a Relationship between Qualitatively and Quantitatively Derived Variables

The purpose of the Castro et al. (2010) article also appearing in the *Journal of Mixed Method Research* differs from those reviewed up to now. Rather than to present the results of a single study, their purpose was to illustrate different ways to conduct integrated mixed methods analysis by using examples from over ten years of research, including about Hispanic men's identification with positive and negative manifestations of concepts of masculinity and family (e.g., machismo). One of the tables presented in the article moves beyond what Mazzola et al. (2011) were able to accomplish by directly juxtaposing qualitative and quantitative data in a way that convincingly demonstrates a significant relationship.

Table 7.4 reproduces Table 3 from the Castro et al. (2010) article. In this case, mixing was accomplished without quantifying qualitative data. The table provides what the authors label as a "contrasting group analysis" (p. 354). It is based on a qualitative approach to extreme case sampling involving outliers. The table contrasts quotes about machismo between five men scoring the highest on a life satisfaction scale and another five men scoring at the lowest end of the same scale.

TABLE 7.4 ■ Contrasting Group Analysis of Qualitative Themes			
Case Number	**Life Satisfaction Score**	**Quoted Statement About Machismo Self-Identification**	**Story Lines**
Highest on Life Satisfaction			*Story Line I*: Men who value and engage in family caretaking exhibit high levels of *caballerismo* (positive machismo) in their male gender role identity, are giving and responsible, and experience high levels of life satisfaction
10133	2.17	"I care about my family" "For me, it's acting like a gentleman"	
10147	1.56	"I'm respectful for women" "I never bring shame to the family"	
10164	1.50	"I do my best to take care of my family"	
10343	1.48	"I treat women with respect and don't beat them"	
10371	1.42	"I bring home money and make sure there is food on the table"	
Lowest on Life Satisfaction			*Story Line II*: Men who do not value or engage in family caretaking exhibit low levels of *caballerismo* (positive machismo) in their male gender role identity, are selfish and irresponsible, and experience low levels of life satisfaction.
10160	−1.15	"I have my flaws, I'm selfish" "I hold a grudge forever" "I'm not afraid to cry in front of others, even strangers"	
10162	−1.21	"I don't identify with working hard or taking care of my family"	
10149	−1.67	"I never had aspirations to have any children or family responsibility"	
10399	−2.58	"In prison, I acted in ways I didn't want to, and even today I still do"	
10370	−2.63	"I'm lazy, I'm selfish, I have a short fuse" "I have low self-esteem"	

Source: Castro, F. G., Kellison, J. G., Boyd, S. J., & Kopak, A. (2010). A methodology for conducting integrative mixed methods research and data analyses. *Journal of Mixed Methods Research*, 4(4), 342–360. DOI:10.1177/1558689810382916.

The linking of qualitative and quantitative data (a satisfaction score) in the same table for analytical purposes makes this a mixing table. The clear alignment of quotes reflecting positive views of machismo with a high life satisfaction score and quotes reflecting negative views with a negative life satisfaction score builds a persuasive case for how the two are interconnected without the use of any statistical procedures. In the example considered next, Young and Jaganath (2013) use a statistical procedure to demonstrate a relationship between qualitative and quantitative data.

Example 3 From Young and Jaganath (2013): Quantifying Qualitative Themes to Show Change Over Time

You will recall that we reviewed features of the article reporting on the results of a study about using social networking to promote HIV prevention among 57 high-risk youths by Young and Jaganath (2013) in Chapter 5. After using qualitative methods to identify themes in the posts made by participants over the course of twelve weeks on a social media site, the authors used a multivariate analysis to demonstrate that participants who ultimately requested HIV testing were significantly more likely to be engaged in conversations related to prevention. None of the other conversational themes were significantly related to this outcome.

One of the figures included in the article by Young and Jaganath (2013) is a good example of how quantifying can be used to demonstrate changes in attitude over time. This is an example of how a mixed methods approach makes it possible to broaden the range of analytical procedures that can be used with qualitative data when the sample size is sufficient. A simple form of mixing during analysis is represented visually in this figure because qualitative themes are compared across a quantitative dimension of time.

Figure 7.1 duplicates Figure 1 from the Young and Jaganath (2013) article. It contains bar graphs for each of six conversational themes and compares change in the percentage of occurrence over each of three 4-week time periods.

Among other things, the graph documents a steady decline over time in what was characterized as friendly conversation and an increase in the proportion of entries about prevention/testing and stigma. Subsequent analysis of the content of 485 conversations that further mixed the qualitative and quantitative data revealed that only the conversations about prevention and testing played a significant role in predicting a request for HIV testing.

Example 4 From Odom et al. (2006): Quantifying Qualitative Themes to Distinguish Groups

It is not uncommon for a researcher in an educational setting to launch a research project with the purpose of distinguishing low- and high-performing groups, classrooms, or schools. Odom and his colleagues (2006) did something similar in an ambitious project that was designed to distinguish the characteristics of 80 socially accepted and socially rejected preschool children with disabilities distributed nationally across 16 programs. The impetus that drove their work was the hope that if early identification was possible, an evidence-based intervention program could be designed to promote social competence for the group of preschool students who had difficulty interacting with peers in a positive manner. Although the multiphase, multilevel design and ambitious

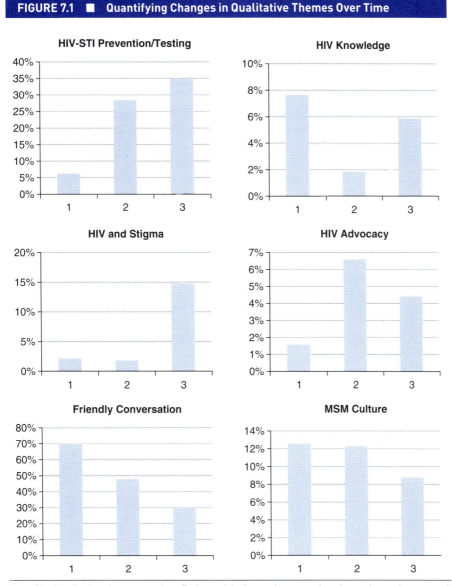

FIGURE 7.1 ■ Quantifying Changes in Qualitative Themes Over Time

Note: The distribution of posts over time. Each graph indicates the proportion of posts in a topic compared to all posts within a 4-week time period.

Source: Young, S. D., & Jaganath, D. (2013). Online social networking for HIV education and prevention: A mixed-methods analysis. *Sexually Transmitted Diseases, 40* (2), 162–167. doi: 10.1097/OLQ.0b013e318278bd12.

scope of data collection make this an unrealistic model to replicate in research that all but the most ambitious graduate student might be willing to undertake, it would be difficult to find another example of an article that better leverages an integrated mixed method approach to both data collection and analysis.

I introduced this article earlier in this chapter because it is a rare example of a single project that used both types of data transformation. During an initial phase of qualitative analysis, a type of qualitization was used as themes were developed from case summaries of observational field notes. Further data transformation occurred through quantitizing as matrices were constructed to distinguish the themes that characterized the accepted and rejected children. These were recontextualized in the final stage by the use of brief vignettes.

Table 7.5 reproduces a table from Odom et al. (2006) that quantifies qualitative data by listing the frequency of the occurrence of eight different themes that distinguished socially rejected children.

Different themes distinguished socially accepted and socially rejected children. The figure that follows the above table in Odom et al. (2006) is a theme cluster by child cluster matrix (Miles, Huberman, & Saldana, 2014) that can be produced by using qualitative software such as NVivo. Both qualitatively and quantitatively derived data were used to construct the matrix (Figure 7.2).

TABLE 7.5 ■ Quantifying Themes That Distinguish Socially Rejected Children		
Social rejection	**Frequency of themes**	**Definition**
Speech-language-communication problems	14	The child does not effectively convey his-her thoughts, ideas, or social goals to others.
Conflict with peers	12	The child commits actions to which another child objects.
Lacks social ski lls	10	The child does not have or use the necessary social skills for engaging other children in positive social internclions.
Disruptive in class	8	The child does not follow teacher directions, does not participate in classroom routines, and/or engages in tantrums or protests when teachers attempt to direct the child's activities.
Socially isolated or withdrawn	7	The child actively withdraws from or avoids interactions with peers.
Physically aggressive toward peers	6	The child hits, pushes, shouts at, or speaks negatively to peers in the class.
Prefers adult interactions	2	The child chooses to talk or play exclusively with adults.
Lacks play skills	1	The child does not have the necessary symbolic play skills to participate in playful activities with peers in the classroom.

Source: Odom, S. L., Li, S., Sandall, S., Zercher, C., Marquart, J. M., & Brown, W. H. (2006). Social acceptance and rejection of preschool children with disabilities: A mixed method analysis. *Journal of Educational Psychology, 98,* (4), 807–823.

FIGURE 7.2 ■ Quantified Themes in Cluster Analysis

Cluster	Child Diagnosis	#	Social Withdrawal				Conflict/Aggression			
			PAI	LPS	SIW	DIC	CWP	PAP	LSS	SLC
R1	MR	11							X	
	MR	14							X	
	HI	9					X			
	DD	15							X	X
	SI	20					X			
R2	SI	10				X				
	SI	12								
	DD	17				X				
	EBD	18				X			X	
	SI	7				X				
R3	EBD	2					X	X	X	
	SI	3					X	X		
	EBD	5					X	X		
R4	A	1			X					
	DD	19								
	A	16			X					
	MR	8			X	X				
	A	6			X	X				
R5	A	13			X					
	DD	22	X		X					
	A	4		X						X
Outlier	MR	21	X						X	

Note: Theme Cluster × Child Cluster matrix for socially rejected children. PAI = prefers adult interactions; LPS = lacks play skills; SIW = socially isolated or withdrawn; DIC = disruptive in class; CWP = conflict with peers; PAP = physically aggressive towards peers; LSS = lacks social skills; SLC = speech–language–communication problems; MR = mental retardation; HI = hearing impairment; DD = developmental delays; SI = speech–language impairment; EBD = social–emotional, behavioral, or attenion-deficit disorder; A = autism–pervasive developmental delay.

Source: Odom, S. L., Li, S., Sandall, S., Zercher, C., Marquart, J. M., & Brown, W. H. (2006). Social acceptance and rejection of preschool children with disabilities: A mixed method analysis. *Journal of Educational Psychology, 98,* (4), 807–823.

The darkened cells in the matrix highlight the point that the behaviors of most of the socially rejected preschoolers were characterized by either social withdrawal or conflict/aggression.

QUALITIZING NUMERIC DATA

Qualitizing is identified as one way to accomplish data transformation in mixed method research (Sandelowski, 2001; Teddlie & Tashakkori, 2009). In its purist form, it is a mixed methods analytical strategy where measures on quantitative instruments are woven together in a narrative form either for intrinsic interest or for the more instrumental purpose of further analysis through cross-case comparison. Qualitized data can be incorporated to create anything from a relatively brief narrative profile (Teddlie & Tashakkori, 2009) to a fully fleshed-out case study that considers the interplay between elements of the context and the phenomenon of interest. One useful, if underutilized, mixed method way to qualitize is to dimensionalize quantitatively derived factors or clusters by developing narrative profiles or summaries that capture those properties.

While much has been written about its counterpart, quantitizing, only the most cursory attention has been given in the method methods literature to qualitizing. In fact, after much searching, I would say with some conviction that examples of qualitizing, where a narrative is constructed based solely on scores on quantitative instruments, is not something that is easy to locate in the published literature. Most case studies either use a qualitative approach to analysis that merges data from multiple qualitative sources (e.g., interviews, observations, and documents) or a mixed method approach that links qualitative and quantitative data. It is possible that narrative profiles of the type described by Teddlie and Tashakkori (2009) are sometime used as steps in the analytical process, but not in ways that are reflected in a published product.

Case summaries played a pivotal role in the mixed methods analytical procedures used in an exceptionally well-crafted study of the social acceptance and rejection of preschool students by their peers conducted by Odom and his colleagues (2006) and described in the previous section. The case summaries of rejected and accepted preschool students used data transformation but are not pure examples of qualitization because they were constructed from both qualitative and quantitative data. They incorporated scores on a quantitative observational instrument measuring interaction between peers, findings from interviews with teachers, and field notes recording observations of peer-to-peer interaction. Analysis of the summaries by three of the members of the team produced themes that later proved effective in distinguishing the behaviors of students who were accepted by their peers from those who were rejected.

While rarely an amalgamation of only quantitative data, the prominence of analytical procedures that integrate multiple sources of data in a narrative is one of the reasons that case study research is so amenable to a mixed method approach.

MIXED METHOD APPROACHES TO CASE STUDY

Although often housed within the family of qualitative approaches, case study research is well suited to a mixed methods approach (Kitchenham, 2010; Luck, Jackson, & Usher, 2006). This compatibility is evident in the definition of *case study*, where it is explicitly situated as an approach that requires the collection of multiple sources of data. This feature is incorporated in Yin's definition of a case study: "an empirical inquiry that investigates a contemporary phenomenon within the real-life context; when the boundaries between the phenomenon and the context are not clearly evident; and in which multiple sources of evidence are used" (2006, p. 23). The types of data collected for a case are often quite diverse. They can include such sources as documents, direct observation, surveys, archival records, interviews, and physical artifacts (Stake, 2003; Yin, 2006). Case studies are presented as narratives that often link qualitative and quantitative data. A key feature that distinguishes a case study from other types of narrative profiles is the philosophical assumption that the analysis depends on an understanding that is embedded within a very specific setting and time frame.

There is surprisingly little that has been published that explicitly explores mixed methods approaches to case study research. In the next section, we explore three different aspects of a mixed methods approach to case study. First, we consider some ways that foundational assumptions of case study research are compatible with a mixed methods approach. Next, we take on the topic of how mixing can occur rather seamlessly in case study research. Finally, we turn to two different examples of research in educational settings to see how a mixed method approach has been used with case study research.

Philosophical Assumptions of Case Study That Are Well-Suited to Mixed Methods

Case study research has been described as "a bridge that spans the research paradigms" (Luck et al., 2006, p. 103). In addition to the expectation that cases are built from multiple types of data, there are other aspects about the philosophical assumptions undergirding case study research that mesh with a pragmatic approach to mixed methods. It is an approach that has been explicitly framed as being suitable to either a quantitative or qualitative approach (Yin, 2003). It is amenable to mixed methods because it is not characterized as either a method or methodology, but as an approach. Stake, a leading spokesperson for case study research, places the emphasis on what is produced rather than a specified set of procedures when he observed, "Case study is not a methodological approach but a choice of what is to be studied. By whatever methods, we chose to study the case" (2003, p. 134). Case study is described as an approach because there is no agreed-upon set of prescribed data collection and analytical procedures nor one set of philosophical or methodological assumptions (Luck et al., 2006). Instead, methods are selected in relation to the nature of the case and the research questions (Luck et al., 2006).

After nearly three decades of writing about it, Stake (2003) continues to see tremendous flexibility in the potential uses of case study. A case can involve a single individual, organization, or group (Stoecker, 1991) or social or political event that is selected as an example or because of its uniqueness. It can also be presented as an amalgamation of more than one organization, individual, or event. When confidentiality is an issue, cases are sometimes fictionalized. The purpose of a case study is often to understand some abstract phenomenon or the interrelationship of a set of constructs.

Stake (2003) classifies case studies into three broad categories: intrinsic, instrumental, and collective. A mixed method evaluation, such as that conducted by Ivankova and Stick (2007), can be an example of an *intrinsic case study*. They are picked purely because of their inherent interest or because they are exemplary in some way. This type of case study is often used for heuristic (e.g., to illustrate a point) or pedagogical and teaching purposes. For example, a case study of a highly effective organization, leader, or school might be used to communicate an ideal worth emulating rather than to imply that it is representative.

What Stake (2003) calls an *instrumental case study* is far more common in the empirical literature than an intrinsic case study. An instrumental case is picked for its potential to add more depth and nuance to the insight about a phenomenon such as a process or a construct. "The case is of secondary interest," according to Stake; "It plays a supportive role because it facilitates the understanding of something else" (p. 136). In contrast to the intrinsic case study, an instrumental case study can be used to test or to build theory or to strengthen explanatory power through divergent perspectives (Eisenhardt, 1989). The variety of ways in which a phenomenon manifests itself can be demonstrated through the comparison of multiple cases.

The *collective case study* is a variation of the instrumental case study (Stake, 2003). This is when a number of cases are studied to understand a wider phenomenon. "They are chosen," according to Stake, "because it is believed that understanding them will lead to better understanding, perhaps better theorizing, about a still larger collection of cases" (p. 137). Cross-case comparisons are a type of mixing that contributes to the rigor and credibility of case study research and facilitates an entirely different level of analysis through synthesis. Researchers (such as Jimenez-Castellanos, 2010, discussed below) conducted a cross-case comparison to identify similarities and differences in the way constructs or variables operated across cases and how these might be explained by differences in context.

The expectation for appropriate sample size in case study research varies by the purpose or aim of the study and carries a decidedly qualitative mindset. Guidelines range from a low of one to a recommended high of 15 (Teddlie & Tashakkori, 2009). When the purpose is to identify an intrinsically interesting case, sample size can be a single individual or an organization. Three to five cases are recommended generally (Creswell, 2002). Eisenhardt (1989) raises the bar for sample size when the goal of case study research is to develop theory. To avoid the risk of building theory that is based on an idiosyncratic situation, she recommends sample size of between four and 10.

In addition to the assumption that the case will be constructed by integrating information from multiple sources of data and that it is adaptable to a variety of different approaches to sampling, data collection, and analysis, the compatibility of case study research to a mixed methods approach extends to the topic of mixing. There are multiple ways that qualitative and quantitative data can be mixed in case study research. These include (a) by linking qualitative and quantitative data in the case report, (b) through sampling procedures, and (c) during analysis, including through cross-case analysis.

Mixing by Linking Qualitative and Quantitative Data in a Case Report

Qualitative and quantitative data can be linked in a case study and across cases in ways that can be considered a form of mixing. **Linking** *is a type of mixed method analytical procedure where qualitative and quantitative data are interwoven in a case narrative.* This is a different analytical approach than compiling a case narrative that summarizes the results from multiple quantitative instruments or measures (i.e., qualitizing). It also differs from an approach that compares cases that vary widely in terms of constructs or themes that emerged from the qualitative analysis.

Accomplishing Mixing Through Sampling Procedures in Case Study Research

In Chapter 5, we talked about the potential to use both probabilistic (e.g., representative) and purposeful sampling in a single study as one of the strengths of mixed methods research. This is a point in the research process where there is a potential for a good deal of creativity. A researcher designing a mixed methods study that will provide access to both qualitative and quantitative data about a group of participants has many options for sampling procedures at his or her disposal. The combination of purposeful and probabilistic sampling procedures serves the dual purpose of adding to overall quality of the research by bolstering the claims that can be made about the transferability of the findings.

The procedures used to select a case for further analysis depend on the purpose or aim of the study and the approach that is used to select them. The choice varies depending on whether the goal is to identify unique or special cases (i.e., an intrinsic case) or to pursue instrumental cases. Instrumental cases include those that are chosen because they are typical or representative of the phenomenon. Cross-case comparisons often involve the analysis of a number of cases that are selected for purposes of revealing variation. Another approach is to compare outlier or extreme cases, such as by picking cases that differ dramatically in their expression of qualitative themes. Others might choose a very targeted form of purposeful sampling (e.g., theoretical sampling) to identify participants to profile in a case study in order to more fully explore the causal mechanisms that might explain the connection between variables. (**Theoretical sampling** *is a type of purposive sampling used in grounded theory to develop theoretical categories by application to a new sample of participants, sometimes in a different location. It is emergent in the sense that the sample is not determined until after the first phase of the analysis.*)

TABLE 7.6 ■ Sampling Procedures in Mixed Methods Case Study Research				
	Type of Case	**Criteria**		
Driving Purpose	**Sampling Procedure**	**Qualitative**	**Quantitative**	**Mixed Method**
Embody uniqueness	Critical case	Select using qualitative themes	Select using scores on a quantitative measure	Select using relative weight of a quantified/ qualitative theme or based on a composite qualitative/ quantitative scale
Representativeness	Average or typical case			
Comparison	Negative case			
	Extreme/Outlier			
	Maximum variation case studies			
Theory development	Theoretical sampling			

Table 7.6 identifies some of the most frequently used sampling procedures in case study research and links them to the purpose that might drive their selection. The types of sampling procedures are derived from typologies summarized by Collins, Onwuegbuzie, and Jiao (2006), Teddlie and Tashakkori (2009), and Teddlie and Yu (2007), among others. It is not an exhaustive list of all types of sampling procedures but a selection of those that are particularly adaptable to mixed method approaches to case study research.

Table 7.6 is designed to illustrate that it is possible to develop criteria for selecting a case study or group of case studies based on qualitative, quantitative, or a mix of qualitative and quantitative criteria. With a qualitative approach, a single case or multiple cases might be purposefully selected because it is a critical case. A critical case might embody all of the major themes that emerged during the qualitative phase of analysis. On the other hand, a researcher might use a similar qualitative approach to choose outlier or extreme cases in order to explore elements of the environment that might explain differences in settings or the phenomenon. A composite measure that combines quantitative score(s) and quantified qualitative scores is a mixed method sampling procedure that could prove useful in case study research.

Exemplars of mixed method sampling procedures in case study research. The two exemplars discussed in the next section used a quantitative approach to identify a sample (i.e., Cooper, 2014; Jimenez-Castellanos, 2010). They illustrate how a well-conceived sampling procedure can provide a form of mixing that bridges the qualitative and quantitative strands of a mixed methods study. Both used a form of maximum variation by combining scores on several quantitative measures to identify between three and five cases for further analysis. In case study research, maximum variation sampling involves intentionally selecting a range of cases that differ on the central dimension of interest in order to facilitate comparison.

The two studies share some additional features. Both deal with issues concerning significant policy implications for public schools in the U.S. One is about practices that promote engagement and involved case studies of five classrooms (Cooper, 2014), while the second developed three case studies to explore the link between physical, fiscal, and personnel resources and student achievement (Jimenez-Castellanos, 2010). Cooper compared the classrooms of teachers with different teaching practices, while Jimenez-Castellanos' unit of analysis was Title 1 and non-Title 1 schools that differed in terms of the number of the percentage of students that were low income and received federal subsidies for a free lunch program. Both authors used a sequential approach to the analysis, with the emphasis placed on the quantitative analysis. Both used multiple sources of data and produced narratives that effectively incorporated both qualitative and quantitative data.

In both of the exemplars, the goal of sampling was to find an explanation for differences across the settings through a cross-case comparison. The sampling logic can be described as quantitative because the goal was not to pick a case for its intrinsic interest or because it modeled a setting considered exemplary but to facilitate comparison across settings with different contexts. In both cases, the parameters for selecting the cases could not be fully anticipated at the onset. Instead, the selection criteria emerged during the first phase of the analysis, when the most salient points of comparison emerged.

The Jimenez-Castellanos (2010) article illustrates a creative variation of what Stake (2003) refers to as the collective case study. Rather than summarizing resource characteristics of a single school, Jimenez-Castellanos contrasted the resource characteristics of more than one school in each case. Case 1, for example, included data from four schools, while Case 2 and Case 3 each summarized information from two schools. Comparison across the cases was facilitated by the organization around three different types of resources issues: fiscal, personnel, and facilities.

One indicator of the quality of the sampling strategy used by Jimenez-Castellanos (2010) is its contribution to the conclusions of the study in the form of meta-inferences. The insertion of data from qualitative interviews with school principals into the case studies highlighted differences between the schools that were directly related to student achievement. These were access to hidden funds, such as those contributed by parent associations; low turnover among experienced teachers; and newer, more flexible space that facilitated small group interaction among students were strongly associated with student achievement. The ability to generate meta-inferences that integrate conclusions drawn from the quantitative and qualitative strands of a study is one of the principal reasons given to support the argument for the value-added of mixed methods research (Tashakkori & Teddlie, 2008).

An ambitious project undertaken by a doctoral student at Harvard and published in 2014 offers an exceptional example of the use of a mixed methods approach with case study research. In order to demonstrate different ways that teaching practices are related to student engagement, Cooper presented case studies of five carefully selected classrooms. The case studies blended quantitative scores produced from student surveys of three different teaching practices (e.g., connected instruction, lively teaching, and academic rigor) with qualitative interviews and classroom observation.

In the next section, we explore how Cooper took advantage of one of the strengths of a mixed methods approach by weaving together the qualitative and quantitative data at many phases of the research project to produce a fully integrated mixed method study. I extend my discussion of this article beyond those of the other examples presented in the chapter because of the detail the authors provide about how mixing was accomplished across multiple stages of the research project.

EXEMPLARY ARTICLE: MIXED METHOD CASE STUDY RESEARCH BY COOPER (2014)

Although the study is more ambitious than most graduate students can realistically undertake, the Cooper (2014) article has a number of exemplary features that are relevant to our discussion up to this point. These include, at the forefront, that the study meets the definition of being fully integrated and that a meta-inference was produced that could not have been developed without the integration or linking of the qualitative and quantitative data, including through sampling. I have labeled the study as having a quantitative emphasis for reasons that include that the author frames the study as testing an *a priori* theory. I first considered this article in a review I prepared for the Mixed Methods International Research Association (Creamer, 2015).

Figure 7.3 uses the standard template to summarize key features of the mixed methods design of the Cooper (2014) study.

Rather than being constructed exclusively as an amalgamation of quantitative data (i.e., qualitization), the case studies provided by Cooper merge qualitative data from interviews and observations with quantitative data about students' perceptions about the extent that they embodied connective instruction, academic rigor, and lively teaching.

The author uses an unusually wide range of mixed methods analytical procedures to identify, compare, and consolidate thematically similar results by using more than one source or form of data.

Fully integrated mixed methods studies mix qualitative and quantitative data and/or analytical strategies throughout the research process. In addition to mixing at the design phase through posing a pair of linked quantitative and qualitative research questions, there were multiple points of interface during data collection and analysis in the Cooper (2014) study. These are described next.

Mixing Across Stages of the Research Process in the Exemplar

Purpose and design. Cooper demonstrates methodological transparency by explicitly labeling her research questions as quantitative and qualitative:

> *Research Question 1*: Quantitatively: If the hypothesized three-factor structure of connective instruction, academic rigor, and lively teaching is consistent with survey data from high school students, what are the main and interactive effects of these types of practices on engagement?
> *Research Question 2*: Qualitatively: How and why do these types of classroom practices individually and collectively engage students? (p. 370)

The combination of a *what* and a *how* or *why* research question is a classic signature of mixing at the design phase.

FIGURE 7.3 ■ Exemplary Article About Teaching Practices That Promote Student Engagement: Summary of Key Features of Cooper (2014)			
Rationale/Purpose	Development		
Priority	Quantitative		
Timing of Data Collection	Sequential		
Timing of Data Analysis	Sequential		
Mixing	Fully integrated: Yes		
	Design	✖	One qualitative, one quantitative research question
	Data collection	✖	Survey data used to select case studies
	Data analysis	✖	Survey data from students integrated into concept maps for each classroom, then into five case studies
	Inferences	✖	Meta-inference
Meta-inference	Characteristics of the teaching approach are much more strongly related to student engagement than to the characteristics of the individual.		
	Qualitative conclusion	Student engagement was not as high in classrooms where connected instruction was not supplemented with academically challenging activities.	
	Quantitative conclusion	Connected learning had a much stronger connection to student engagement than other teaching practices.	
Value-added	• "The case study enhances our understanding of the nuanced relationship between teaching practice and student engagement" (p. 392), showed ranges of practice within a single classroom (p. 384)		
	• "Survey data were integrated into each concept map to situate individual classrooms within school-wide student perceptions, shedding greater light on classroom practice than teaching individually and collectively related to engagement" (p. 384)		
	• Graphic displays (Venn diagrams, concept maps, conceptually clustered matrices) facilitated cross-case comparisons		

Eighty percent of the students in 581 classrooms with 106 different teachers at a comprehensive high school in Texas completed multiple survey forms designed to evaluate the extent that teachers in their different classes used three sets of teaching practices. These were *connected instruction* (personally meaningful), *lively teaching* (promoting active engagement through games and activities), and *academic rigor* (academically rigorous assignments and conveying a passion for the content). In addition to the quantitative data, qualitative observations and interviews were organized into five case studies in order to illustrate variations in classroom practices related to engagement.

The research questions parallel the way the analyses were conducted. The statistical procedure confirmatory factor analysis was used to document the reliability of the three-factor structure and regression analysis was used to confirm a significant relationship between teaching strategies and student engagement. Case studies confirmed and expanded the quantitative results by revealing that there was a range of practices within and across classrooms.

Data collection and analysis. Data for the qualitative and quantitative phases of the study were collected separately but connected by a mixing strategy that falls under the development type of mixed method design identified by Greene, Caracelli, and Graham (1989) from their content analysis of evaluation studies using mixed methods. Quantitative survey data were collected from 1,132 students who reported on the prevalence of a range of teaching practices in the classes they attended. To further explore the contextual factors conducive to engagement, classrooms were selected based on mean survey scores for each of the three types of teaching practices.

Mixing of multiple sources of qualitative data. Similar to the Mazzola et al. (2011) example reviewed earlier in the chapter, this exemplar has an additional type of mixing that not all researchers see as part of their definition of mixed methods. During the qualitative phase of the analysis, the author mixed a variety of types of qualitative data (e.g., interviews and observations) and from a variety of sources (e.g., students, teachers, and administrators) to develop case studies of five classrooms where students had above-average levels of engagement. She introduced an alternative hypothesis, an analytical strategy strongly associated with quality, by using data from interviews with teachers and administrators to "confirm or challenge the findings of the student interviews" (Cooper, 2014, p. 377). Bazeley (2009) joins Small (2011) in embracing the idea of mixing multiple qualitative data collection techniques as a type of mixing.

Mixing at the stage of drawing inferences. Meta-inferences link or integrate conclusions drawn from the qualitative and quantitative strands of a study. Results from Cooper's study indicated that characteristics of the class were much more strongly related to engagement than characteristics of the individual student. The quantitative analysis led to the conclusion that connected learning had a much stronger relationship to student engagement than the other categories of practice. The conclusions from the qualitative case studies linked to the quantitative results by indicating a wide variation in the way that teachers promoted connected learning. Student engagement was not as high in classes where connected instruction was not supplemented with academically challenging activities.

One clue to the ambitious nature of Cooper's (2014) research is that it was clearly a struggle for her to fit all that was needed to describe the methods and results within the boundaries of the traditional journal article. Were it not for the meta-inference that bonds the principal conclusion of the study and links the sequential quantitative-followed-by-qualitative approaches, it would have been far more feasible for the author to disentangle the two strands of the study and publish them separately.

Value-added. There is considerable value-added by the use of mixed methods in this study. The author pegs her reasons for using mixed methods primarily in terms of confirmation and triangulation, but the case studies add nuance to the understanding of classroom practices that promote engagement. They demonstrate that engagement is maximized when connected learning strategies are used within the context of a demanding academic environment where there are many opportunities for active involvement. The discussion section is exemplary in that it provides a well-developed explanation for the findings that interweaves or mixes insights from both the qualitative and quantitative analyses. Science, technology, engineering, and mathematics (STEM) educators will be heartened to know that three of the five case studies illuminate teaching practices that promote higher-than-average levels of student engagement in science classrooms.

CONCLUSIONS

A stark contrast exists between the possibilities for creative data transformation and the reality that in the mixed method research that appears in journals, there is very little diversity in the way that data transformation is utilized. It is rarely used for purposes other than to report on the results of quantifying qualitative data or themes. Most surprising is the limited use of avowedly mixed method approaches to case study research.

The reality that may underlie the limited ways that data transformation has been used may reflect not only the paradigm issues that raise red flags among journal editors and reviewers about quantifying qualitative data but the hardcore reality that except for a project generously funded by outside sources, the sample size for qualitative data that is required to execute even the most basic of descriptive statistical procedures is beyond that which can be realistically accomplished by the lone researcher. New generations of qualitative software that move beyond mechanistic counting of words may offer more analytical options in the future. While the individual mixed methods researcher may well continue to be hampered by what analytical procedures he or she can use legitimately with transformed data because of sample size issues, we are likely to find that the team-based interdisciplinary research that is so characteristic of mixed methods research is likely to push the frontier of data transformation forward.

Graphics and visualization such as those I have highlighted in this chapter are one of multiple dimensions of guidelines to evaluate the overall quality of mixed methods research. The issue of evaluating the quality of mixed methods research is a topic we take up in the next chapter.

Summary of Key Points

1. Many, but not all, mixed methods analytical procedures utilize data transformation.

2. Quantifying qualitative data to report on the prevalence of themes or categories is a type of data transformation, but it involves counting, not mixing.

3. It is not the least unusual to find a case study that links both qualitative and quantitative data, but it is very unusual to find one that qualitizes by exclusively using quantitative data.

4. One way that mixing occurs in case study research is through the synthesis produced by a cross-case analysis.

5. Qualitative and quantitative data can be linked in a case study without either qualitizing or quantitizing.

6. In mixed methods case study research, separate qualitative and quantitative strands are often linked through sampling procedures.

Key Terms

- Data transformation
- Linking
- Theoretical sampling

Supplemental Activities

1. Imagine that you are in charge of campus safety at a large urban college and you decide to conduct a mixed methods study to triangulate data about the location of campus crimes in the last three years with students' perceptions about the characteristics of safe and unsafe locations on campus. In small groups, discuss different strategies you could use to collect and analyze data for this kind of study.

2. The critical incident technique is highly adaptable to a mixed methods approach. It has been used to understand types of occupational or workplace stress, the factors related to it, and the types of physical and social symptoms it produces. One of its great advantages as a qualitative method is that the unit of analysis is brief descriptions of real-life events provided by participants that can be collected through interviews or online surveys. Each description of an incident can be coded in ways that allow a comparison of the source of stress and the symptoms associated with it by severity.

3. This activity can be done alone or with a small group of other students. Begin by writing a paragraph that describes a stressful event you experienced related to your work that occurred within the last 30 days. Describe how stressful you found the event and explain why you found it stressful. Follow

this with a list of three adjectives that describe the emotional and physical reactions, if any, you experienced during the incident. Now repeat this activity by following the same format to describe a second example of a stressful experience at work. Experiment with coding each paragraph you have written, just as you would if you were using the critical incident technique in your own research.

a.   Label the type or source of the stress you reported. This might be something such as *interpersonal conflict* or *a too-heavy workload*.

b.   Identify the underlying reason for why the event was stressful.

c.   Apply a form of intensity coding and rate how stressful the event seemed to be using a scale of 0–5 (0 = not at all stressful, 1 = slightly stressful, and 5 = highly stressful).

Recommended Reading

Cooper, K. (2014). Eliciting engagement in the high school classroom: A mixed methods examination of teaching practices. *American Educational Research Journal, 51*(2), 363–402.

EVALUATING QUALITY

PART THREE

8

EVALUATING QUALITY IN MIXED METHODS RESEARCH PUBLICATIONS

PRINCIPAL PURPOSES OF THE CHAPTER

1. To introduce the Mixed Method Evaluation Rubric (MMER) as a tool to evaluate the quality of a mixed method publication

2. To review evidence about the links between design features and overall quality in mixed method research

As is the case in the world of entrepreneurs in the private sector, a novel idea or approach to the design of a study is what garners recognition and wins awards in the academic arena. The ambition to make a name for oneself for a novel idea has to be weighed against the need to be sure an original finding is not an anomaly or the result of researcher bias (Makel & Plucker, 2014). The urge to publish novel results has to be juggled against other principles that guide the practice of science, including, most notably, the expectation that results can be replicated. **Replication** *conveys an expectation that others using the same data and methods can duplicate the results of a study.* A defining feature of science, the expectation that results can be replicated invites skepticism until the same results can be confirmed in multiple studies. It includes communicating the results of a study with enough precision and clarity to allow reproducibility (Open Science Collaboration, 2015) and giving readers enough information to evaluate the merits of the research procedures and results.

A 2015 study conducted by the Open Science Collaboration reinforces the idea that science requires a critical mindset by challenging the assumption that much of the science that appears in journals meets the standard of replicability. This large group of researchers conducted replications of 100 experimental and correlations studies appearing in three top-tier psychology journals. Ninety-seven percent of the original studies reported statistically significant results.

When members of the research collaborative reran the analysis of studies conducted by other researchers, only about one third of them produced a statistically significant result. The majority of the replications produced much weaker evidence to support original results using materials provided by the researchers. The articles with the most surprising findings were the least readily replicated, while those with strongest correlations or effect sizes were the most likely to be replicated. The authors from the Open Science Collaboration urged caution about placing too much confidence on the results from a single study.

Persuasive evidence that it is often very difficult to reproduce the results of empirical research, even when it is published in a prestigious outlet, points directly to one reason why many graduate programs put forward as one of their principal goals to educate students in becoming informed consumers of research. This requires adopting a skeptical attitude toward research. It also involves developing the critical thinking skills to determine if a research study has been grounded in the appropriate literature, systematically conducted according to the expectations associated with the method, and produces results that are clearly supported by the data and analysis. Only after these kinds of judgments are made can the reader make a decision about whether the research is credible enough to warrant using it as the basis for further action. This action might be the decision to develop a new program or set of activities based on solid evidence or to add to the knowledge base by making a deliberate choice to build on its results through replication.

Despite a strong level of consensus about its defining features, there is no agreement about what criteria should be used to evaluate a mixed methods publication (Heyvaert, Hannes, Maes, & Onghena, 2013). Sale and Brazil (2004) and O'Cathain (2010) are among the authors who have attempted to catalog the comprehensive array of criteria that have been put forward to evaluate quality in the methodological literature. Several authors have proposed their own set of evaluation criteria and subsequently tested their efficacy with a set of articles (e.g., Dellinger & Leech, 2007; Leech, Dellinger, Brannagan, & Tanaka, 2010; O'Cathain, Murphy, & Nicholl, 2008; Pace et al., 2012; Pluye, Gagnon, Griffiths, & Johnson-Lafleur, 2009). While there is consensus about some features, such as the importance of evaluating the way mixing is accomplished, authors hold diverse views about the core features of a systematic way to evaluate mixed methods research.

Differences in paradigmatic or philosophical assumptions partially explain why there is such a proliferation of viewpoints about what should be at the core of a framework to evaluate mixed methods research. The quality criteria that seem most relevant depend on a researcher's philosophical and political paradigm (Bryman, 2006). For example, a researcher who operates from a realist stance is likely to give priority to evaluation criteria related to replicability and include how systematic and well-documented the procedures are (Maxwell & Mittapalli, 2010). On the other hand, a researcher operating from a transformative or emancipatory paradigm is likely to award greater emphasis on the importance of reflexivity about paradigm and the utility of the research to impact social change in the set of evaluation criteria they put forward.

Authors such as Sale and Brazil (2004), who see qualitative and quantitative approaches as being grounded in fundamentally different paradigms, are very likely to belong to the group that advocates for a framework that contains a separate set of evaluation criteria for the qualitative, quantitative, and mixed components of a mixed method study. Such frameworks are invariably cumbersome to implement. The conventional assumption that evaluating a mixed method study requires a three-part framework probably explains the argument that the onus to demonstrate that results are warranted is even greater than usual for those conducting mixed methods research. Opting for the term *legitimation* to refer to the quality and rigor of the conclusions and inferences made, Collins, Onwuegbuzie, and Jiao (2007) articulated this position when they observed,

> The challenge of legitimation is greater in mixed methods studies than in mono-method studies (i.e., quantitative or qualitative research alone). The challenge of legitimation refers to the difficulty in obtaining findings and/or making inferences that are credible, trustworthy, dependable, transferable, and/or confirmable. (p. 269)

Pluye and his colleagues are among those who have taken the stance that evaluating a mixed method publication requires a framework with a separate set of criteria for the qualitative, quantitative, and mixed strands of a study (Pace et al., 2012; Pluye et al., 2009; Pluye & Hong, 2014). This group of authors developed and tested a framework that contains 19 criteria to evaluate the quality of a mixed methods research, only three of which concentrate on the mixing portion of the study.

It is my view that elaborate evaluative frameworks that contain more items to judge the quantitative and qualitative strands than the components related to mixed methods contribute to the derisive label of "mixed up" methods. They implicitly communicate the view that a mixed methods approach is one whose principal purpose is to combine qualitative and quantitative approaches to data collection and analysis and that a strategy for mixing is the only feature that distinguishes it. This is in contrast to the position that mixed methods provide the opportunity to use distinct ways to approach the design, data collection, sampling, analytical, and inferential stages of a research project. I share the view that research paradigms are adaptable to more than one paradigmatic position and, therefore, that many core quality criteria apply in equal measure to a variety of approaches and methods.

One place there is consensus in the community of authors writing about ways to evaluate mixed methods research is around the topic of mixing. Results of a content analysis of mixed methods publications conducted by O'Cathain et al. (2007a) indicate that a focus on mixing is effective in distinguishing mixed and multiphase studies. Their application of a rubric that tabulated at what phase in the research process mixing occurred revealed that only a small percentage of studies (16% of 49) conceived as mixed methods actually resulted in publications that integrated the qualitative and quantitative strands. Despite assertions to the contrary, authors of almost two thirds of the publications separated out the qualitative and quantitative strands or documented only one strand.

O'Cathain et al.'s (2007a) analysis of a body of mixed method publications underscores the idea that one of the first jobs of a rubric to evaluate quality in mixed methods research is to single out published studies that purport to be mixed methods but execute and report on the qualitative and quantitative strands so separately as to suggest that two, rather than one, studies were conducted. Although this type of study sometimes adopts the label of a *parallel* or *concurrent design* conducted for the purpose of triangulation or confirmation, this is a situation where elements of the design can interfere with opportunities for meaningful mixing.

PURPOSE, GOALS, AND CONTRIBUTION OF THE CHAPTER

My principal purpose in writing this chapter is to cut through the bewildering array of frameworks and terminology that has appeared in the literature by proposing a streamlined rubric to evaluate the quality of a mixed methods publication that I refer to as the Mixed Methods Evaluation Rubric (MMER). My purpose is consistent with the argument put forward by Small (2011) that one way for mixed methods to be officially recognized as a distinct methodology in its own right, rather than simply a buffet line of other methods, is to develop a set of standards that are unique to mixed methods. The rubric consists of criteria related to methodological transparency, the amount of mixing, engagement with diverse perspectives, and grounding in the methodological literature. As compared to the frustration of trying to apply a rubric that contains a long list of items that are a strong indicator of poor quality but only rarely present, the criteria in the MMER are rarely absent in a publication declaring a mixed methods purpose.

The main rational for proposing a rubric is to provide the novice researcher with a tool to systematically single out exemplary mixed methods research publications from the rapidly expanding body of literature. The rubric provides a systematic way to identify the weaknesses in a research publication as well as its strengths. It is designed with a set of criteria that are fundamental to distinguishing mixed methods from other approaches, including by the intentionality of an overriding mindset to engage with differences that emerge from the analysis of data from different sources. While informed judgment is required to apply any rubric, my goal has been to create a rubric that is relatively easy to apply.

The goals of the chapter are to (a) introduce a rubric for evaluating the quality of a mixed method publication, (b) illustrate how to apply the rubric by using an exemplary publication, and (c) consider evidence about the links between design features and overall quality in mixed method research.

Specific goals for the chapter include the following:

1. Consider differing viewpoints about evaluating quality in a mixed method report or publication.
2. Identify expectations for design transparency.

3. Acknowledge some of the challenges mixed method researchers face to provide adequate documentation that supports replication.
4. Summarize the design features of an exemplary publication.
5. Provide a rationale and document support from the methodological literature for four evaluation criteria.
6. List ways that a mixed method way of thinking is exhibited in a research report.

My ambition in this chapter is not to overtax the reader by providing a comprehensive review of the literature about evaluating quality in mixed methods. Even as a reader that is well versed in the methodological literature about mixed methods, I find it challenging to identify commonalities between the frameworks that have been proposed.

Organization of the Chapter

The next part of the chapter begins with a summary of some of the design features and results of the mixed method article that is used as an exemplar in this chapter. That is followed by a detailed discussion of the MMER, a definition for each criterion, and a rationale for its selection. The section about each criterion closes with an explanation of the rating of the chapter's exemplary publication on each criterion.

CHAPTER EXEMPLAR: McMAHON (2007) STUDY ABOUT THE ENDORSEMENT OF RAPE MYTHS AMONG COLLEGE ATHLETES

This 2007 article by Sarah McMahon of Rutgers University reported on the contradictory results from the analysis of quantitative survey data and qualitative interview data concerning collegiate athletes' perceptions about commonly held views about victim blaming for sexual assault. While the author casts her work as multimethod, Hesse-Biber (2010c) first identified this article, along with two others (e.g., Fuentes, 2008; Torres, 2006), as an example of a mixed method article with a qualitative priority that reflects a feminist, transformative paradigm. As has been my habit with other exemplars, I singled this article out for attention primarily because of its methodological transparency. Despite some methodological weaknesses, I prioritized it because it is a good example of how contradictions between qualitative and quantitative data can generate powerful meta-inferences. This is part of a mixed methods way of thinking, the intention to engage multiple points of view that can be effective in producing a more nuanced explanation than would be possible with a single method alone.

McMahon's study was executed sequentially in three phases, with two phases of data collection through interviews following the analysis of the quantitative data. The author explicitly addressed the rationale for the study in ways that

FIGURE 8.1 ■ Exemplary Article About Rape Myths Among Athletes: Summary of Key Features of McMahon (2007)			
Rationale/Purpose	Complementarity		
Priority	Qualitative		
Timing of Data Collection	Quantitative ➔ Qualitative ➔ Qualitative		
Timing of Data Analysis	Quantitative ➔ Qualitative		
Mixing	Fully integrated: No		
	Design	✖	
	Data collection	✖	Qualitative samples overlap
	Data analysis		
	Inferences	✖	Qualitative mixing
Meta-inference	Participants ascribed to subtle rape myths as a strategy to avoid acknowledging vulnerability.		
	Qualitative conclusion	Men and women athletes from all teams expressed victim-blaming beliefs in subtle ways.	
	Quantitative conclusion	Low acceptance of rape myths among student athletes	
Value-added	• Qualitative methods captured views about rape myths that are specific to student athlete culture. • Interviews produced "rich, descriptive data that could not have been discovered from the survey" (p. 368). • Qualitative methods offset weaknesses in the quantitative instrument.		

are consistent with what Greene, Caracelli, and Graham (1989) referred to as a *complementarity design*. An additional reason put forward for the use of multiple methods was to offset limitations of the survey instrument whose completion was plagued by the influence of social desirability. This is neither a fully integrated nor a mixed priority study because there is no explicit mixing through analytical procedures that combined quantitative and qualitative data. As with most articles reporting on mixed methods research, mixing occurred only at the stage of drawing inferences.

Key features of the design of this mixed methods study are summarized using the standard template incorporated in the preceding chapters (see Figure 8.1).

The strength of this article lies in the power of the insight that was gained by trying to explain inconsistencies between the qualitative and quantitative results. While quantitative results showed low acceptance of traditional rape myths, qualitative data from focus groups and individual interviews showed that virtually all of the male and female participants held views that "there are certain situations in which violence is acceptable, unintentional, or the fault of the victim" (McMahon, 2007, p. 366). The author moved her reasoning to the level of a meta-inference by proposing different purposes for male and female athletes for victim blaming. For male athletes, the reasoning justified concerns about false charges. For female athletes, the victim blaming provided a form of self-protection against feelings of vulnerability.

We shift our attention now to a discussion of the MMER and how it informs our understanding of the exemplary publication.

MIXED METHOD EVALUATION RUBRIC (MMER)

The MMER provides a streamlined tool to evaluate the methodological quality of a mixed methods publication. It is a rubric that is intended to help novice researchers distinguish exemplary publications that can serve as models on two fronts: first as a model to design and execute a mixed method study, second as a model to present the results of a mixed methods study in a report or publication. A rubric serving these purposes is different from one designed with the intent to evaluate the overall quality of a proposal for a multiphase research project that produces multiple interlinked publications. This is where inconsistencies between the rationale, plans for analysis, and actual execution are most likely to occur.

Both frameworks and rubrics specify criteria for evaluating quality of a research publication. The distinction between the two is that a framework (such as that proposed by Dellinger & Leech, 2007; O'Cathain, 2010; and Collins, Onwuegbuzie, & Johnson, 2012) does not present concrete benchmarks that enable assigning a numeric score to a publication. Criterion in a rubric need to be mutually exclusive and to address the most important aspects of quality in mixed methods publications (Heyvaert et al., 2013). A rubric can supply a set of hierarchical scales that make it possible to assign a score that distinguishes levels of quality. This type of scoring can facilitate mixing and the type of cross-case comparison that is seen in systematic reviews of the literature.

The MMER is briefer than most other frameworks that have been proposed. It contains four mutually exclusive criteria that provide a way to judge the quality of the inferences or conclusions. These relate to the process used to generate the inferences and attributes of the inferences themselves (Teddlie & Tashakkori, 2009). The four criteria in the MMER are (a) transparency about the reason for using mixed methods, (b) the amount of mixing across the four phases of the research process (i.e., design, data collection and sampling, analysis, and inferential phases), (c) engagement with diverse perspectives (i.e., interpretive comprehensiveness), and (d) methodological foundation. The rubric probably tips the hat in favor of fully integrated mixed methods studies and those that have a mixed priority. Mixed priority studies are distinguished by the attention they award to mixing during analysis and multiple, iterative phases of data analysis that often reflect an emergent component.

With the exception of the criterion about diverse perspectives that is scored as a binary yes/no variable, the three other criteria in the MMER are each scored on either a three- or four-point scale. Total scores on the MMER can range from a low of zero to a top score of 12. A coding sheet to apply the MMER to rate an empirical publication appears in Table 8.1.

There is stronger support in the literature for some aspects of the MMER than for others. Table 8.2 lists examples of leading figures that have offered frameworks for evaluating quality in mixed methods research that contain criterion that overlap with those in the MMER.

The data displayed in Table 8.2 supports the idea that despite the persistent argument that there is no general consensus about the criteria that should be applied to evaluate mixed methods research, there is general support in the literature for at least two criteria that are fundamental to mixed methods. These are the centrality of methodological transparency and the amount of mixing. Four of the seven authors listed in the table singled out different types of methodological transparency and six of the seven pointed to mixing as an important dimension of quality. While none of the authors refer to the construct by the same name (i.e., interpretive comprehensiveness), Collins et al. (2012) and Onwuegbuzie and Johnson (2006) are two examples of authors who support the emphasis on plurality and comprehensiveness that is so integral to the mixed method way of thinking that Greene (2007) has advocated. Only Dellinger and Leech (2007) provide support for the last item in the rubric, the foundational element. This is the part of a publication that identifies links to a wider body of mixed methods literature through the pattern of referencing the methodological literature.

We now transition to closer scrutiny of each of the criterion in the MMER and how they apply to the McMahon (2007) article.

DEFINING AND ILLUSTRATING THE EVALUATION CRITERIA IN THE MMER

The application of the MMER to the exemplary article selected for this chapter by McMahon (2007) reveals that it is not without its weaknesses. It scores 8 of 12 potential points on the MMER. The article earned the maximum possible points on two of the criterion in the MMER: transparency about rationale and engagement with different viewpoints (referred to as *interpretive comprehensiveness*). The low score on the foundational element discloses a major weakness of the article.

Table 8.3 summarizes the scoring of the McMahon (2007) article using the MMER.

TABLE 8.1 ▪ Mixed Methods Evaluation Rubric (MMER)

| Evaluation Criteria | Rating Scales | |
	Quality Definitions	Quality Score (Circle Score)
Transparency	No reason for using mixed methods is implicitly or explicitly stated.	0
	Speaks about the value of mixed methods generally but not specifically for this study	1
	Implicitly suggests a reason(s) for using mixed methods	2
	Explicitly states one or more reasons why mixed methods were used in this study or about what was gained from using mixed methods	3
Amount of mixing during the design, data collection or sampling, analytical, and/or interpretive phases	No mixing occurs in the study.	0
	Mixing occurs in one phase.	1
	Mixing occurs in two phases.	2
	Mixing occurs in three phases.	3
	Mixing occurs in four phases.	4
Interpretive comprehensiveness	No indication is given that multiple explanations were considered.	0
	Inconsistencies between the qualitative and quantitative data are identified but not explained.	
	The qualitative and quantitative phases are not integrated into a meaningful meta-inference.	
	Negative or extreme case analysis is utilized.	1
	Inconsistencies between the qualitative and quantitative data are identified and explained.	
	Alternative explanations are weighed to explain inferences drawn from the analysis.	
	Inconsistencies between the results and previous literature are identified and explained.	
	Other:	
Methodological foundation	No references are given to any methodological literature.	0
	Two or more methodological references are identified but only to one of the methods used (qualitative, quantitative, or mixed).	1
	Two or more methodological references are supplied for at least two of the methods used (qualitative, quantitative, or mixed).	2
	Three or more methodological references are supplied and they cover all three methods used (qualitative, quantitative, and mixed).	3
	Three or more methodological references are made to the mixed methods literature.	4

Note: I am indebted to doctoral students enrolled in my advanced mixed methods class (fall 2015) for input about the rubric, most particularly to Sarah Steelman, a student in Marriage and Family Therapy, for the suggestion for a way to construct the rubric for the foundational element and to Sreyoshi Bhaduri from Engineering Education, for giving me the idea to add the element related to a mixed methods way of thinking to the rubric.

TABLE 8.2 ■ Authors That Include MMER-Related Criteria in Their Evaluative Frameworks

Authors	MMER Criteria			
	Transparency	Mixing	Interpretive Comprehensiveness	Methodological Foundation
Bryman, Becker, & Simpik, 2008	X	X		
Collins, Onwuegbuzie, & Johnson, 2012		X	X	
Dellinger & Leech, 2007				X
Creswell & Tashakkori, 2007	X	X		
O'Cathain, Murphy, & Nicholl, 2007a	X	X		
Onwuegbuzie & Johnson, 2006		X	X	
Pace et al., 2012	X	X		

TABLE 8.3 ■ MMER Scoring of the Chapter Exemplar (McMahon, 2007)

Evaluation Criterion	Quality Feature	Score
Transparency	Explicitly identifies a reason for using mixed methods	3 of 3
Amount of mixing during the design, data collection or sampling, analytical, and/or interpretive phases	Mixing occurs at three or four phases	3 of 4
Interpretive comprehensiveness	Contradictions between the qualitative and quantitative data are identified and explained	1 of 1
Methodological foundation	Two or more methodological references are identified, but only to one of the methods used. No references to the mixed method literature	1 of 4
TOTAL SCORE		**8 of 12**

Criterion #1: Transparency

There is a strong level of consensus about the centrality of methodological transparency to evaluating research in the social and applied sciences for the purposes of replication and being able to substantiate the results. Many authors have included items related to methodological transparency in the frameworks they proposed to evaluate mixed methods research (e.g., Bryman, Becker, & Simpik, 2008; Collins et al., 2012; Creswell & Tashakkori, 2007; Dellinger & Leech, 2007; Onwuegbuzie & Johnson, 2006; Pace et al., 2012). First introduced in Chapter 2, *methodological transparency* is defined as promoting replication by providing explicit detail about the steps taken to complete data collection and data analysis as well as by delineating the link between results and the source of data.

Transparency is the criterion that has received the most attention in professional standards and the manuscript guidelines for the leading journal publishing mixed methods articles, the *Journal of Mixed Methods Research* (*JMMR*). Transparency is one of two overarching principles in the professional standards for reporting on empirical research put forward by the leading professional association in education, the American Educational Research Association (AERA). Emphasizing its role in enabling others to use the work, the following wording about transparency appears in these standards:

> Reports of empirical research should be *transparent*; that is, reporting should make explicit the logic of the inquiry and the activities that led from development of the initial interest, topic, problem, or research questions; through the definition, collection, and analysis of data or empirical evidence; to the articulate outcomes of the study. (AERA, 2006, p. 33)

The editorial guidelines for the *JMMR* share the emphasis on transparency. The guidelines specify the expectation that a publication contain sufficient details to understand the findings: "The manuscripts need to be well-developed in both quantitative and qualitative components, each complete with its own questions, data analysis, and inferences" (Creswell & Tashakkori, 2007, p. 108). The prominent role of methodological transparency in the MMER reflects the priority I have given throughout the book to it as one of two features for selecting exemplars. Along with inadequate attention to mixing, a lack of transparency has been a principal reason for why I have had to discard hundreds of potential exemplars.

Methodological transparency is one aspect of quality that crosses all phases of a research project from its inception during a planning stage through its execution during the implementation phase and, finally, to the reporting stage and the stage of judging its utility (O'Cathain, 2010). In her comprehensive review of frameworks that have been proposed, O'Cathain listed at least one type of transparency associated with each of the design phases: (a) design transparency, (b) data transparency, (c) interpretive transparency, and (d) reporting transparency.

There is the strongest level of consensus about the expectations for design transparency. These include the expectation to clearly identify the priority of the methods (e.g., primarily qualitative, quantitative, equal, or mixed), the purpose of mixing methods, the sequence of the methods (e.g., concurrent or sequential), and the stage of integration of both types of data (e.g., during data collection, data analysis, and/or interpretation). This type of documentation is crucial to an assessment of quality because it clarifies the alignment between mixed methods to the purpose of a study and its research question.

Many other types of methodological transparency have been addressed in the literature as being central to reaching a judgment about the quality of a research publication. The relevance of several criteria related to methodological transparency, such as using explicit wording to address the strengths and limitations of the methods used (Onwuegbuzie & Johnson, 2006) and philosophical clarity (Collins et al., 2007), could prove useful in an all-encompassing rubric designed with the intent to provide a means for comparing qualitative, quantitative, and mixed methods research articles.

Problems concerning insufficient transparency about steps taken to execute research are common in all methods but perhaps even more pronounced in mixed methods publications, where the demand to fully document the qualitative, quantitative, and mixing phases of a research project can prove challenging in the face of the restrictions to page limits in most journals. That obstacle may be particularly significant in fields such as health services that are driven by the expectation for evidence-based practice. The absence of sufficient methodological transparency has been attributed to the underrepresentation of mixed methods studies in systematic reviews of the literature (Wisdom, Cavaleri, Onwuegbuzie, & Green, 2012). Wisdom et al. concluded their content analysis of the frequency of mixed methods research in health services with a criticism of the overall quality of mixed method publications. They noted, "Many mixed methods studies did not include the level of detail that likely would be required for a qualitative or quantitative paper to be accepted in these high-ranking journals" (p. 738).

Application to the Exemplar

Even though it lacks any reference to conventional features of the design of a mixed method study, such as timing and priority, the exemplary article for this chapter by McMahon (2007) scores the maximum number of possible points (3 of 3) on the criterion for methodological transparency. Table 8.4 extracts this portion of scoring on the MMER.

One reason for the high score on the methodological transparency in the MMER transparency is that the author included clear language about the rationale for using mixed methods as well as what was gained by its use. Referring to her research as multiple rather than *mixed methods*, McMahon described the purpose of her study as "to use a multiple-method approach to understand the definition, function, and salience of rape myths within the student athletic community at one university" (p. 358). The link between this purpose and the goal of creating a richer, more comprehensive and nuanced picture is made clear by language in the last two sections of the article:

TABLE 8.4 ■ Scoring of the Chapter Exemplar on the MMER Criterion "Transparency"		
Evaluation Criterion	**Quality Feature**	**Score**
Transparency	Explicitly identifies a reason for using mixed methods	3 of 3

Three methods of data collection—a survey, focus groups, and individual interviews—were used to provide a rich, comprehensive look at student athlete culture and to dig deeper into the issue of rape myths. Each of the three data-gathering methods produced key findings, although the examination of the integration of the findings from all three sources provide the richest and most telling analysis. (p. 366)

The reference here to integration is what repositions this article as a mixed rather than simply multimethod study.

Criterion #2: Amount of Mixing

There is little doubt that the amount and quality of the integration of the qualitative and quantitative strands of a mixed methods study play a central role in any evaluation rubric or framework. Extending the strategy applied by O'Cathain et al. (2007a) to distinguish if mixing occurred at the design, data collection or sampling, analysis, and/or interpretation stages of a research project is a useful way to single out publications that self-advertise as mixed methods but fail to integrate the qualitative and quantitative strands in any meaningful way. The amount of mixing documented in a mixed methods publication is ranked in the MMER on a scale from one to four. Studies earning the highest score meet the definition of being fully integrated because they provide evidence of mixing at all stages of the research process.

Application to the Exemplar

Even though it is one of the few exemplars that is not fully integrated, the study reported by McMahon (2007) scores well on the mixing criterion in the MMER. It scored three of a possible four points on the mixing criterion because it provides documentation of mixing in all but one phase of the research process. Table 8.5 shows the article's scoring on this portion of the evaluation rubric.

Consistent with its label as a mixed method study that has a qualitative priority, the mixing occurred during data collection and analysis not through a back-and-forth exchange between the qualitative and quantitative strands of the study but by the interaction of findings from two qualitative phases of sampling and data collection. Mixing at sampling occurred because the qualitative samples for the focus group and

TABLE 8.5 ■ Scoring of the Chapter Exemplar on the MMER Criterion "Amount of Mixing"		
Evaluation Criterion	**Quality Feature**	**Score**
Amount of mixing during the design, data collection or sampling, analytical, and/or interpretive phases	Mixing occurs at three or four phases.	3 of 4

individual interviews overlapped. The analysis between the two qualitative forms of data collection was linked because the author sought to use individual interviews to clarify some issues raised in the focus groups.

The author returns to a type of mixing that is more conventional and quite common in mixed methods studies. Mixing occurred at the interpretation phase as the author summarized the analysis by pointing to the meta-inference that, as she hypothesized, the qualitative data told a different story than did the quantitative data. This is a case where the meta-inference provided the glue that linked the qualitative and quantitative strands of the study. There would be no ready way to make this point and explain it in a research publication without packaging the research as mixed methods.

Criterion #3: Interpretive Comprehensiveness

The third criterion in the rubric to evaluate the quality of a mixed methods research publication, **interpretive comprehensiveness**, addresses what many consider to be a defining feature of mixed methods research. It is defined as involving the *different ways that consideration of more than one viewpoint is incorporated, not only during the process of drawing conclusions but also throughout other phases of the research process.* Greene (2008) refers to a similar construct that she calls *independence/ interaction* as one of the key dimensions of the design of a mixed methods study. She defines it as "the degree to which the different methods are conceptualized, designed, and implemented independently or interactively" (p. 14).

Like mixing, interpretive comprehensiveness is a criterion that is unique to mixed methods and, consequently, may not be particularly useful when the task at hand is to compare publications using different methods. This criterion downplays the role of mixed method for the singular purpose of gathering multiple types of data for enhancing the credibility and transferability of findings through triangulation and confirmation and instead foregrounds its potential to advance analytical power by the generation of powerful meta-inferences.

This argument is at the heart of what Greene (2007) famously coined as "a mixed method way of thinking" that she maintains is the paradigmatic grounds for mixed methods. It is a position that coincides with her unconventional assertion that "convergence, consistency, and corroboration are overrated in social inquiry" (Greene, 2007, p. 144). This requires a paradigmatic mindset that deliberately acknowledges the complexity of social phenomenon and the human experience by intentionally maintaining a multiplistic mental model. Referring to it as *dialectical mixed methods*, Greene and Caracelli (2003) noted, "Dialectic mixed methods inquiry is envisioned as one way of intentionally engaging with multiple sets of assumptions, models, or ways of knowing toward better understanding" (p. 97). The view of reality as socially constructed and inherently multiple is a fundamental assumption of more than one paradigm, including a social constructivist and critical realist perspective (Maxwell & Mittapalli, 2010).

The MMER criterion, interpretive comprehensiveness, casts more light on the quality of the inferences or conclusions drawn than do the other criteria in the rubric.

Although both serve the purpose of bolstering the potential to generate meaningful meta-inferences, this MMER criterion is broader than what Teddlie and Tashakkori (2009) refer to as *interpretive rigor* and others default to by references to different types of validity. I depart here from my predecessors by arguing that the multiplistic mindset behind interpretive comprehensiveness is not merely a matter of drawing warranted or credible inferences. It can be manifested in a number of different ways and at multiple points of the research process.

A number of ways that interpretive comprehensiveness can be manifested at different phases of the research process are included in the MMER. These include the following:

1. *During the design phase* by framing the study with what Greene et al. (1989) referred to as an *initiation design*. This is the way, for example, that the purposes of two of the exemplars were framed (e.g., Chapter 2 Durksen and Klassen [2012] article about preservice teachers, Chapter 3: Gasson and Waters [2013] article about online collaborative behaviors). In these cases, the initial framing was directly tied to meta-inferences that reconciled what initially appeared to be counterintuitive results.

2. *During data collection or sampling* by the use of extreme or negative case sampling. Elliott, Gale, Parsons, Kuh, and the HALCyon Study (2014) used this sampling strategy in one of the exemplars featured in Chapter 6 in order to explain that the added mobility offered by cars after the second world war explained cohort differences in how older adults conceptualized social cohesion.

3. *During data analysis* by pursuing strategies to test alternative explanations. In one of the exemplars associated with Chapter 6, Jang, McDougal, Pollon, Herbert, and Russell (2008) prepared case studies to detect differences in school practices that were suggested by the qualitative data but not evident in the survey data. Gasson and Waters (2013), the exemplar in Chapter 3, provide an unusual example of analytical insight that can be gained by a deliberate strategy to consider what is missing in the data or what is not happening that might be expected.

4. *During the interpretation phase* through the construction of warranted or substantiated inferences or meta-inferences.

The manner of scoring interpretive comprehensiveness differs from the other three criteria. Rather than on a hierarchical scale, with higher values associated with increasing quality, it is scored as zero when absent and one when present. The different approach to scoring is taken because I can find no grounds to award greater weight to one strategy of engaging multiple viewpoints over another. Each can make a powerful contribution to supporting the credibility of a meta-inference that meaningfully integrates the qualitative and quantitative strands of a study.

It can be seen from Table 8.2 that several authors have included a construct similar to interpretive comprehensiveness in their discussion of an approach to evaluate the quality of a mixed method research publication. For example, while opting for the term *legitimation* over the more conventional but controversial term *validity*, Onwuegbuzie and Johnson (2006) first generated a typology of nine legitimation types related to the production of quality meta-inferences that was later reproduced in an article by Collins et al. (2012). An emphasis on multiple perspectives is woven throughout multiple criteria in Onwuegbuzie and Johnson's (2006) legitimation framework. One criterion in their legitimation framework explicitly highlights the benefits of multiple points of validation. Another legitimation criterion, referred to as *political legitimation*, is defined as addressing "the interests, values, and standpoints of multiple stakeholders in the research process" (p. 857). Yet a third criterion in the legitimation framework considers mixing of diverse perspectives in another way. It identifies an expectation for reflexivity about paradigmatic mixing as another strategy for legitimation.

Application to the Exemplar

The exemplar scored the maximum possible points on this criterion because it is framed with an overriding purpose of explaining differences between the ways that student athletes at a single research university responded to quantitative and qualitative approaches to assessing acceptance of stereotypical victim-blaming statements about sexual assault. Table 8.6 highlights scoring of the exemplar on this portion of the MMER.

A type of mixing occurred at the inference stage as the author found a way to reconcile the differences between results from survey data that indicated a low acceptance of rape myths and findings from focus groups and individual interviews that revealed that most athletes implicitly subscribed to subtle yet pervasive rape myths among student athletes. A distinguishing feature of the research approach adapted by the author is that she chose to pursue findings that emerged during focus group discussions with a second qualitative data collection strategy that involved individual interviews with many of the participants in the initial focus groups.

TABLE 8.6 ■ Scoring of the Chapter Exemplar on the MMER Criterion "Interpretive Comprehensiveness"		
Evaluation Criterion	**Quality Feature**	**Score**
Interpretive comprehensiveness	Contradictions between the qualitative and quantitative data are identified and explained.	1 of 1

Criterion #4: Methodological Foundation

The final criterion in the MMER is one that involves displaying familiarity with the literature about qualitative, quantitative, and mixed methods. The foundational element refers to the expectation that the author of any empirical publication document has prior understanding of the construct or phenomenon under study (Dellinger & Leech, 2007; Leech et al., 2010). The criterion of **methodological foundation** in the MMER refers to *the expectation for the authors of a mixed methods publication to demonstrate expertise in the research methods employed, including mixed methods.* Situating the research in the appropriate body of literature provides initial evidence of construct validity (Dellinger & Leech, 2007; Leech et al., 2010), establishes the credentials of the authors to conduct the research, and is necessary to establish the credibility of the conclusions (Beach, Becker, & Kennedy, 2007). In addition to signaling level of expertise, references to the mixed methods literature are a way to establish the audience for a piece of work and to communicate with members of a like-minded community of practice.

An unusual layer of expectation for documentation is evident in an editorial about developing publishable mixed method manuscripts prepared by Creswell and Tashakkori (2007) for the inaugural issue of the *JMMR*. They refer to an expectation about documenting the foundational element that is consistent with the purposes of the journal to publish original research that advances the field and is consistent with the inclusion of this criterion in the MMER. According to them, a strong mixed methods manuscript "includes mixed method components that adds to the literature about mixed methods" (p. 109). It requires some familiarity with the mixed methods literature to be able to defend an argument that a manuscript makes an original contribution. Explicit wording that identifies the contribution of the study to the literature requires an unusual level of confidence by the manuscript author but greatly aids reviewers on journal editorial boards and researchers in gauging the quality of a manuscript.

Reflecting on affinity with the movement toward evidence-based practice in health-related fields, Dellinger and Leech (2007; Leech et al., 2010) have been the chief proponents of awarding the foundational quality of a research publication a central place in what they refer to as a *validation framework* for evaluating mixed method research. They see its role as an element of construct validity that is more pervasive than simply pinpointing the contribution of the research in terms of the content area. They observed, "The foundational element provides evidence of construct validation through evaluation of relevant research that may offer insight into the meaning of data, interpretation of data, uses of data, and consequences of data" (Dellinger & Leech, 2007, p. 319). Laying out a comparison between findings and those reported elsewhere, including by providing an explanation for why the results may differ, can invite creative thinking and alternative explanations. Such references can add credibility to an itemization of the implications for practice.

There is some overlap between this criterion and the transparency criterion. As is likely to have been the case with the chapter's exemplar, it would be sheer happenstance for an author unacquainted with any of the foundational mixed methods literature to format his or her purpose statement in a way that is consistent with the communities' expectations about transparency. O'Cathain, Murphy, and Nicholl (2007a) specify, for example, that transparency is expected in the introductory portion of a manuscript where the purpose statement is provided by explicit reference to four dimensions of the design: (a) the priority of methods (primarily quantitative or primarily qualitative), (b) the purpose or rationale for using a mixed methods approach, (c) the sequence of the methods (qualitative first, quantitative first, or simultaneous), and (d) the stage of integration of both types of data (data collection, analysis, and/or interpretation). This type of transparency adds to the credibility of the author by serving to demonstrate a level of expertise sufficient to execute a mixed method project with some level of sophistication.

Application to the Exemplar

The foundational element is the part of the rubric that reveals the most significant weakness in the McMahon (2007) exemplar. The article scored only one of four possible points on this criterion. Table 8.7 summarizes the scoring on this portion of the MMER.

A commitment to social justice may explain the focus on implications for practice in the section of the manuscript that is used to discuss the results. An emphasis on implications may also explain the unusual failure to situate the results within the wider body of literature about victim blaming for rape. Similarly, the reference list includes one generic qualitative reference and one reference to a leading book about feminist research. The lack of references to any of the methodological literature about mixing methods seems at odds with the careful attention the author gave to being transparent about the value-added of using multiple methods. It is possible that many authors with little knowledge of the mixed method literature may be drawn to it as an approach because of its sheer usefulness and practicality in dealing with real-world issues.

TABLE 8.7 ■ Scoring of the Chapter Exemplar on the MMER Criterion "Methodological Foundation"		
Evaluation Criterion	**Quality Feature**	**Score**
Methodological foundation	Two or more methodological references are identified, but only to one of the methods used. No references to the mixed methods literature.	1 of 4

USING EVALUATION CRITERIA TO DEMONSTRATE A LINK BETWEEN DESIGN AND QUALITY

Up to this point, the discussion about the uses of the MMER has been framed to emphasize its use as a tool by the novice researcher to single out exemplary publications for the purposes of finding a model for his or her own study. Similar to other rubrics that use scales to produce an overall numeric score, the MMER can be used for an additional important purpose: to provide an analytical strategy for comparing mixed methods research articles in order to answer a question that is of a compelling interest to mixed methods researchers. That is, what design features are most strongly associated with overall quality in mixed methods research? An analytical strategy that made it possible to answer this question would provide a way to judge if the design features of the exemplars featured in the book differ in important ways from those of a less-selective body of mixed methods research literature. Any answer to this question would be instructive to researchers as they begin to flesh out the design for a mixed method study.

Despite a bountiful cross-disciplinary body of literature using content analysis to categorize mixed method publications by design features, few authors have taken the analysis far enough to test whether a link between design features and quality can be demonstrated. Rather than use a rubric that contains items that address elements of quality related to both the process and product of the research process, those who have broached the task have done so by developing a single quantitative measure of quality. Collins et al. (2007), for example, narrowed their focus to sampling strategy as a way to evaluate the quality of the inferences drawn. O'Cathain and her colleagues attacked the issue by looking at the amount of mixing that occurred and by judging if opportunities for mixing had been maximized. They leave unaddressed the challenge of confirming the widely held assumption that greater levels of integration produce stronger results.

The analytical strategy used in a content analyses conducted by O'Cathain et al. (2007a) is singular in that it made it possible to address the question about

Table 8.8 ■ A Comparison of the Design Features of Mixed Method Chapter Exemplars With Others From the Literature					
Authors (Sample Size)	**Design Rationale**				
	Triangulation	**Development**	**Complementarity**	**Initiation**	**Expansion**
	Percentage (Number)				
O'Cathain, Murphy, & Nicholl (2007a) (N=48)	6% (3)	35% (17)	40% (19)	0% (0)	44% (21)
Chapter exemplars (N=9)	0	11% (1)	44% (4)	22% (2)	22% (2)

design features of mixed methods studies that facilitate mixing of the qualitative and quantitative data. These authors extracted data from 48 final reports of funded mixed methods health services research projects in the United Kingdom. Each article was coded for a number of design features, including its purpose and whether mixing of the qualitative and quantitative data occurred at the design, data collection, analytical, and/or inferential stage.

Results of the analysis conducted by O'Cathain et al. (2007a) confirm the legitimacy of the widespread concern that many studies that collect both qualitative and quantitative data fail to take advantage of opportunities for mixing. Their analysis led them to conclude that there was no evidence of mixing in more than half of the reports (51%). Mixing across multiple phases of the research project, of the type that is evident in a fully integrated study, was very unusual. Mixing was most likely to occur at the inferential stage (81%) and least likely to occur at the design phase (10%). The type of mixing most instrumental to produce strong conclusions, mixing during analysis, was only documented in 17% of the cases. The authors judged that 28% of the studies failed to optimize opportunities for mixing.

There are fairly stark differences between the body of literature examined by O'Cathain and her colleagues in 2007 and the articles that I have featured as exemplars throughout various chapters in this textbook. Table 8.8 is used to summarize data in order to compare the design purposes of the exemplars and the publications analyzed by O'Cathain and her colleagues. Table 8.9 considers differences in how much and when mixing occurred in the two datasets.

Some of the differences between the two datasets are not entirely surprising, as one of the principal reasons I used for selecting the exemplars was because of thoroughness of the way that mixing was integrated into the different phases of the design.

The first of the two comparison tables reveals that there is considerable variation in the purposes identified by the exemplars and those of the studies analyzed by O'Cathain et al. (2007a). Most notably, only one of the exemplars fits under the

Table 8.9 ■ **A Comparison of the Stages of Mixing between Exemplars and Others From the Literature**					
	Stages When Mixing Occurred				
Authors (Sample Size)	**Design**	**Sampling**	**Analysis**	**Inference**	**Average**
	Percentage (Number)				
O'Cathain, Murphy, & Nicholl (2007) (N=48)	19% (9)	40% (19)	17% (8)	81% (39)	1.5*
Chapter Exemplars (N=9)	89% (8)	100% (9)	89% (8)	100% (9)	3.8

Note: Of the 48 studies, 27 mixed at more than one stage.

two design types that O'Cathain et al. found least conducive to mixing. None of the exemplars identified triangulation as a principal purpose of using mixing methods, though it is one of the longest-standing purposes of using mixed methods. Triangulation of qualitative and quantitative data on the same construct is important for confirmatory purposes. Similarly, only one of the exemplars, as compared to 35% of the studies in health sciences, was classified as having a development design. Differences between the prevalence of the expansion design is probably explained by the fact that the exemplars report results from a study in a single article, while the other datasets involved reports from funded projects, which might span multiple publications.

The second table provides strong evidence that the nine chapter exemplars differ from a wider body of literature in the way that strategies for mixing were incorporated across multiple stages of the research process. Mixing was spotted only at one stage in most of the health studies and this was most likely to be at the inferential stage. The largest indicator of a quality difference between the two databases is that strategies for mixing during analysis occurred in all but one of the exemplars (89%) as compared to only 17% of the health research studies.

Table 8.10 identifies when mixing occurred in the chapter exemplars. With a highest possible score of four for both datasets, the large difference between the means of the amount of mixing in the health reports (1.5 for 48 articles) and those of the exemplars (3.78 for 9 articles) reflects my emphasis on singling out articles that maximize the potential for mixing.

TABLE 8.10 ■ Scoring of the Chapter Exemplar on the MMER Criterion "Amount of Mixing"

Authors	Stages of Mixing				
	Design/Research Questions	Data Collection/ Sampling	Analysis	Inferences	Fully Integrated
Durksen & Klassen, 2012	X	X	X	X	X
Gasson & Waters, 2013		X	X	X	
Catallo, Jack, Ciliska, & MacMillan, 2013	X	X	X	X	X
Young & Jaganath, 2013	X	X	X	X	X
Jang, McDougall, Pollon, Herbert, & Russell, 2008	X	X	X	X	X
Elliott, Gale, Parsons, Kuh, & The HALCyon Study, 2014	X	X	X	X	X
Creamer & Ghoston, 2012	X	X	X	X	X
Cooper, 2014	X	X	X	X	X
McMahon, 2007	X	X		X	
	8 of 9 (89%)	9 of 9 (100%)	8 of 9 (89%)	9 of 9 (100%)	7 of 9 (78%)

Another set of authors add to the evidence that the chapter exemplars can better be understood as critical cases that exemplify certain design qualities than as typical or representative cases. Critical cases are chosen because their inclusion provides a researcher with compelling insight about the phenomenon of interest (Collins et al., 2007). Collins et al. conducted a content analysis of 121 articles from disciplinary journals in nine different fields, including education. Their analysis targeted sampling strategy and sample size to create an indicator of the quality of interpretations, recommendations, and meta-inferences made in the discussion section of an article that could be justified as being warranted.

In comparison to the results reported by Collins et al.'s (2007), the chapter exemplars share some qualities about sampling strategies that further distinguish them. Whereas the majority of the mixed methods studies analyzed by Collins et al. collected qualitative and quantitative data concurrently (81 of 121 or 66.1%), less than half of the nine chapter exemplars (44%) used this approach. Similarly, the two sets of articles also differ on another dimension of sampling strategy that creates opportunities for mixing, particularly during analysis. A greater percentage of the exemplars used an identical or nested sample for both their qualitative and quantitative data (7 of 9 or 77.7%) than those in the sample analyzed by Collins et al.

CHALLENGES AND FUTURE USES OF THE MMER

All too frequently, mixed methods research is executed in ways where the logic of mixing is not embedded in an overriding methodological and philosophical mindset. In such cases, the qualitative and quantitative strands of a study are often kept separate. Two people with quite different levels of expertise could team up to conduct such a study and never engage in a substantive conversation about ways to link what they have found. Separate research questions dealing with different but related phenomenon can drive the qualitative and quantitative strands. The data can be collected separately and the sampling plan designed to recruit two distinct groups of participants. The analysis can be executed separately, either concurrently or sequentially. Studies undertaken with this kind of mindset can readily be packaged into two separate articles reporting on the qualitative and quantitative strands because it is likely that no overarching meta-inference provides a comprehensive framework to explain the findings in a way that makes it impossible to disentangle the two strands. This is not the mindset that ultimately has much chance of producing a fully integrated mixed methods study.

This all-too-frequent approach to conducting and reporting mixed methods research is compatible with the widely shared assumption that the only way to evaluate it is by first using criteria that are specific to qualitative and quantitative approaches and then to add on a component to determine if any type of mixing occurred. This logic minimizes the influence of mixing throughout the research process and sets an impossibly high bar for mixed methods. It is based on the assumption that a study can achieve the designation of being a model for mixed methods research only after it first demonstrates that it satisfies the highest standards for both qualitative and quantitative methods.

There is not a good fit between the conventional, three-part approach to evaluate mixed methods research and the type of fully integrated mixed priority study that has been at the center of attention in this text and that would achieve top marks in the scoring system in the MMER. The logic behind the MMER coincides with the proactive stance taken by Creswell and Plano Clark (2007):

> Our stance is that while mixed method research must be responsive to both qualitative and quantitative criteria, there is a separate set of expectations for a mixed method study beyond those needed for qualitative and quantitative research. (p. 267)

The MMER takes this argument one step further by setting out to identify an interrelated set of evaluation criteria to apply to a mixed methods publication that embraces a set of basic criteria that are also central to standards for evaluating other types of research. An expectation for transparency about choice of methods, fidelity between the methods selected and the purpose of a study, consideration of multiple possible interpretations before reaching final conclusions, and solid grounding in relevant methodological literature are expectations for all types of research.

In addition to offering a streamlined way to evaluate mixed method research publications that is usable by someone who has only begun the process of claiming expertise as a mixed method researcher, the MMER makes a number of contributions to the body of literature that catalogs quality criterion important to attesting to the credibility, trustworthiness, and transferability of findings of mixed methods studies. In contrast to the more traditional approach of concentrating on the quality of inferences or conclusions, the four criteria are all encompassing because they stretch across different phases of the research process. The scoring system for three of the four criteria in the MMER is more nuanced than in other appraisal frameworks that rely on assessing the presence or absence of a quality, such as the use of appropriate conventions for naming the design and priority of study. The fact that the MMER produces a quantitative score facilitates its use in content analysis and systematic reviews.

There are many challenges to creating and applying a rubric to evaluate quality such as the MMER. These include avoiding items, such as *sample size*, that would unavoidably award greater weight to results emerging from mixed methods studies with a quantitative priority where the sample size is almost always larger than in qualitative priority mixed method studies. Assigning a higher score to studies using random assignment to groups and control groups would have the similar effect of denigrating findings emerging from studies that maintain a more equitable balance between the qualitative and quantitative strands.

A second major challenge in developing a rubric such as the MMER is to reduce it to criteria that are widely supported by professional standards but where there is the potential to devise a meaningful way to systematically apply a scoring system. Originality of the insight produced or methods used, for example, is an intuitively attractive criterion but one that is not amenable to a manageable scoring system. The test of a rubric such as the MMER is to determine the level of agreement that can be achieved when more than one rater applies it to a mixed method article. The topic of the MMER is picked up again at the end of the following chapter.

Summary of Key Points

1. There are many different views about what criteria should be included in a framework to evaluate the quality of mixed methods research.

2. The conventional view is that a framework to evaluate mixed methods research should include a separate set of criteria for the qualitative, quantitative, and mixing strands of the study.

3. An alternate viewpoint is that a framework to evaluate mixed methods research should focus on dimensions that are unique to the approach.

4. There is a strong level of consensus about the centrality of methodological transparency in evaluating research in the social and applied sciences because it is so instrumental to the ability to confirm or replicate the results.

5. There is widespread agreement that any evaluation framework designed to assess the quality of mixed methods research should include a measure of when and how much mixing occurred.

6. There is evidence in the literature to support the link to overall quality of two features of mixed methods studies (a) the amount of mixing and (b) the use of nonparallel or concurrent designs for purposes other than triangulation or confirmation.

Key Terms

- Interpretive comprehensiveness
- Methodological foundation
- Replication

Supplemental Activities

1. Score a mixed methods article that is in the reference list you have been accumulating using the evaluation rubric that is introduced in this chapter. Reflect on what types of judgments you had to make to score the article and what additions you would recommend to make the rubric more effective.

2. Follow the model set by the MMER to create an additional criterion that you can score with between three and four hierarchical levels of quality. The criterion might be about philosophical transparency or reflexivity about paradigm, for example. It could also be about validity. Pick something that matters to you when you are reading a research article.

3. Work with a partner to use the MMER to score two or three of the mixed method articles that have been identified as exemplars in this textbook. Score each article independently and then compare your scores to see where the scores you assigned are similar and different.

Recommended Reading

Dellinger, A. B., & Leech, N. L. (2007). Toward a unified validation framework in mixed methods research. *Journal of Mixed Methods Research, 1*(4), 309–332.

McMahon, S. (2007). Understanding community-specific rape myths. *Affilia: Journal of Women and Social Work, 22*(4), 357–370.

DESIGNING AND REPORTING A FULLY INTEGRATED MIXED METHODS RESEARCH PROPOSAL OR DOCTORAL DISSERTATION

PRINCIPAL PURPOSES OF THE CHAPTER

1. To suggest practical strategies for a graduate student with foundational knowledge of the mixed methods literature to consider during the process of planning for the design of a mixed method dissertation

2. To provide guidelines for organizing a mixed methods manuscript to reflect a methodological commitment to mixing

Although some faculty members trained in an earlier era express skepticism that it is possible to design a mixed methods study that is doable within the time frame, resources, and expertise of the typical graduate student, there are ample examples of high-quality studies that managed to accomplish just that task. Two of the chapter exemplars (i.e., Catallo, Jack, Ciliska, & MacMillan, 2013; Cooper, 2014) report on dissertation projects. Many students in applied disciplines such as education and health services are driven by a pragmatic interest to search for a combination of methods that have the best chance of producing the type of information that will be effective in addressing real-world problems. Members of this group are likely to be methodologically eclectic (Teddlie & Tashakkori, 2012) and committed to the idea that when combined, qualitative and quantitative research will produce a richer, more nuanced explanation for complex social phenomenon.

Foundational expertise in research methods is essential for anyone undertaking a research project. One of the principal challenges to the idea that it is feasible for a novice researcher to undertake a mixed method research project is the necessity to demonstrate expertise that spans multiple areas. In addition to content area expertise, this includes a basic knowledge of qualitative, quantitative, and mixed methods research approaches and the software that is compatible with these approaches (Leech, Onwuegbuzie, & Combs, 2011). Along with the scarcity of mentors or supervisors with training in mixed methods (Halcomb & Andrew, 2009), the lack of graduate programs offering courses in mixed methods adds to the challenges associated with using a mixed methods approach in a dissertation (Capraro & Thompson, 2008). Teddlie and Tashakkori emphasized this expansive skill set when they observed, "We believe that mixed methods researchers *must* be competent in a full spectrum of research methods and approaches to select the best paths for answering their research questions" (2012, p. 777).

Every graduate student must develop a foundational level of expertise in research methods to undertake the independent research project that is the penultimate phase of a doctoral program. Poth (2014) refers to the need for methodological expertise with the term *methodological literacy*. Applying to research conducted using any type of method, she defines methodological literacy as "possessing the knowledge and skills necessary for making informed decisions during the research process" (p. 74). During the planning phase, this requires the knowledge necessary to develop research questions and to select a design as well as to identify paradigmatic frameworks, select data collection instruments, and develop a plan to analyze the data.

Throughout this text, I have referred to the image of an architectural arch as a way to conceive a single mixed methods study as being constructed with a qualitative, quantitative, and integrative component. It is an apt way to capture the type of study undertaken by a newcomer with limited time and resources and working within the expectations of his or her program to earn a degree.

This metaphor can be extended to consider an unusual type of bridge that is constructed with either multiple arches or a single, extended arch. This offers a way to punctuate the difference between the design of a single study undertaken by an independent researcher to fulfill the requirements of a graduate degree in applied, human, and social science fields with the type of real-world research that is launched by more experienced researchers. This type of initiative is generally conceived as a research project rather than a research study. Particularly when there is an ambition to be competitive for external funding, a research project is generally initially framed as a series of interrelated studies. In this situation, a mixed methods piece may well be just one of several studies that are imagined at the onset.

A well-known example of a bridge that consists of a single, extended arch is not far from my home in southwest Virginia (http://www.nps.gov/neri/index.htm). It is shown in a photo in Figure 9.1.

FIGURE 9.1 ■ New River Valley Gorge Bridge

© iStock/Kenneth Keifer

A haven for bungee jumpers, the bridge that spans the New River Valley gorge is considered to be both a feat of engineering and an aesthetic marvel. It remains one of the longest arches in the world. At 1,700 feet longest, the arch comprises more than half of the expanse of the entire bridge. Completed in 1977, the bridge is ranked by some sources as one of the top ten arches in the world.

A researcher more advanced in his or her career may envision a project in a way that is similar to the extended arch that spans the New River Valley gorge. The goal of the novice researcher who has chosen a mixed methods approach to designing a research project is the equivalent of a constructing a single arch. It is clearly and narrowly conceived in its purpose.

COMMUNICATING PRIORITY

The widespread adaptation of a single standard to structure an empirical research article across academic fields belies the fact that there yet remain many choices about the ways to organize it. The amount of space devoted to each of the methods, along with the figures, tables, and headings, communicate the priority awarded to the quantitative, qualitative, and mixed methods phases of the research process (Creswell & Plano Clark, 2011). Researchers with the ambition to design a fully integrated mixed method study are faced with the challenge of designing and presenting their work in a way that is consistent with the overriding purposes of mixed methods.

Using mixed methods is not simply about collecting and analyzing multiple types of data but includes intentionality about wedding the two in meaningful ways. This is best reflected when attention to mixing is incorporated throughout the different sections of a research report.

PURPOSE, GOALS, AND CONTRIBUTION OF THE CHAPTER

The approach I take in this chapter is one that reflects the priority I have placed in this textbook on fully integrated mixed methods studies that attends to mixing throughout the various phases of the research process. This is consistent with an overriding purpose of mixed methods research that is undertaken not solely for collecting multiple sources of data for triangulation or confirmation, but with attention and forethought to integrating them in ways that extend or advance understanding of the phenomenon being studied.

The central purposes of the chapter are twofold. These are, first, to suggest practical strategies for a graduate student with foundational knowledge of the mixed methods literature to consider during the process of planning the design of a mixed method dissertation and, second, to provide guidelines for organizing a mixed methods manuscript to reflect a methodological commitment to mixing. The contribution of the chapter lays in the explanation and illustration of ways to design a mixed methods study and to structure a mixed methods research publication in order to communicate a priority on mixing. This is when attention to meaningful strategies and outcomes of mixing are interwoven throughout the research process and in the way it is represented in the form of articles, presentations, and other types of publications.

As has been my approach in the previous chapters, my focus in this chapter is largely on issues that are specific to mixed methods. The principal audience for the chapter is doctoral students and those who begin with the intention to design an empirical study that has the potential to make a contribution to knowledge or to advance policy or practice. Many publications are available that describe the content and order for organizing a research proposal and the generic challenges, including political ones, faced by the novice researcher. I refer readers to helpful books by Bazeley about the use of software in qualitative data analysis (2013; Bazeley & Jackson, 2013).

It is not my intent in this chapter to provide a comprehensive review about what has been written about reporting in mixed methods studies, nor is it to offer examples of creative alternatives to write up a mixed methods research project. I refer the reader to earlier chapters to consider the implications of paradigmatic assumptions on study design. Instead, it is my goal to illustrate how to attend to the central features of mixed method research to embrace multiple types of data and points of view through the conventional, linear approach to structuring a mixed methods publication. This begins with an introduction, moves to the literature review and a description of methods, and ends with results and discussion. With intentionality about the integration of the qualitative and quantitative strands, the conventional format has proven adaptable to the growing diversity and creativity shown in mixed method publications.

The principal goals of the chapter are to

1. acknowledge practical challenges faced by graduate students who find a mixed methods approach to be compatible with the nature of the research questions they would like to pose;
2. identify types of studies where the multimethod label is more appropriate than a mixed method label;
3. distinguish the qualities of the chapter exemplars that are feasible and less feasible for a newcomer to research;
4. introduce content analysis as a realistic option for graduate student research;
5. present strategies for organizing a mixed methods manuscript;
6. summarize different ways that mixing can be incorporated through all stages of the research process;
7. explore the way figures can be used to depict the steps in the research process, including how mixing was accomplished; and
8. identify reporting guidelines for methodological transparency.

Organization of the Chapter

The chapter is organized into two main sections. The first section is devoted to the planning or design phase of a research project. In an ideal world, this is when many decisions are made about the design and execution of a mixed methods study, including about how and when the qualitative and quantitative data will be integrated. Uses of mixed methods that are better adapted to a multimethod approach are singled out here. The suggestion that content analysis can be suitable for graduate student research is pursued next. Characteristics of chapter exemplars that are realistic for graduate students with a foundational knowledge of mixed methods research are explored, as are effective strategies for designing a study that promotes mixing.

The second portion of the chapter addresses the topic of reporting and presenting the results of a mixed method study. There are strong linkages between this section and the discussion about evaluating quality in mixed methods in Chapter 8. In the last section, I use a single exemplar to demonstrate how to add to the credibility of reporting through different types of methodological transparency.

The quality of a research study is as much about the thought that goes into the initial planning stage as it is about its execution. As the new researcher goes through the process of fine-tuning a purpose statement, research questions, and the types of procedures that will be used, attention to design features of the study can help to create a stronger context for mixing. Before considering qualities that make a mixed method approach feasible for a dissertation, we will address types of designs that are not particularly conducive to meaningful mixing.

SITUATIONS WHEN THE MULTIMETHOD LABEL IS APPROPRIATE

There is little doubt that there is considerable interest in mixed methods as a research approach, particularly among graduate students. Plowright (2013) demonstrates that the enthusiasm for it, particularly among students in applied fields such as education, is at a level that merits its characterization as a trendy option. Ninety percent of the 93 doctoral students Plowright surveyed used or intended to use mixed methods in their research. The vast majority of the doctoral respondents believed that the problem being investigated drove the choice of methods. The majority downplayed the concern that qualitative and quantitative approaches operate from a set of opposing paradigmatic views. Only 15% of the doctoral respondents expressed the view that the philosophical or paradigmatic position of the researcher is the most important factor when it comes to planning or designing research.

The trendy nature of mixed method approaches has some consequences. It is very likely to lead the newcomer to research to appropriate the label without giving thoughtful attention to the types of studies where the multimethod label is a better way to characterize the research. The multimethod label communicates the intent to use more than one procedure to collect data. It implies no promise to include a genuine inductive or qualitative component that contributes to the analysis. There is no commitment to explore how multiple sources of data interface for purposes of building a more comprehensive picture of a phenomenon.

Centering mixing in the decision to use a mixed methods approach is a methodological choice that can help a novice researcher make an informed decision about the appropriateness of mixed methods label as compared to multimethod label. Several types of empirical studies minimize the role of mixing. These include a common design of surveys to include open-ended questions, considering counting of themes or codes from the qualitative analysis as mixed methods, and classic uses of both a concurrent and two-phase design that only modestly bridge data sources.

As early as 2003, Sandelowski voiced a concern that the mixed method label is being applied simply because it is "methodologically fashionable" (p. 323). She spelled out a list of types of studies where the mixing of the qualitative and quantitative sources of data is so trivial that she challenges the appropriateness of its affiliation with mixed methods. Sandelowski questioned the meaningfulness of labeling two types of studies as mixed methods:

1. Projects where one or two open-ended questions are added to a questionnaire or survey without any intent to analyze the data independently. Quotes from open-ended responses are often used simply for purposes of illustration or to flesh out or to enliven dryer statistically derived results.
2. Treating projects that involve counting of qualitative codes or themes as data transformation and a form of mixing.

The multimethod label may well be a more accurate descriptor of these two types of studies because they lack the meaningful strategies for mixing that is communicated by a mixed methods label.

An important figure in the field, Bazeley (2009) raised further questions about the assumption that the single most frequent use of mixing will continue to be sufficient to warrant the mixed method label. She challenged the idea that simply mixing at the interpretation stage—generally a topic raised in the discussion section of a publication—justifies the application of a mixed methods label. As informative as a statement about the differences and similarities between the results is, the failure to produce results that are embedded in an analytical procedure reduces the credibility of the conclusions. Bazeley's question should motivate new researchers to be more creative during the early phases of planning to build in nontrivial opportunities for mixing.

Two widely used designs are not particularly conducive to mixing and, consequently, might be more suitable for a multimethod study. Both are probably widely used because they are so well suited to collaborative initiatives in which team members divide up responsibility for a project and each contributes a specialized expertise. One of these is the classic concurrent approach to data collection and analysis. The second is the two-phase development design. Limitations in both of these designs can be overcome by drafting research questions in a way that requires the interlinked analysis of both qualitatively and quantitatively derived variables.

A concurrent design where the qualitative and quantitative data are collected and analyzed separately is the single most frequently used mixed method design. Eighty-percent of the 677 mixed method publications reviewed in a cross-disciplinary content analysis of mixed methods publications in 17 subject areas were executed using a concurrent design (Ivankova & Kawamura, 2010). None of the exemplars use this approach. The bifurcation of the analytical procedures into separate qualitative and quantitative phases probably goes a long way to explain why most mixed methods studies only mix at the final, interpretive stage.

Because the two strands are so distinct, the development design shares many of the design features of a concurrent design. The development design is an umbrella term to describe two types of studies. This is when qualitative data, often from interviews, are collected in an initial phase in order to develop an instrument or intervention in the second phase. The two phases are only loosely linked. The second most frequent use of the development design is for purposes of sampling, when indicators from the first phase are used to identify members of a sample for the second phase. The weakness in this design is that the mixing that contributes to the analytical insight is often absent.

Studies with either a concurrent or development design are appealing because they can be executed quite efficiently and in distinct rather than interlocked phases. They may well be so widely used because they are compatible with packaging into separate publications. The limitations in the way these two types of studies have conventionally been conceived can readily be offset, however. There are many ways to promote the meaningful integration of qualitative and quantitative sources of data throughout the research process.

Intentionality About Incorporating Design Features That Promote Mixing

In earlier chapters, I placed a good deal of emphasis on unexpected opportunities for mixing that often emerge over the course of the research process, particularly when the analysis is allowed to become iterative and further analytical strategies are employed to pursue extreme or negative cases or contradictions or unexpected or counterintuitive results. Pursuing these through further analysis not only adds to the credibility of the findings but also adds to the potential to reach sophisticated, nuanced inferences that make an original contribution to research and practice.

Without downplaying the contribution of serendipitous opportunities for mixing that emerge during the process of conducting research, there are strategic ways to incorporate intentionality about mixing during the early phases of designing a study. Table 9.1 provides a generic list of eleven strategies to facilitate mixing that are useful to consider during the planning stage of a research project. The emphasis in this table is on strategies that have an effect on data collection and analysis rather than two other features of a mixed methods design—timing and priority—that have figured so prominently in the mixed methods literature.

Table 9.1 provides a checklist of items to consider during the planning stage of a project. It offers a full range of examples of the ways that multiple types of data can be integrated in meaningful ways. It is unlikely, however, that all these ways would be used in a single study.

TABLE 9.1 ■ Examples of Different Ways That Mixing Can Be Incorporated at All Stages of the Research Process	
Stage of the Research Process	**Examples of Strategies for Mixing**
1. **Design research questions**	Qualitative and quantitative data are collected about the same or overlapping constructs.
	Separate qualitative and quantitative research questions (one that is descriptive and a second that is intended to answer the why and how questions).
2. **Data collection**	Analysis of results from the first phase of a sequential or multistage study shapes the data collected in the second phase.
3. **Sampling**	Qualitative and quantitative samples are the same or overlap.
	Both purposeful and probabilistic sampling strategies are used.
	Extreme or negative case sampling is used.
4. **Analysis**	Qualitative and quantitative data on the same constructs are merged into one quantitative variable.
	Case profiles are used to explore nuances in the quantitative data in different settings or for different individuals or entities.
5. **Interpretation and conclusions**	An explanation is offered for inconsistencies between the results from the analysis of qualitative and quantitative data.
	Results from the qualitative and quantitative analysis are explicitly linked and explained by a meta-inference.
6. **Reporting**	An explanation is offered for consistencies and inconsistencies between the results and the literature.

Up to this point in the chapter, we have attended to generic features that can be considered during the planning of a research project that are incompatible and compatible with an approach to mixed methods that incorporates mixing in every stage of the research design. We shift our attention now to other practical factors that need to be weighed as a study is conceptualized and the relative merits of a mixed method approach is determined.

DESIGNING A MIXED METHODS STUDY IN WAYS THAT ARE FEASIBLE FOR A NEWCOMER TO EMPIRICAL RESEARCH

The characteristics of a realistic or feasible research project for a graduate student depend on a myriad of factors. These include the student's long-range goals, expectations of the program, and negotiations that ensue with a research mentor or advisor and other committee members. The choice of appropriate methods is quite a different matter for a student who is working independently and generating a topic of his or her own volition than for a student working in a team. This was the case, for example, with the chapter exemplar reporting on Catallo's dissertation research about the reporting of intimate partner violence in emergency rooms (Catallo et al., 2013). Catallo had the benefit of conducting a study that emerged from within the context of a large, externally funded research team. Feasibility may be weighed differently by a student who is motivated by the desire to lay the foundation for a future career as an academic.

There are many facets to the feasibility of a research topic. Sufficient expertise, the potential for timely completion, adequate resources, and the support of an experienced and trained mentor who is engaged with the literature in mixed methods would have to be at the top of any list of issues that merit a coolheaded appraisal. Projects that utilize existing databases, streamlined instruments that already have a demonstrated record of reliability, and access to an extant body of data that is publicly accessible at minimal or no charge (as are now increasingly available through the Internet) greatly enhance the potential to carry a mixed method project to fruition in a timely manner.

A minimum of foundational knowledge of quantitative, qualitative, and mixed methods is widely acknowledged as one of the principal challenges a new researcher encounters when weighting the merits of utilizing a mixed methods approach. Some methods that are philosophically compatible with a mixed methods approach, such as content analysis and case study, require a foundational knowledge that is not unduly ambitious to acquire. Although it is not pursued here, Ivankova demonstrated that evaluation research is achievable in a dissertation (Ivankova & Stick, 2007).

More sophisticated expertise and prolonged exposure to the methodological literature is likely necessary to pursue more advanced designs, such as those explored by Plano Clark (2010) and Plano Clark et al. (2014). It is also likely to be necessary to produce research that would be of interest to an audience of methodologists. Some newly emerging, innovative uses of mixed methods, such with social network analysis (see Cross, Dickmann, Newman-Gonchar, & Fagan, 2009, for an example) and geospatial analysis (see Hites et al., 2013, for an example), require knowledge of specialized software that is likely to require additional training.

In the next section, I incorporate references to the chapter exemplars to distinguish models that are most likely to be appropriate for an independent researcher attempting to craft a dissertation that is not unduly ambitious or beyond the scope of expertise that can be expected of a scholar in his or her first long-term foray in the arena of academic research and publishing.

Chapter Exemplars That Are the Most Feasible as Models for Doctoral Research

Some of the chapter exemplars are more realistic models than others for graduate students undertaking their first independent research project. Table 9.2 summarizes the design characteristics of five of the nine exemplary articles featured in the preceding chapters as being designed in a way that is feasible for a graduate student operating without the benefit of the additional resources and support that comes from being

TABLE 9.2 ■ Chapter Exemplars That Are the Most Feasible for Graduate Student Research				
Chapter: Author(s) (Date)	**Topic**	**Rationale**	**Sample**	**Timing/Scope Issues**
Chapter 2: Durksen and Klassen (2012	Preservice teachers	Initiation	Identical	Qualitative and quantitative data collected simultaneously over the course of one term
Chapter 4: Catallo et al. (2013)	Disclosure of intimate partner violence	Complementarity	Nested	Sequential, qualitative data collection following an intervention to answer a why question
Chapter 5: Young and Jaganath (2013)	HIV education	Complementarity	Identical	Use of a private Facebook page to collect qualitative and quantitative data simultaneously over the course of 10 weeks
Chapter 6: Creamer and Ghoston (2012)	Mission statements of colleges of engineering	Complementarity	Identical	Qualitative and quantitative data collected from publicly available, free online sources
Chapter 9: McMahon (2007)	Endorsement of rape myths	Complementarity	Nested	Uses standardized publicly available instrument for survey followed by two phases of qualitative interviewing

embedded in a research team (i.e., Catallo et al., 2013; Creamer & Ghoston, 2012; Durksen & Klassen, 2012; McMahon, 2007; Young & Jaganath, 2013).

The five studies I have distinguished as feasible for graduate student research vary in the priority they awarded to the qualitative, quantitative, and mixing phases. Topic areas and disciplinary home were also quite diverse. All of the studies integrated the qualitative and quantitative components in multiple ways throughout many, if not all, of the phases of study, including during analysis. In addition, these examples share these design features:

1. An identical or overlapping group of participants for the qualitative and quantitative phases.
2. Research questions that provide for a comparison during analysis of the same or overlapping qualitative and quantitative constructs.
3. A rationale for using mixed methods that falls under what Greene, Caracelli, and Graham (1989) referred to as a *complementarity rationale*. This rationale reflects the goal of creating a more nuanced, complex understanding of a phenomenon.
4. Publicly available data and/or instruments are utilized.
5. Qualitative and quantitative data are collected simultaneously and over a relatively efficient time frame.

These five features reinforce the argument that it is indeed possible for a graduate student to craft a mixed method research project that includes meaningful opportunities for mixing within a reasonable time frame, set of resources, and requirement for methodological expertise.

Four of the nine articles featured as mixed method chapter exemplars have design features that are less likely to be realistic for a graduate student to pursue independently without unusual motivation or access to resources, including time (i.e., Cooper, 2014; Elliott, Gale, Parsons, Kuh, & the HALCyon Study, 2014; Gasson & Waters, 2013; Jang, McDougall, Pollon, Herbert, & Russell, 2008). Two characteristics distinguish these: first, the requirement for access to data that would not typically be available to a graduate student. Gasson and Water's (2013) research about engagement in an online class that I reviewed in Chapter 3 is an example of this. Replicating the study would only be feasible for someone who has access to data about students' patterns of usage and access to an online class.

The second feature of the chapter exemplars that would be challenging for most graduate students to undertake are those associated with what Greene et al. (1989) referred to as the *expansion rationale or design*. This type of design applies to studies where data are collected from multiple constituencies at different levels of a school or organization. It is characterized by the iterative, multiphase cycle of data collection and analysis that Teddlie and Tashakkori (2012) identified as one of nine core characteristics of mixed method research. Even though the article summarizes the results of her dissertation, the multilevel nature of the process of data collection is the reason I categorized Cooper's (2014) research as being challenging for another graduate student to replicate.

Some methods or approaches, such as content analysis and case study, are more compatible than others with mixed methods. Feasible applications of a mixed method approach to several qualitative dominant methods are considered in the next section.

METHODS THAT ARE ADAPTABLE TO A MIXED METHODS APPROACH

Some methodologies, such as ethnography, have their own prescription for specialized methods for collecting and analyzing data that are so deeply rooted in an overarching philosophical framework that the intent to integrate qualitative and quantitative data that is so integral to the philosophical grounding of mixed methods inevitably plays an ancillary role. This is a method where Plowright's (2013) radical idea that methodology dictates paradigm comes in to play. The challenge of reconciling two strong methodological orientations make it difficult to frame ethnographic research as mixed methods.

A similar argument has traction with the exemplar by Catallo et al. (2013) in Chapter 4. It has many strong reporting features but uses grounded theory in a way that is decidedly secondary to the dominant methodological orientation of the randomized controlled clinical trial. A qualitative component inevitably plays a secondary role in this type of quantitative-dominant study that is the gold standard in medical and health fields. It is a struggle to adapt this method to the context of research in many applied fields, including education.

There are several other research traditions that have been widely used with qualitative strategies for data collection and data analysis that are readily adaptable to a mixed methods dissertation. Studies executed using grounded theory, content analysis, and case study can fall in this group. Though I have said that the breadth of its data collection would make it a challenge for others to replicate, Cooper's (2014) research about the effectiveness of different teaching strategies in promoting student engagement is an example of the meaningful merger of qualitative and quantitative data through case study in a dissertation.

Content analysis is a method that is widely used by mixed methods practitioners. Bryman (2006) estimated that about 8% of the mixed methods articles in the social sciences utilize a form of content analysis. Although the analysis of textual data is thought by some to be inherently a qualitative act, content analysis is a method that is readily adaptable to mixed method approaches. Features in qualitative software make it possible to extract data to analyze posts in social media or entries in online forums.

Content Analysis

Content analysis *is an empirical research method for systematically analyzing data that are in textual or visual form.* It first emerged as a research method in the field of communication studies (Weber, 1985, 1990), where it has been used to study patterns of usage of texts in mass media using materials as diverse as advertisements, greeting cards, blogs, newspaper editorials, magazine advertisements, and film. Text includes written or printed materials such as transcripts of interviews or conversations, diaries, reports, books, written or taped responses to open-ended questions, media, and verbal descriptions of observations (McTavish & Pirro, 1990). Not solely restricted to written materials, content analysis can be extended to objects that carry meaning, including art, photographic images, maps, sounds, signs, symbols, and numerical records (Krippendorff, 2004). Arts-informed mixed methods approaches have been used to analyze drawings produced by participants (Shannon-Baker, 2015). The recent digitization of library holdings by members of a nationwide consortium to encourage free and open access to the public offers a trove of opportunities for innovative approaches to content analysis of different types of textual and media data, including historical maps and restaurant menus (Schuessler, 2016).

Content analysis is a method that is particularly adaptable to a mixed methods approach (Downe-Wamboldt, 1992; McTavish & Pirro, 1990; Weber, 1985, 1990). Weber argued, "The best content analytic studies utilize both qualitative and quantitative operations on texts" (1985, p. 10). One quality that makes content analysis particularly suitable to mixed methods is that it is a research method that is not deeply wedded to a single paradigm, worldview, or philosophical orientation. That is why it is best characterized as a method rather than a methodology. Its largely pragmatic philosophical grounding is adaptable to a quantitative or qualitative priority as well as to an integrated approach that balances the two. A mixed methods approach to content analysis can juggle inferences drawn from analyses that quantify the explicit occurrence of words, phrases, or sentences with those constructed from analyses that are more overtly interpretive of the meanings underlying the text (Graneheim & Lundman, 2003).

Content analysis has tremendous advantages as a method for use by a novice researcher. One reason for this is that it is eminently doable without advanced expertise in mixed methods or specialized software. A second feature that contributes to its feasibility is its use of existing publicly accessible data that are both free and almost unlimited. Because these data are in the public domain, there are no issues of securing access to the data. An additional advantage is the potential to assemble a relatively large database of data that is amenable to statistical analysis. The potential to generate multiple publications from a single database adds to the list of advantages of a mixed method approach to content analysis.

Organizations, schools, colleges, clubs, or corporations almost always provide readily accessible statements that announce their central mission. These offer many opportunities for a mixed method content analysis.

Using content analysis to analyze mission statements. Analyzing mission statements is another application of content analysis that is highly suitable for doctoral research using mixed methods. Mission statements "represent an important summation or distillation of an organization's core goals represented by concise and simple statements that communicate broad themes" (Stemler, Bebell, & Sonnabend, 2011, pp. 391–392). A shared sense of mission has been widely shown to be associated with school effectiveness. Mission statements would be expected to differ markedly between colleges that, for example, place a high value on public service from those with an emphasis on entrepreneurship. This type of textual data has the advantage of being publicly available at no cost and readily accessible in this age of online data collection. Mission statements can be systematically and reliably coded into thematic categories. An additional advantage is that the large and varied nature of a number of entities producing mission statements makes it possible to adapt mixed method or quantitative sampling strategies that extend the argument for the generalizability of the findings.

The Creamer and Ghoston (2012) study foregrounded as one of the exemplars in Chapter 6 is an example of a type of mixed methods content analysis of mission statements that could readily be undertaken by a newcomer to research. Interested in issues related to gender diversity, Creamer and Ghoston initially inductively coded mission statements from colleges of engineering for the types of outcomes expected of graduates. The same approach could be used to identify the types of values explicitly and implicitly endorsed in mission statements. Creamer and Ghoston shifted to a quantitative approach in a second stage of analysis, where they identified differences in the demographic characteristics of the colleges that emphasized values related to diversity in a mission statement.

Uses of content analysis to study the characteristics of mixed methods research published in a field. One of the principal uses of a mixed method approach to content analysis is as a tool to analyze the prevalence and design features of mixed methods studies reported in journal articles in a field. This includes analysis of patterns of usage of rationales, designs, mixing, and sampling strategies. Data for this type of study are collected at a single point in time through a process of a systematic keyword search of databases and/or selected journals. Analysis begins only after all the articles are collected and carefully scrutinized for relevance.

There are many examples of content analyses conducted to assess the prevalence and characteristics of mixed methods articles in a field that can serve as models for graduate student research. These include analyses of the mixed methods literature in many subfields in education (e.g., general education, Truscott et al., 2010; gifted education, Leech, Collins, Jiao, & Onwuegbuzie, 2011; math education, Ross & Onwuegbuzie, 2012, and Hart, Smith, Swars, & Smith, 2009). Results from these analyses are reported in Table 10.1. Doctoral students in my mixed methods class have published content analyses of the use of mixed methods when studying topics in their own disciplines (e.g., literature in family studies, Gambrel & Butler, 2013; literature in engineering education, Kafir & Creamer, 2014; and science education, Schram, 2014).

Some interrelated publications by a faculty member at a university in Spain further demonstrate my argument that content analysis of a body of published research using mixed methods approaches is well within the scope of what can be accomplished in a reasonable period of time. Molina-Azorin appears as lead author in at least four content analyses of the mixed methods literature in different subfields in business (e.g., organizational research, management research, strategic management, and entrepreneurial research) in a two-year span between 2010 and 2012 (Molina-Azorin, 2010, 2011, 2012; Molina-Azorin, López-Gamero, Pereira-Moliner, & Pertusa-Ortega, 2012). The tally notches up to five published content analyses of the methodological literature in a two-year span when an article he appeared in as a second author is added (López-Fernandez & Molina-Azorin, 2011).

Content analyses that are conducted with the purpose of analyzing how mixed method approaches have been used to study a topic or academic field are frequently guided by a similar set of readily replicable research questions. For example, a team of researchers from Georgia State University (Truscott et al., 2010) undertook a project to examine the prevalence rate of mixed methods in eleven prominent educational journals in literacy, mathematics, social studies, and science. These authors posed the research questions for their study this way:

1. How many mixed methods research articles were published in this collection of journals during a specific time period?
2. How did the numbers of mixed methods research articles vary by year, by journal, and by educational domain? (p. 319)

The addition of a qualitatively oriented research question about the value-added of a mixed method approach would enhance the contribution of this kind of content analysis.

Other authors pursuing content analyses of the mixed method literature in a discipline or topic provide examples of research questions that look more deeply into the issue of how different designs or mixing have been used by authors publishing in that field. These could include coding articles for purpose or rationale for using mixed methods, timing of data collection and analysis, and type and amount of mixing. This approach is evident in one of the research questions posed by López-Fernandez and Molina-Azorin (2011) in a content analysis of interdisciplinary educational journals. By focusing on analyzing how mixing was accomplished, these authors model a research question that could readily be adapted by others:

What are the characteristics in terms of purpose of mixing and design in mixed methods articles identified in three journals over the period 2005 to 2010? (p. 270)

A research question about type and amount of mixing appears in many content analyses of mixed methods publications, including quite recently by Cameron, Sankaran, and Scales (2015) in a study of the literature in management research. An interest in how mixing was accomplished is at the center of multiple interlinked publications produced by O'Cathain and her colleagues from the United Kingdom about research proposals from the area of health sciences (O'Cathain, 2010; O'Cathain, Murphy, & Nicholl, 2007a, 2007b, 2008).

Content analyses that consider quality. Consideration of the quality of publications in the sample is not something that is routinely addressed by content analyses of mixed method publications. One way this can be done in a dissertation is by systematically applying an existing rubric designed to measure quality, such as those introduced in Chapter 8. Developing an original rubric is another way to approach the task.

Authors of two relatively recent mixed method content analyses used guidelines about expectations for reporting in mixed methods in order to address a research question about the quality of these publications (i.e., Cameron et al., 2015; Schram, 2014). Schram scored articles on a four-item rubric she devised, while Cameron and her colleagues extracted a few items from a comprehensive evaluative framework for reporting produced by Morse and Niehaus (2009) to single out exemplary publications for further case analysis. Neither of these authors leveraged the potential of a strong qualitative component to identify other ways the articles might have been original or innovative.

Schram's (2014) content analysis makes a significant contribution to the literature by demonstrating the way a rubric about reporting standards can be incorporated in a mixed methods analysis. She devised a four-item rubric to create a quantitative score to answer a research question related to quality: "What articles from the sample best reflect contemporary assumptions about mixed methods research methodology"? (p. 2621). She created a scale to systematically score each article on aspects of reporting related to methodological grounding in the literature, clarity about rationale for using mixed methods, and two items related to mixing. Schram's approach to evaluating quality shares some of the features with the Mixed Method Evaluation Rubric (MMER) introduced in Chapter 8.

Cameron et al. (2015) also included a research question about the quality of the reporting in their analysis of the use of mixed methods in the research literature in project management. They singled out exemplars by applying a comprehensive set of reporting guidelines developed by Morse and Neihaus (2009) about issues that should be addressed in a mixed method publication.

A mixed method content analysis that might be conducted by a graduate student to fulfill the requirements of a dissertation requires a set of empirical procedures to systematically identify, screen, code, and analyze a body of literature. The use of an auditable protocol is what distinguishes a content analysis from a systematic review (Sandelowski, 2008). An auditable protocol is simply a data collection form that facilitates the systematic coding of the data. This type of protocol can be applied to many types of questions that are suitable for a mixed method dissertation, including considering values addressed in mission statements, themes emerging from posts on social media sites or in threaded conversations that occur in online forums, and analyses intended to categorize the methodological and thematic qualities of a body of literature.

We shift our attention now from the type of issues that are considered during the planning stage of a research project to the essentials of organizing a mixed methods research publication that communicates a priority on mixing.

ORGANIZING A MIXED METHODS RESEARCH MANUSCRIPT

Conventions about the major sections for organizing a research proposal or publication were first introduced in the 1940s and are now universally used (Sollaci & Pereira, 2004). This includes an introduction, literature review, description of the procedures used, summary of findings or results, and discussion or interpretation of results. Dahlberg, Wittink, and Gallo (2010) provide a checklist of the structure of an empirical article with a detailed itemization of what is routinely included in each section of a conventional research report. This is the same style advocated by the American Psychological Association (2010) and is evident in the multiple versions of a style manual that is widely adopted by many academic disciplines.

McGill (1990) considered a standardized format for reporting to be an aspect of the rhetoric of science. He argued that demonstrating familiarity with it is a prerequisite for entry into scientific circles. Using a standardized format makes it easier for a reader to zero in on what most interests them in a publication and, consequently, makes it more likely they will read it. Adhering to the conventional reporting format sends a message that the study was conducted scientifically. A distinct advantage of the standardized format is that "readers tend to assume scientific rigor as long as everything is presented the way it should be" (McGill, 1990, p. 131).

The choice about how to present information about the different phases of a mixed methods project within the conventional reporting format is no trivial matter. Like the tables and figures, these influence the amount of space that is devoted to the qualitative, quantitative, and mixed methods phase of a study in the methods, results, and discussion section of a manuscript. The amount of space and the way it is organized communicates if priority has been awarded to the qualitative, quantitative, or mixing phase. The underlying concern in reporting is to be attentive to strategies for organizing the manuscript in ways that clearly communicate the centrality of an ongoing interaction between the qualitative and quantitative phases.

O'Cathain (2009) catalogued two major approaches to organizing information in a publication about the qualitative, quantitative, and mixing phases of a mixed method study. She referred to these as a *segregated* and an *integrated* approach. Both are linked to the design of the study and the timing of how the phases are executed. The segregated approach to reporting is used most frequently. It occurred in almost two thirds of the grant proposals she analyzed. Authors using a segregated approach organize their manuscript in a way that is well-suited to a multimethod rather than mixed method approach. They separate out the discussion of the qualitative and quantitative phases of the study either into two different chapters or two different sections of the manuscript.

The integrated model to reporting is more consistent with a methodological perspective centered on mixing. Authors using this format weave references to the interaction between the qualitative and quantitative strands throughout the major sections of the manuscript (Bazeley, 2012; Leech, 2012; O'Cathain, 2009).

Table 9.3 builds on O'Cathain's (2009) work but suggests four approaches to organizing a mixed method manuscript, rather than two. The approaches are, in effect, a continuum that ranges from completely segregated to segregated to integrated to completely integrated.

Commentary about the interplay between the qualitative and quantitative analyses is relegated to a separate section in all but the completely integrated approach.

The segregated approach to organizing a mixed method manuscript is the one that raises the most concerns. It organizes a manuscript into two loosely linked sections: one section that details the methods and results from one phase and a second that uses the same procedure for a second phase. This type of organizational strategy often signals two

TABLE 9.3 ■ Ways to Organize a Mixed Methods Manuscript			
Completely Segregated	**Segregated**	**Integrated**	**Completely Integrated**
The article is divided into two parts: one with the methods and results of the qualitative strand and a second with the methods and results of the quantitative strand. No separate section for mixing is available.	Discussion about the qualitative and quantitative strands is organized into two different sections in the methods, results, and discussion sections of the manuscript.	References to the qualitative and quantitative strands are woven throughout the methods, results, and discussion section of a manuscript. It includes a separate section that describes mixing.	References to the qualitative, quantitative, and mixing strands are woven throughout the methods, results, and discussion section of a manuscript.

very loosely connected studies. The concern about the suitability of a mixed method label for this type of study is that it misrepresents the underlying logic of the inquiry.

Stemler and his colleagues (2011) used an extreme variant of the segregated approach to report the results of research about school mission statements that I have referred to as *completely segregated* in Table 9.3. While the authors display convincing evidence of their content area expertise, the organization of the manuscript communicates unfamiliarity with the conventions in mixed methods. The article is divided into one section that describes the methods and results from the first phase of the study and a second that does the same for the second phase. Language that links the two is left to the concluding section. The omission of any references to the foundational mixed methods literature is a tip-off that the authors may well be operating without knowledge of the expectations and conventions for reporting mixed methods research.

Being mindful that the organizational structure of a mixed method manuscript communicates the priority of the qualitative, quantitative, and mixing strands extends to other aspects of reporting, including to the visuals and graphics that are included. In the next section, we return to the topic of the indicators of methodological transparency in reporting. These are valuable for the new researcher to keep in mind as he or she begins the process of organizing and drafting a publication.

EXTENDING THE QUALITY OF REPORTING

Strategies for reporting play a pivotal role, if not a singular role, in the way that the quality of the research is judged (O'Cathain, 2009). Most typologies or guidelines, such as the Good Reporting of a Mixed Methods Study (GRAMMS) presented by O'Cathain et al. (2008), are simple checklists for what should be included in the write-up of a study that are all reflections of methodological transparency. These routinely include such items as justification for the study, description of design features, and a description of when and how mixing occurred. These differ from the types of issues addressed by a rubric such as the MMER, which is framed in order to get at the twin issues that underscore the importance of both documenting the research process and indicators of the quality of the outcomes.

The credibility of the conclusions is warranted or supported by documentation present in a report about the process used to reach the conclusions. O'Cathain and the colleagues that joined her after she completed her dissertation have published extensively about reporting standards that reflect quality (O'Cathain, 2010; O'Cathain et al., 2007a, 2007b, 2008). The six items in the GRAMMS (O'Cathain et al., 2008) are widely acknowledged elsewhere, including in the manuscript guidelines for the *Journal of Mixed Methods Research* and an instrumental document produced for the National Institute for Health, *Best Practices for Mixed Methods Research in Health Services* (O'Cathain et al., 2010). The GRAMMS is practical in that it is brief and it is relatively easy to apply. Cameron and her colleagues (2015) used the GRAMMS in their content analysis of the literature in management research.

Table 9.4 is a considerably more detailed list of expectations for transparency than that first reported by O'Cathain et al. (2008) in the GRAMMS but is more reflective of what is itemized in a later publication by O'Cathain (2010). I have aligned the type of transparency with the section of a conventionally organized research article. I have added a seventh type of transparency in reporting, foundational transparency, to the section about transparency in the literature review. I include it because it contributes to making a judgment about the credibility of a manuscript by adding a measure of the author's expertise in research methods. Absence of this type of transparency often accompanies low levels of other types of transparency. It often introduces doubt about the quality of mixed method studies with two strands that are, at best, only minimally interconnected.

In this table, I make it easier for the researcher new to mixed methods to use these guidelines to organize a manuscript by aligning the criteria to the section in a manuscript where it is most likely to appear. I illustrate the different types of methodological transparency using one of the chapter exemplars in Table 9.5.

Visual displays such as tables and figures are important tools for researchers using any methods to document both the process of and product of the analytical procedures.

Process-Oriented Graphics

In mixed methods, visual displays can provide evidence of causality, demonstrate change over time, and, most importantly, integrate or compare qualitative and quantitative evidence. They contribute to methodological transparency and thus are included in the Guidelines for Methodological Transparency in Mixed Methods by Research Phase adapted from O'Cathain (2010) and listed in Table 9.4. In mixed methods, an effective process-oriented figure provides a map that links the results and conclusions of a research project to its qualitative, quantitative, or mixing source.

TABLE 9.4 ■ Guidelines for Methodological Transparency for Reporting in Mixed Methods by Research Phase		
Location in Research Report	**Type of Transparency**	**Definition**
1. Introduction	Rationale	Identifying the rationale or justification for using mixed methods
	Design	Describing key aspects of the design of the study, including the timing, priority, and design and/or illustrating them in a figure
2. Literature review	Foundational	Grounding demonstrated use of the relevant content and methodological literature
3. Methods	Data	Providing details about the sample, data collection, and analytical procedures for the qualitative, quantitative, and mixed elements of the research project
	Mixing	Using language that explains when and how mixing occurred
4. Results	Interpretive	Providing clarity about what results emerged from the qualitative, quantitative, and mixed analysis; also includes demonstrating the link between the meta-inference and qualitative, quantitative, and mixed results
5. Discussion	Value-added	Explaining the anticipated and unanticipated contribution of mixing methods to producing inferences and meta-inferences

Source: Adapted with modifications from O'Cathain (2010).

Visuals are a key aspect to communicating the credibility of any empirical study (O'Cathain, 2009). With careful ordering, visuals that represent the results of the analysis can allow the reader to follow the development of an argument (McGill, 1990). Demonstrating the link between a result, conclusion, or meta-inference with its data source is a type of interpretive transparency, what Teddlie and Tashakkori (2009) refer to as *interpretive rigor*. This is a type of reflexivity that contributes to methodological transparency by explicitly linking the source of data to a conclusion or inference. According to McGill, who no doubt was reflecting a positivist paradigm, "They communicate the simple yet powerful message to the reader that one is in the presence of science" (2010, p. 141).

It is common practice in mixed methods to include a figure in the methods section of a proposal or publication that maps the steps in the process of data collection and analysis. As a streamlined summary of steps in the analytical process, these are particularly instrumental in helping a reader understand how a complex, multiphase study was executed. It is conventional to depict a two-phase study where data were collected and analyzed separately with horizontal orientation, while sequential designs are drawn with a vertical orientation. Because mixing is so often relegated to the final inference stage and the stages only loosely linked, this type of process-oriented figures rarely highlights an ongoing interaction between the qualitative and quantitative phase.

In the chapter exemplar reporting on an ambitious, multiphase study of resource-poor schools in urban settings, Jang et al. (2008) provided an exemplar of a process-oriented figure that highlights what they described as the messy process of executing mixed method analytical procedures. By *messy*, I expect they meant it was part of the process that had an emergent quality that was not anticipated.

Figure 9.2 is a reproduction of Figure 3 (p. 230) from Jang et al. (2008). Its three-column format that delineates how mixing occurred is innovative.

The centrality of mixing is what distinguishes this figure and puts it forward as a model for others to follow. The figure is organized into three columns that depict what was originally conceived as an independent and parallel analytical process. The left column is devoted to the qualitative steps in the process and the right column to the steps taken to execute the quantitative portion of the study. The originality in this figure is in the rectangles aligned vertically down the center column. This is what the authors refer to as the messy part of the analysis. The six rectangles in the center column depict procedures that were used to mix the qualitative and quantitative data. They are labeled: member checking, data comparison, consolidation into themes, correlational analysis of the consolidated themes, identifying cases, and case narratives of the schools.

The process-oriented graphic in Jang et al. (2008) meets the expectation of interpretive transparency because it provides an explicit acknowledgment of the data sources used to construct the conclusions. It is useful as a model because it captures the type of mixed methods study where different strategies for mixing are embedded at multiple points during the analysis.

Illustrating the Guidelines for Methodological Transparency With an Exemplar

To add to the overriding practical purpose of this textbook, I pursue the utility of the guidelines for methodological transparency presented in Table 9.4 in two different ways. The first is to demonstrate its utility for identifying methodologically credible mixed methods studies by showing how it applies to dissecting one of the previously featured chapter exemplars. The second is to compare the way this article scores on the GRAMMS (O'Cathain et al., 2008) and the MMER. This makes it possible to see if anything can be gained by a rubric that extends the reporting standards to include criteria related to the validity or interpretive rigor of inferences. The latter criterion is considerably harder to evaluate.

Although it may be no easy task to find another manuscript where the author has been conscientious about meeting reporting guidelines, Table 9.5 applies the set of expectations for transparency in reporting shown in Table 9.4 and demonstrates how each one is manifested in the mixed method article by Catallo et al. (2013). The table also includes information that specifies in which section of the document each appeared.

FIGURE 9.2 ■ Figure Illustrating Steps

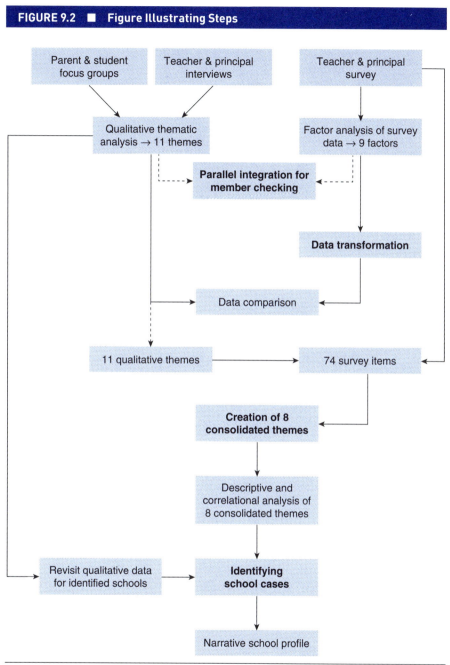

Source: Jang, E., McDougall, D. E., Herbert, M., & Russell, P. (2008). Integrative mixed methods data analytic strategies in research in school success in challenging circumstances. *Journal of Mixed Methods Research*, *2*(3), 221–247. doi: 10.1177/1558689808315323.

TABLE 9.5 ■ Types of Methodological Transparency Unique to Mixed Methods by Research Phase as Applied to a Chapter Exemplar by Catallo, Jack, Ciliska, and MacMillan (2013)			
Type of Transparency	**Section of Document**	**Page Number**	**Quote From Document**
Rationale	Introduction	2	"The purpose for this sequential mixed methods design was to enhance initial quantitative results by using follow-up qualitative methods."
Design	Introduction	1	"Our goal is to describe the process of implementing a sequential explanatory mixed methods study involving a randomized controlled trial (RCT) with a sub-analysis of quantitative data and a qualitative grounded theory approach."
Foundational	Introduction and Literature Review	1–3	Multiple references to mixed method grounded theory methodological literature
Data	Methods	4	Figure 1 depicting the two phases and describing the mixing
Mixing	Results	7	(a) Figure 1 depicting the two phases and describing the mixing (b) section of results labeled with heading "Integrating of Quantitative and Qualitative Data" (c) Table 3 showing one type of mixing
Interpretive	Results	7	"Participants with high scores [on a quantitative measure of violence exposure] were most concerned with being judged by health care providers for remaining in an abusive relationship." Those with high scores for emotional abuse had more difficulty identifying the relationship as abusive.
Value-added	Discussion	9	Adhering to sampling strategy and principle of randomizing from the randomized controlled trial phase reduced selection bias in the qualitative phase

Table 9.5 demonstrates a credit-worthy thoroughness in documenting the seven indicators of reporting quality in this exemplar. Its framing within a methodological purpose and the documentation of immersion in the mixed methods literature evident by the reference list probably offer some insight into why the authors so ably met the expectations outlined in the reporting guidelines.

CONCLUSIONS

In a summary of the core characteristics of mixed methods research, Teddlie and Tashakkori (2012) made the observation that it is necessary to be a methods connoisseur to do mixed methods research. By that, I think they meant that it is important that anyone seeking to make a contribution to knowledge or to advance practice through research must present evidence of not only content- or topic-related expertise but also expertise in the methods they have chosen to use. Authors of two of the chapter exemplars demonstrate that this task is more doable by a novice researcher than it might seem at first (e.g., Catallo et al., 2013; Cooper, 2014). Both of these authors were able to simultaneously demonstrate sufficient expertise in their content areas and in mixed methods to produce a credible mixed method research article from dissertation research.

There are many ways a newcomer to the research enterprise with foundational knowledge in mixed methods can craft a dissertation that is doable within the context of limited resources and time. Several methods are well suited to a mixed approach that can be adapted to fulfill the requirements of a degree. In this chapter, I have proposed several ways to adapt content analysis to graduate student research. Other chapters include discussion of exemplars worth replicating that use grounded theory and case study. The critical incident technique (Butterfield, Borgen, Amundson, & Maglio, 2005) and various kinds of systematic literature reviews (Heyvaert, Hannes, & Onghena, 2017) are additional methods that lend themselves to research that a graduate student might undertake.

Most advanced degree students frame their thinking about a research topic in a way that is compatible with the metaphor of an architectural arch. Their priority is to work through the logistics of planning and executing a single study. Students who aspire to a career that involves research are likely to be motivated by a more ambitious agenda. This is akin to the metaphor of the bridge introduced at the front of this chapter because of the ambition to design an initial study that can serve as a way to build a long-term research agenda. A mixed methods publication might be only one of the publications produced from projects conceptualized in this way.

In addition to empirical publications and presentations, students completing a mixed methods dissertation are likely to find that they have much to say about the methods and what they did to adapt them to their particular research problem and context. Packaging these in a methodological article can widen the impact and audience of one's research. This type of publication is designed to describe the process used in an original empirical research project in ways that might be helpful to other researchers undertaking projects with the same methods. That, for example, is what Jang et al. (2008) set out to do in an article that appeared in the *Journal of Mixed Methods Research* with the stated purpose of using insights learned from a mixed methods study of urban schools to illustrate the messy process of using of mixed methods data analytical strategies. Even for someone who does not aspire to become an expert in mixed methods, this type of methodological article has the distinct advantage of generating entirely new, and often unexpected, publication and presentation venues.

Choosing to describe a research study as mixed methods carries an expectation for methodological transparency that is not associated with research identified as multimethod. At minimum, mixed methods require that the author acknowledge foundational literature, explain the rationale for using mixed methods, describe the design and timing of the data collection using conventional language, and identify matters related to how and when mixing occurred. Methodological conventions are less demanding for studies framed as multimethod.

We close the chapter with a summary of its key points and the consideration of what the next and final chapter of the book will bring.

Summary of Key Points

1. The credibility of a study rests almost wholly on the way it is reported.

2. The way a mixed method publication is organized reflects the priority awarded to the qualitative, quantitative, and/or mixed method phases.

3. The multimethod label is appropriate for studies that lack research questions that require analysis involving interlinked variables.

4. There are features of the design of a mixed method study that facilitate meaningful mixing.

5. The design features that are most feasible for a mixed method study undertaken by a graduate student include the same or overlapping qualitative and quantitative participants and data collection using publicly available instruments or data.

6. Content analysis is a method that is especially adaptable to a mixed methods approach and to research that a graduate student might pursue.

7. It is common practice in mixed methods to include a figure in a publication that maps the steps taken in the process of data collection and analysis.

8. Visual displays, such as tables and figures, are important tools for the researcher to use to document both the process of and product of the analytical procedures.

There is no doubt that the topic of quality in mixed methods and how to assess it will continue to engage mixed methods practitioners as emerging technologies create innovative opportunities for interlocking different sources of data in ways that could not be imagined when the movement first began to cohere ten to fifteen years ago. The final chapter reviews the shifts in views among experts about the most controversial aspects of mixed methods research and considers new directions that promise to keep the field moving forward.

Key Term

- Content analysis

Supplemental Activities

1. Apply the guidelines for methodological transparency listed in Table 9.4 to the article by Stemler et al. (2011) about school mission statements to determine if the lack of foundational grounding in the mixed methods literature is reflected in other ways throughout the article.

2. Compare the qualities and what is communicated about mixing in three or four mixed methods publications that include a process-oriented figure that maps steps in the process of data collection and analysis. Compare what is communicated about mixing in these visual displays with the one discussed in the chapter from Jang et al. (2008), which designated a third column to itemize the steps that involved mixing.

Recommended Reading

Catallo, C., Jack, S. M., Ciliska, D., & MacMillan, H. L. (2013). Mixing a grounded theory approach with a randomized controlled trial related to intimate partner violence: What challenges arise for mixed methods research? *Nursing Research and Practice*, 1–12.

Jang, E., McDougall, D. E., Pollon, D., Herbert, M., & Russell, P. (2008). Integrative data analytic strategies in research in school success in challenging circumstances. *Journal of Mixed Methods Research, 2*(3), 221–247.

O'Cathain, A., Murphy, E., & Nicholl, J. (2008). The quality of mixed methods studies in health services research. *Journal of Health Services Research and Policy, 13*(2), 92–98.

CONTROVERSIES AND FUTURE DIRECTIONS

PART FOUR

10

CONTROVERSIES AND FUTURE DIRECTIONS

PRINCIPAL PURPOSES OF THE CHAPTER

1. To offer a way to conceptualize the priority of the qualitative, quantitative, and mixing strands of a mixed methods study by using inferences and meta-inferences

2. To address ongoing controversies about mixed methods, including by challenging the assumption that mixed methods research is simply a combination of qualitative and quantitative approaches

In the preceding chapters, I have returned on a number of occasions to the metaphor of the architectural arch as a way to conceptualize design features of mixed methods research. In this use of the metaphor, one arm of the arch visualizes the qualitative data and methods and the second arm visualizes the quantitative data and methods. The keystone at the apex of the arch mirrors the principal goal of a mixed methods approach: to integrate qualitative and quantitative inferences in ways that produce meaningful conclusions.

There is another, entirely different way to conceptualize the arch as a metaphor for mixed methods research. It shifts the focus from design features to the product or outcome of mixed methods research or its inferences as the central point of interest. The arch metaphor is compatible with both conceptualizations. One attends more to the mechanics of how the research is executed and the second gives priority to the value-added of mixing and the inferences or conclusions produced.

Figure 10.1 is used to depict this reframing of the arch as a metaphor that gives priority to identifying the inferences produced rather than the design employed.

FIGURE 10.1 ■ Conceptualizing the Conclusions of a Mixed Methods Study

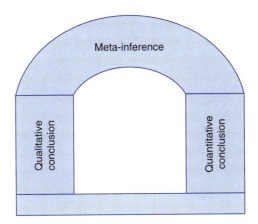

This depiction of the arch offers a way to highlight the conclusions drawn from the qualitative and quantitative phases of a mixed methods study and provides a way to substantiate their role to producing an overarching meta-inference.

This second mindset for visualizing and deconstructing a mixed methods research article shifts attention away from the long-standing attention that has been awarded in the methodological literature to design features such as priority and timing. This reenvisioning of the arch metaphor bears some relationship to one of the overriding controversies about mixed methods research that will be addressed in this chapter: the concern that too much attention has been devoted to a prescribed set of designs and too little to its products (Guest, 2012), which are generally conceived as the inferences and meta-inference.

This reconceptualization of the arch metaphor and shift away from a preoccupation with initial design features has strong implications for the way that mixed methods designs are conceptualized and for the way that quality is conceived. It is consistent with Teddlie and Tashakkori's (2009) argument that while inference quality is related to the process used to generate it, an overall assessment of the quality in mixed methods rests on the quality of the meta-inferences produced. They expressed this viewpoint in an expansive way in observing, "Obviously, the quality of the entire research project depends on the degree to which integration, blending, or linking of QUAL [qualitative] and QUANT [quantitative] inferences is achieved" (p. 292). A promising by-product of this argument that I will pursue in this chapter is that an emphasis on the conclusions generated in a mixed methods study invites innovative ways to diagram or visualize it. Such visualization can highlight the link between the knowledge generated and its qualitative, quantitative, or mixing source.

PURPOSE, GOALS, AND CONTRIBUTION OF THE CHAPTER

In this final chapter, I pursue the idea of conceptualizing a mixed methods research project in terms of the inferences and meta-inferences that are produced rather than trying to capture the way it is designed or executed. We revisit issues raised in preceding chapters by reviewing some persistent controversies and criticisms about mixed methods research, including the concern about the overreliance on a small set of conventionally conceived designs.

The principal contribution of the chapter is to offer an innovative way to conceptualize the insight gained from a mixed method approach. The following goals guide the chapter:

1. Weigh evidence about the prevalence of mixed methods across fields against the concern that has been expressed about its emergence as a dominant discourse.
2. Explore some ambiguities inherent in the way the mixed methods research designs have been conceptualized, including about how timing and priority have been defined.
3. Address the criticism that mixed methods researchers have been overly preoccupied with a small set of preconceived designs and design features.
4. Explore ways to visualize mixed methods research designs that highlight mixing.
5. Reconceptualize priority in terms of inferences and meta-inferences.
6. Challenge the assumption that mixed methods research is simply a combination of qualitative and quantitative approaches.

There are several topics that figure prominently in lists of controversies about mixed methods research that I am not going to revisit. One of these is uncontestable: the accuracy of the charge that there is a proliferation of terminology introduced by different authors of the methodological literature that newcomers to the field understandably find incredibly frustrating (Creswell, 2011; Tashakkori & Teddlie, 2010; Teddlie & Tashakkori, 2012). A second one is the charge that mixed methods devalues qualitative research or uses it in a decidedly secondary role (Giddings & Grant, 2007; Hesse-Biber, 2010a, 2010b). This argument is reflected in the focus on fully integrated mixed methods designs that have been at the center of this textbook and the emphasis that has been placed on the value-added of an emergent element. Fully integrated mixed method studies are executed through an ongoing iterative exchange between the qualitative and quantitative strands that invites an engagement with the unexpected and often paradoxical results that cannot emerge when the mindset is driven by a singular hypothesis-testing framework and a linear approach to analysis.

An additional controversy I do not pursue at length in this chapter is one that I devoted an entire chapter to in the first section of the book: the topic of paradigms and the concern that qualitative and quantitative approaches are incompatible. Both Creswell (2011) and Tashakkori and Teddlie (2010) recognize this as an ongoing controversy. Literature about this topic continues to emerge despite the claim of a cease-fire in the paradigm wars. It is a topic that is of seemingly endless fascination to methodologists, but not one that many pragmatically oriented students find engaging.

Contribution of the Chapter

This chapter departs from conventional wisdom in several ways. It adds to the controversies raised about mixed methods by addressing the concern that too much attention has been devoted to design features at the expense of the principal value-added of a mixed approach, which lies in the power of the knowledge it generates. It deconstructs the logic of combination that underlies so much of the discourse about mixed methods. Further innovation in this chapter is evident in suggestions about ways to visualize the centrality of mixing in figures and flowcharts. An additional contribution of this chapter is to introduce the idea that meta-inferences provide a window into how a study was designed as well as its purpose.

Organization of the Chapter

The chapter is organized in three major sections. In the first section, we will direct an eye to the past in order to consider controversies and points of contention about mixed methods research. This includes the perception that there is a proliferation of mixed methods research to the point it amounts to a new heterodoxy. A second controversy is about the amount of attention that has been awarded to distinguishing design features of mixed methods studies and the viability of the small cadre of designs that have become the mainstay of the mixed methods literature. In the second section of the chapter, we cast our eyes in a more forward-thinking direction by considering the implications of conceptualizing mixed methods studies in terms of their outcomes rather than the way they are executed. At the close of the chapter, I revisit the exemplars by considering what they have to tell us about mixed methods in practice and consider future directions.

LOOKING BACK: CONTROVERSIES ABOUT MIXED METHODS RESEARCH

There is little doubt that since 1990, there has been a surge in the rhetoric about mixed methods and their potential contributions (Guest, 2012; Truscott et al., 2010). Some attribute the popularity of mixed methods to funding agencies, such as the National Institute of Health (Giddings & Grant, 2007). Denzin echoed this assumption when he pronounced, "Mixed, multiple, and emergent methods are everywhere today," (2010, p. 419). Another skeptic shares the same viewpoint about the expansive presence of mixed methods: "There is little doubt that the dissemination of mixed methods research has increased and that the presentation and representation of the discourse is now far reaching" (Freshwater, 2007, p. 138). Both support the assertion by pointing to support from funding agencies, the growing audience for mixed methods research at professional meetings, and the emergence of the *Journal for Mixed Methods Research*. Perceptions about the proliferation of mixed methods research has generated concern that the movement is so strong that it is eroding interest in qualitative and quantitative approaches.

Prominent skeptics have charged that mixed methods are emerging as the dominant discourse in the methodological literature. Freshwater is among this group. She asserts, "I would argue that mixed methods research text has become a discourse and is nearing becoming a meta-narrative" (2007, p. 139). She charges that a mixed methods approach was intended to offer a creative alternative to a positivist mindset but has been adopted as a "mindless mantra" (p. 135) that has become "bland" in its recipe-like aspirations for certainty. Authors of a recent publication grounded in the context of political science expressed a similar concern that the growth of mixed methods research has been so explosive that it is tantamount to becoming a gold standard. These authors observed, "[Mixed methods research] is no longer simply an option for pragmatically coping with emergent challenges and opportunities in advancing a research agenda. It is increasingly viewed as disciplinary best practice and as a rationale for promoting standardized multi-method skill sets" (Ahmed & Sil, 2012, p. 948).

Underlying their concern is the impact of the proliferation of mixed methods on professional practice and the perception that mixed methods research comes at the expense of downplaying the importance of deep methodological expertise, particularly in quantitative research methods. Denzin (2010) shares a similar concern that mixed methods is a type of "methodological poaching" (p. 420).

Evidence About Prevalence

Available evidence does not entirely confirm the alarm that mixed methods has become the gold standard or best practice in research in the social, human, and applied sciences. A synthesis of content analyses of the characteristics of the mixed methods literature conducted in a variety of disciplinary contexts do not support the idea that there has been an explosive growth in articles reporting on mixed methods research. Such analyses do support, however, an impressive breadth of utilization across many disciplinary domains.

A seminal piece by Alise and Teddlie (2010) based on Alise's ambitious content analysis of 600 publications in 20 prestigious journals in applied and non-applied disciplines dispels the notion that mixed methods have overtaken all other methodological approaches in popularity. Their analysis shows that quantitative approaches continue to retain their hold on the majority of publications (69.5%). Qualitative research was used second most prominently (19.5%), followed by mixed methods research, representing about 11% of all research publications. Figure 10.2 summarizes the results from the analysis conducted by Alise and Teddlie in a pie chart.

Mixed methods approaches were more than twice as likely to be used in applied disciplines, such as education and nursing (15%), than in less practically oriented and more theoretically driven fields, such as psychology and sociology (6%).

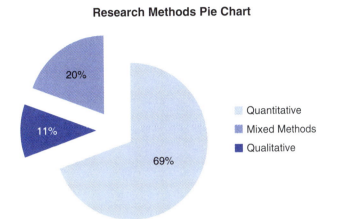

FIGURE 10.2 ■ Research Methods Used by Pure and Applied Disciplines as Reported by Alise and Teddlie (2014)

Although such comparisons are mitigated by differences in the operational definition of mixed methods, Table 10.1 provides a compilation[1] of content analyses that report on the prevalence of mixed methods research in nine different fields. These include business, marketing, education, health sciences, family science, school psychology, library science, counseling, and sports management.

Despite the wide variations in the prevalence rates reported, the message communicated most clearly by the summary table is the breadth of the reach of mixed methods across disciplines that extend far beyond education and nursing and that include fields as diverse as library science, multiple fields in business and marketing, tourism, and sports management. Mixed methods have been adopted in fields yet to be reported in the prevalence literature, including political science and applied fields such as agricultural education.

Truscott et al. (2010) expressed surprise that the prevalence of mixed methods approaches that is documentable from the literature does not match the rhetoric advertising its explosive growth since the 1990s. After analyzing 2,381 studies published in 11 national and international journals in education between 1995 and 2005, these authors calculated a prevalence rate of identifiable mixed methods studies that matches that of Alise and Teddlie (2012) of 14%. Truscott et al. detected little variation across years or areas within education in the number and percentage of articles identifiable as mixed methods. Communicating that the data did not support their initial assumption, these authors concluded, "Mixed methods, although

---

[1] Cherie Edwards, a doctoral student in educational research and evaluation at Virginia Tech, assisted with the compilation of data presented in this table.

TABLE 10.1 ■ Prevalence Rates of Mixed Methods Research in Different Academic Fields						
Field	Authors	Year of Publication	Time Period of Review	Total # of Pub.	# of MM Pub.	% MM Pub.
Business						
Strategic Management	Molina-Azorin	2011	1997–2007	1330	152	11.4%
Entrepreneurship	Molina-Azorin	2012	2000–2009	955	81	8.4%
International Business	Hurmerinta-Peltomäki & Nummela	2006	2000–2003	484	68	14%
Marketing	Hanson & Grimmer	2007	1993–2002	1195	105	8.8%
Education						
Math Education	Hart, Smith, Swars, & Smith	2009	1995–2005	710	207	29.2%
Math Education	Ross & Onwuegbuzie	2012	2002–2006	87	27	31%
Inter. Education Journal	López-Fernandez & Molina-Azorin	2011	2005–2010	171	28	16.4%
Gifted Education	Leech, Collins, Jiao, & Onwuegbuzie	2011	2005–2009	434	19	4.3%
Health Sciences						
Health Services	Wisdom, Cavaleri, Onwuegbuzie, & Green	2012	2003–2007	1502	47	2.85%
Health Services	O'Cathain, Murphy, & Nicholl	2007	1994–2004	119	647	18.4%
Funded Health Science Proposals	Plano Clark	2010	1997–2008	272	226	83.1%
Family Science	Plano Clark, Huddleston-Casas, Churchill, Green, & Garrett	2008	1996–2005	2142	19	0.9%
School Psychology	Powell, Mihalas, Onwuegbuzie, & Daley	2008	2001–2005	873	60	6.9%
Library Science	Fidel	2008	2005–2006	465	22	5.0%
Counseling	Ray et al.	2010	1998–2007	4457	171	3.84%
Sports Management	Van Der Roest, Spaaij, & van Bottenburg	2015	1966–2011	2536	43	1.7%

considered uniquely suited to complex educational issues, does not seem to be an increasingly popular research method" (p. 317).

There are a half a dozen possible explanations for the gap between the documented prevalence rate of mixed methods research and the rhetoric about its emergence as a meta-narrative or dominant discourse. Much of the difference in prevalence rates across time and disciplines is probably attributable to definitional and labeling issues. Since the practice of adopting the mixed method label is a fairly recent phenomenon (Guest, 2012; Hesse-Biber, 2010a), many studies that combine both qualitative and quantitative approaches are not labeled as mixed methods (Truscott et al., 2010). Using the conventional language about design features such as timing and priority was not widely adopted until after 2005 (Ivankova & Kawamura, 2010).

The explanation about the gap between the perception that mixed methods is emerging as a dominant approach to research and the prevalence rates reported in content analyses of the literature is probably a bit more complicated than can simply be reduced to differences in the application of the mixed method label. The growth of the popularity of mixed methods is hard to disentangle from the wider shift to more team-based and large-scale research that is, in part, fueled by technological advancements and shifting disciplinary boundaries. It is also related to the ever-expanding role of external funding sources in shaping the agendas of research scientists. The growth in team-based research and the use of large datasets also can be linked to increasing interest in mixed and multimethod approaches, as can be the ever-higher levels of competition to secure access to publication space in the most highly ranked journals. Technological innovations, such as software that allows for the analysis of data generated from social media or that pinpoints geographical location, have also opened the door for the investigation of more multilayered and innovative research questions about social phenomenon.

There is room for skepticism about the accuracy of the 14% prevalence rate of mixed methods approaches that has been reported in the literature. Consider a fictional, multivoiced exchange that offers two different arguments to explain the gap between the number of empirical publications using a mixed methods approach and the perception that mixed methods has become the dominant discourse:

Argument 1. The growth in discourse about mixed methods has been explosive, but a good portion of it can be explained by what could be called *advocacy literature*. This is a large body of methodological literature appearing in textbooks, handbooks, and journals that excavates different aspects of the way these studies are designed. This kind of methodologically oriented article creates an opportunity for cross-disciplinary dialogue. It can serve as a venue to salvage research that might otherwise be unpublishable because the results proved insignificant or contradictory.

Argument 2. The growth in the discourse has been explosive, but in this age marked by a growth of team-based and large-scale funded research, the impact has more to do with the way research projects are being conceptualized than with the way they are executed and reported. The preeminence awarded to quantitative research, restrictions in word counts, limited publication venues devoted entirely to mixed and multiple methods approaches, and the academic reward structure all explain why the most common practice continues to be to produce separate articles to report on the qualitative and quantitative results of a research project. The gap between the way research projects are often conceptualized (i.e., as mixed methods) and the way they are reported (i.e., in separate publications) confounds attempts to estimate the prevalence of mixed method approaches across academic fields.

The lack of attention to procedures that support the integration of qualitative and quantitative data is an emerging issue in mixed methods (Tashakkori & Teddlie, 2010). This matches a growing concern about the overreliance on a small, narrowly defined set of designs that may no longer be useful and that may inadvertently mask the potential for mixing in ways that enhance explanatory power. I consider this charge in the next section and then shift our gaze toward future directions by exploring ways to visualize designs that highlight both the process and product of mixing.

REFRAMING DESIGNS TO EMPHASIZE MIXING DURING ANALYSIS

More than a half a dozen typologies have been proposed that categorize different types of mixed methods designs (Creswell & Plano Clark, 2011). These types of classification systems serve multiple purposes. They can simplify the landscape and give the inexperienced researcher confidence in his or her ability to conceive a mixed method study. A common set of research designs offers a way to establish a common language in the field, to provide structure to the field, and to legitimize the field (Guest, 2012). Historically, design-oriented classification systems have prioritized features related to the way a research project is initially conceptualized. This same priority is mirrored in quality frameworks, such as proposed in the Good Reporting of a Mixed Methods Study (GRAMMS; O'Cathain, Murphy, & Nicholl, 2008), that specify that aspects of the design, including priority and timing, be acknowledged.

As we know from previous chapters, two features have been used to characterize mixed methods designs: timing and priority. The timing of mixed methods studies is almost always presented as either sequential or concurrent. The multiphase design has received less attention. Both the concurrent and sequential designs often have been conceptualized in a way that assume that the qualitative and quantitative strands are produced quite separately. In concurrent designs—sometimes referred to as *parallel* designs—qualitative and quantitative data are collected and analyzed separately and only linked at the inference stage. The qualitative and quantitative phases are more directly linked earlier in the process in the conventional sequential design. This is when data analyzed in the first phase influences, for example, the sampling procedures utilized in the second phase.

A principal criticism of the way that timing has been conceptualized is ambiguity about whether the sequential or concurrent label applies to when the data are collected or when they are analyzed (Guest, 2012). For example, neither the concurrent or sequential label is easy to apply to a study with a longitudinal component when both the qualitative and quantitative data are collected simultaneously but over time. This was the case for example, in the exemplar featured in Chapter 5 by Young and Jaganath (2013) that collected qualitative and quantitative data to evaluate the effectiveness of using a peer moderator and online social networking for HIV education over a ten-week period. Ambiguity in the language about timing is why I have chosen to distinguish the timing of data collection in the templates and summary tables I provide about the chapter exemplars.

The conventional distinctions between a concurrent and sequential design are most readily applied to studies executed in two phases. They are less useful with multiphase designs or when there is an ongoing iterative interaction between the qualitative and quantitative strands that is more characteristic of mixed methods research today (Teddlie & Tashakkori, 2012). Team-based and interdisciplinary research is often multiphase. "The complexity and fluidity of many contemporary research studies can further confuse the indistinct borders of a typology," Guest observed (2012, p. 143).

Conceiving Mixed Priority Designs

Most reporting standards for mixed methods research identify priority as a second feature of the design of a mixed method study that is important to acknowledge. This involves a judgment about the relative weight of the qualitative and quantitative strands to the overall conclusions. Only the most broadly conceived guidelines have been offered to evaluate the priority or weighting of the qualitative, quantitative, and mixing strands. It is not clear if the judgment rests primarily on the design, execution, or results of a study. Indicators of priority can be interpreted from the title, reflexive statements about paradigmatic position, the purpose statement or research questions, and/or the space allocated to the qualitative and quantitative strands in the results and conclusions (Creswell, Shope, Plano Clark, & Green, 2006).

It is my argument that priority has been conceived of in a way that is consistent with a definitional framing of mixed methods as principally about the combination of qualitative and quantitative approaches or phases. From this perspective, only three priorities have been conceptualized: one when the qualitative phase is dominant, a second when the quantitative phase is dominant, and a third when the two phases are given equal attention in the research report.

I have argued throughout this text that the conventional approach to gauging priority overlooks the possibility of yet a fourth priority or strand, a *mixed priority*. This is a label that I have used throughout the textbook to characterize many of the exemplars. The label is most likely to apply to studies with a fully integrated mixed methods design where strategies for mixing are thoroughly embedded in both the logic and execution of a study.

Contrary to prevailing wisdom, Guest (2012) challenges the idea that priority or weighting of the qualitative, quantitative, and (I would add) mixed methods strand can be fully envisioned during the planning stages of a research project. Placing more emphasis than is conventional on the fluidity of research and the potential for unanticipated findings, Guest suggests that the relative weighting of the different approaches can only be ascertained after the data interpretation and reporting have been completed.

Inserting a Third Column: Visualizing Designs in Ways That Highlight Mixing

The timing and priority of mixed methods research designs have been conceptualized in three standard formats. Figure 10.3 reproduces a graphic that is typical of many methodological articles advocating for the adoption of mixed methods approaches in an academic field. It provides a succinct and accurate reproduction of the three basic variants of a mixed methods design that derive from a textbook by Creswell and Plano Clark (2007, 2011). The three different flowcharts encapsulated within the figure envision the sequential explanatory design where the quantitative phase occurs

FIGURE 10.3 ■ Type of Mixed Methods Designs

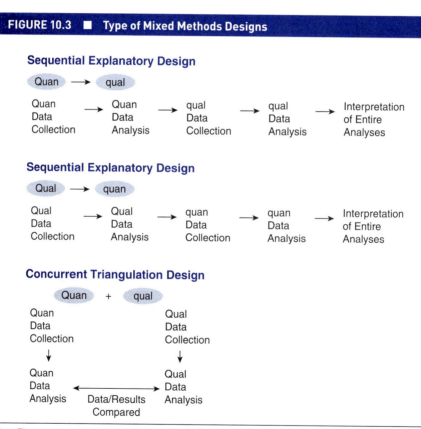

Sequential Explanatory Design

Quan ⟶ qual

Quan Data Collection → Quan Data Analysis → qual Data Collection → qual Data Analysis → Interpretation of Entire Analyses

Sequential Explanatory Design

Qual ⟶ quan

Qual Data Collection → Qual Data Analysis → quan Data Collection → quan Data Analysis → Interpretation of Entire Analyses

Concurrent Triangulation Design

Quan + qual

Quan Data Collection ↓ Quan Data Analysis

Qual Data Collection ↓ Qual Data Analysis

Data/Results Compared

Note: The second design listed in this figure is usually referred to as the Sequential Exploratory Design.

Source: Rauscher, L., & Greenfield, B. H. (2009). Advancements in contemporary physical therapy research: Use of mixed methods design. *Journal of American Physical Therapy Association, 89,* 91–100. Reproduced with permission.

first, the sequential exploratory design where the qualitative phase occurs first, and the concurrent or triangulation design where the data are collected and analyzed separately.

The visualizations of the different designs show the qualitative and quantitative phases as quite self-contained. In each of these designs, mixing is represented in a way that is incompatible with a fully integrated design. It is depicted as occurring at a single point in time, during the interpretation stage. The distinctiveness of the phases is conducive to teamwork and to the bifurcation of the research into separate qualitative and quantitative publications.

The ramifications of the widespread application of these conventionally conceived designs may well provide an explanation for the universal conclusion from numerous content analyses of bodies of literature that, regardless of labeling, most studies that combine qualitative and quantitative data are best described as multimethod because of the lack of meaningful mixing between the strands. For example, Alise and Teddlie (2010) characterized nearly half of the published studies in education that they reviewed as using a quasi-mixed design. This is a design in which two types of data are collected, but there is little or no integration of the findings or inferences (Teddlie & Tashakkori, 2009).

Authors of a few contemporary visualizations of mixed methods designs have found creative ways to highlight the role of mixing during the research process. One example comes from a figure in Wesely's (2010) methodological reflection about how she struggled to make sense of a counterintuitive conclusion that emerged from her dissertation research about the motivation of students who left a language immersion program in Canada. In a flowchart showing the steps in the research process, Wesely used gradients of black and white shading and an oval shape to highlight when mixing occurred.

Visual depictions of the stages of the research process in ways that highlight ongoing interface between the qualitative and quantitative strands make an important contribution to practice by providing models worthy of replication. Such a figure appears in the article by Durksen and Klassen (2012) about preservice teachers (featured as an exemplar in Chapter 2). Figure 10.4 reproduces Figure 1 from that article (p. 34).

The figure is unusual in that its focus is on the details of the process used during data analysis. What makes this figure commendable is that it brings to life a type of interactive exchange between the qualitative and quantitative data during analysis. This type of exchange can never be fully anticipated at the onset of a project. The figure captures the iterative nature of the exchange between the qualitative and quantitative phase that is becoming more typical in contemporary mixed methods studies.

A third example of a visualization that highlights the role of mixing during analysis is derived from a figure from the exemplar authored by Jang, McDougall, Pollon, Herbert, and Russell (2008) and described in Chapter 6. Similar to the figure reproduced from Durksen and Klassen (2012), this figure omits references to the timing of data collection. Figure 10.5 is my generalization of Jang et al.'s flowchart that was so effective in capturing central elements of a complex, multiphase research project in a succinct way.

Similar to the preceding figure, this flowchart deviates from the standard way mixed methods designs have been depicted by focusing on mixed methods analytical procedures. The centering of strategies for mixing in a separate column is what is most innovative about this visualization.

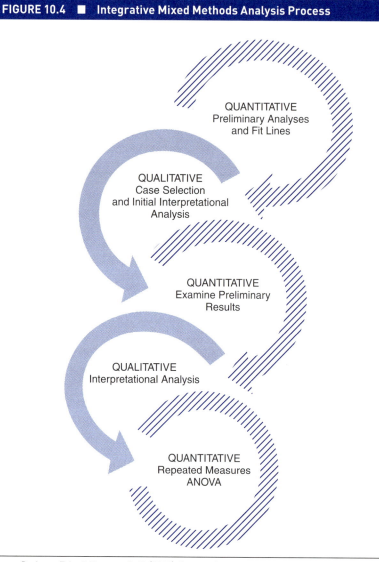

Source: Durksen, T. L., & Klassen, R. M. (2012). Pre-service teachers' weekly commitment and engagement during a final training placement: A longitudinal mixed methods study. *Educational and Child Psychology, 29* (4), 32–46.

Up to this point, I have kept with standard practice by attending to issues related to the procedures used to execute research as they might be reported in a research publication. In the next section, we shift our attention away from process and design features of a mixed methods study to explore more forward-thinking ways that centers the discussion on its product.

FIGURE 10.5 ■ A Flowchart That Highlights Mixing

Example of a Map of Mixing

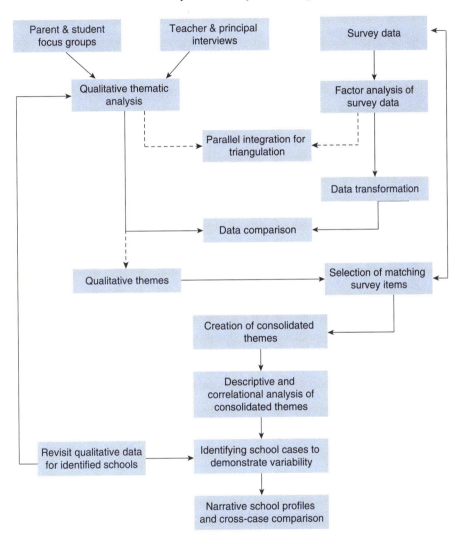

RECONCEPTUALIZING PRIORITY IN TERMS OF INFERENCES AND META-INFERENCES

Guest's provocative 2012 article in the *Journal of Mixed Methods Research* mirrors concerns voiced by others, including Tashakkori and Teddlie (2010), that the field has inadvertently over-attended to classification systems that isolate, and possibly codify, features of five or six mixed methods designs. These are designs that I am now convinced inadvertently downplay opportunities for mixing, particularly during analysis. Guest proposed recentering the discourse away from conventionally conceived designs to ways of conceptualizing that are centered on the interface between the qualitative and quantitative strands.

Linked to an alternative way to conceptualize the arch as a metaphor for mixed methods research that shifts attention from the process used to execute a research project to its outcomes, I experiment with a nontraditional way to conceptualize and map mixed method research project that highlights the value-added of mixing qualitative and quantitative approaches. This way of conceptualizing mixed method studies builds on my interest in demonstrating the value-added of mixed methods research by comparing the types of inferences that are produced by mixed method and single method research (e.g., Creamer, 2016; Creamer, Edwards, & Musaeus, 2015; Creamer & Tendhar, 2015). This type of figure does not replace the need for a design-oriented figure that provides a flowchart of the methods used for data collection and analysis.

The visualization I propose is an attempt to capture the value-added of mixed methods research by offering a way to decide whether the principal conclusions or meta-inferences are largely derived from either the qualitative or quantitative strands or if the two strands merely reinforce each other. It offers an alternative way to evaluate priority and may shed light on studies where the yield or value-added is something greater than the sum of the qualitative and quantitative data or analytical procedures.

At least two types of meta-inferences can be imagined: one that is a sum of the parts and a second that creates a conclusion that is more than the merging or combining of the inferences from the qualitative and quantitative strands. Table 10.2 offers a preliminary way to imagine two basic types of meta-inferences.

Although not a characteristic of the group of exemplars I have selected, there are no doubt many examples of qualitative and/or quantitative dominant mixed method studies that produce no meta-inference that links the qualitative and quantitative strands. This might be the case, for example, when major conclusions are linked to a single strand and only confirmed in the second strand.

There are several implications to producing a visualization that dissects the contribution of the qualitative, quantitative, and mixing strands of a mixed methods

TABLE 10.2 ■ Conceptualizing Different Types of Meta-Inferences		
Type of Meta-inference	**Illustrative Exemplar**	**Purpose or Rationale**
Sum of parts (consists of linked qualitative and quantitative inferences)	Catallo et al., 2013	Complementarity (linked by different constructs)
Synergistic (sum is greater than the sum of parts)	Gasson and Waters, 2013	Initiation

study to its conclusions. The first is that it offers an alternative strategy to evaluate the priority or the relative weighting of the qualitative, quantitative, and mixing strands that is based on the inferences and meta-inferences that are drawn. The absence of a meta-inference, for example, is likely to signal that the major conclusions of a study were drawn from one of the monomethod strands. This might be the case, for example, in a quantitative-dominant study where the principal conclusions are derived from a clinical trial in which the qualitative component played an important role in shaping the intervention but almost no role in constructing the conclusions.

A visualization that provides a way to capture the source of a meta-inference also has implications for ways to evaluate quality of a mixed method publication. While the traditional emphasis has been to demonstrate quality through careful documentation of purpose, rationale, and procedures, supplementing this with a way to dissect the source of the conclusions adds a dimension referred to as **inferential transparency** (*a type of methodological transparency that explicitly links the contribution of the qualitative, quantitative, and mixing strands to the conclusions drawn from a study*). This requires language in the discussion and conclusion sections of a report that explicitly links an explanation to its qualitative, quantitative, or mixing source.

We can consider the insight gained about the value-added of mixed methods research by applying an inference-oriented template to two of the chapter exemplars with two different rationales for using a mixed methods approach. The template is structured to resemble an arch with two sides. It reveals different things about the inferences drawn in the two exemplars.

Applying a Template to Visualize Meta-Inferences

Figure 10.6 applies an inference-oriented template to an exemplar from Chapter 3. This is the study by Gasson and Waters (2013) about collaborative behaviors in an online learning environment. The study fits what Greene, Caracelli, and Graham (1989) referred to as an *initiation purpose* in that it was deliberately undertaken in order to understand an unexplored and possibly paradoxical phenomenon of learning among those who appeared not to be participating in discussion forums in an online class. The template distinguishes the inferences derived from the qualitative and quantitative strands and identifies the meta-inference that links the two.

FIGURE 10.6 ■ Applying the Inference Template to Gasson and Waters's (2013) Study of Online Collaborative Behaviors		
Meta-inference: *There are both visible and invisible learning strategies.*		
Quantitative conclusion:		Qualitative conclusion:
Identified level of involvement of class members and opinion leaders		"Lurkers," those who did not appear to be active, experienced vicarious learning

The template clearly documents that Gasson and Waters (2013) produced a meta-inference that is above and beyond the inferences from the qualitative and quantitative strands. That the meta-inference could be said to reflect a situation where the sum is greater than the parts is revealed in the authors' statements about the value-added of the research. They maintain that the approach helped them to develop an innovative and substantive theory of action in online learning communities.

The inference-oriented template tells a different story when it is applied to a second exemplar. This is the exemplar featured in Chapter 4 by Catallo, Jack, Ciliska, and MacMillan (2013) from the medical field. These authors combined analysis of data from a larger randomized controlled trial with the analysis of interview data about the reporting of intimate partner violence in emergency rooms. Their purpose fits the *complementarity rationale*. Studies with this rationale are often directed by research questions that address different but related phenomenon. They sought to construct a more holistic or complex picture by exploring different aspects of the same phenomenon. Catallo et al. make clear the priority of the quantitative strand and the secondary role of the qualitative strand in their purpose statement: "to enhance the initial quantitative results by using follow-up qualitative methods" (p. 3).

Figure 10.7 summarizes the inferences drawn by Catallo et al. (2013). The content of this template differs from the preceding one in that no overriding meta-inference that is greater than the sum of the parts was produced.

In this case, the inference template revealed two linked inferences that matched the purpose and complementarity rationale. The quantitative inference is descriptive and answers the *what* question, while the qualitative strand extends understanding of the same phenomenon by providing an explanation for the *why*. The lack of an overarching meta-inference adds to the conviction that these are two loosely linked studies with a quantitative priority. The qualitative phase is decidedly ancillary.

We extend the discussion about future directions for mixed methods research by shifting our attention from meta-inferences to a summary of major themes and speculation about future directions. In the next section, we consider what insight the nine exemplars offer about contemporary practice. The interweaving of mixing through many phases of the research project that is evident in all the exemplars offers some indication of the ways that the field is shifting, possibly to expand the emphasis to a more diverse array of strategies that promote mixing.

FIGURE 10.7 ■ Applying the Inference Template to the Catallo et al. (2013) Study of Intimate Partner Violence		
Meta-inference: *No separate overarching meta-inference*		
Quantitative conclusion: Women who experienced the most violence were least likely to attribute it to a partner.		Qualitative conclusion: Reluctance to disclose was associated with fear of stigmatization.

SUMMARIZING MAJOR THEMES

The chapter exemplars that I singled out from the ever-expanding body of research using mixed methods each displays qualities worth emulating. By and large, they reflect the complexity and fluidity Guest (2012) referred to in his work. Viewed as a group, they are a testament to the diverse applications of mixed methods approaches evident in practice today. The exemplars appearing in print most recently have strengthened my conviction to downplay a prescribed set of designs that were probably conceived to reflect practice when mixed methods were first adapted. Practice seems to have outpaced the methodological literature, as the exemplars are far too diverse to fit snugly into widely used classification schemes about mixed method research designs.

Lessons From the Exemplars

A review of the characteristics of the exemplars featured in this textbook reiterates a point made earlier in the chapter: that mixed methods approaches have reached audiences in diverse and emerging disciplines and have been used to address content-oriented questions in a wide array of topics. Table 10.3 lists the exemplary articles and summarizes the topic, rationale for using mixed methods, priority, and level of integration for each.

The exemplary publications reflect an applied focus. Three are on topics related to K–12 teaching (collaborative behaviors in an online course, the experience of preservice teachers, characteristics of successful schools in low-resource environments). Several are health related, including one about the effectiveness of delivering HIV education through social media, another about the link between community affiliation and healthy aging, and a third about the disclosure of intimate partner violence to emergency room personnel.

Specialized and methodologically oriented journals, such as the *Journal of Mixed Methods Research* and the *Journal of Multiple Methods*, are not the only venues for mixed methods research. Other than the two exemplars that appeared in the *Journal of Mixed Methods Research* (i.e., Creamer & Ghoston, 2012; Jang et al., 2008), all of the remaining exemplars appeared in content-oriented (rather than methodologically oriented) journals. The journal titles are an indication of how useful mixed methods have proven to be in many content areas: *Journal of Science and Medicine, Journal of Sexually Transmitted Diseases, Educational and Child Psychology, American Educational Research Journal, European Journal of Information Systems, Nursing Research and Practice,* and *Affilia: Journal of Women and Social Work.* The selection of exemplars understates the innovative work that is being done with mixed method in the nursing field, such as addressed in a textbook by Curry and Nunez-Smith (2015), and in the international arena, as seen in *The Oxford Handbook of Multi-method and Mixed Methods Research Inquiry* (edited by Hesse-Biber and Johnson, 2015).

There are some design features of the exemplars that distinguish them from the larger body of empirical mixed methods research. The stated purposes for using a mixed

TABLE 10.3 ■ Exemplary Publications by Chapter, Topic, Rationale, Priority, and Level of Integration					
Chapter	**Authors**	**Topic**	**Rationale**	**Priority**	**Fully Integrated**
2 (Purpose)	Durksen & Klassen, 2012	Preservice teachers	Initiation	Mixed	Yes
3 (Paradigm)	Gasson & Waters, 2013	Collaborative behaviors online	Initiation	Qualitative	No
4 (Designs)	Catallo, Jack, Ciliska, & MacMillan, 2013	Intimate partner violence	Complementarity	Equal	Yes
5 (Mixing Prior to Analysis)	Young & Jaganath, 2013	HIV education	Complementarity	Equal	Yes
6 (Analytical Procedures)	Jang, McDougall, Pollon, Herbert, & Russell, 2008	School effectiveness	Complementarity	Qualitative	Yes
	Elliott, Gale, Parsons, Kuh, & The HALCyon Study, 2014	Healthy aging	Expansion	Mixed	Yes
	Creamer & Ghoston, 2012	Mission statements	Complementarity	Mixed	Yes
7 (Mixing through Data Transformation)	Cooper, 2014	Promoting classroom engagement	Development	Quantitative	Yes
8 (Quality)	McMahon, 2007	Rape myths	Complementarity	Qualitative	No

method approach by and large align with several of those first identified by Greene et al. (1989) (i.e., complementarity, initiation, triangulation, and expansion) that are more conducive to mixing by virtue of promoting an iterative, multiphase approach to data collection and analysis. Many of the exemplary studies are distinguished by a strong emergent quality. Three of nine articles are marked as awarding priority to the qualitative phase. Only one showed a distinctive quantitative priority. Most are grounded in larger studies and, consequently, reflect the value-added of mixed methods in generating nuanced and complex explanations.

Because of the attention awarded to mixing, the exemplars defy the general characterization of mixed methods research in that they are definitely not articles that warrant a multimethod label. They stand in contrast to most published mixed methods research in that all but one (i.e., McMahon, 2007) incorporated strategies for mixing during analysis. The authors of many of these articles seem to have found ways to mix the qualitative and quantitative strands using strategies that probably emerged somewhat spontaneously from ongoing interaction on a team of people with different areas of content expertise.

The exemplars shed light on another question that arises from time to time in mixed methods. That is the question about whether mixed methods require an unusually high level of methodological expertise. It is noteworthy that other than the exemplar I chose from my own work, an examination of the publications of the authors of the exemplars reveal that none use mixed methods exclusively. By and large, mixed methods are only one of several research approaches reflected in their list of publications. Further evidence that a mixed methods approach is a suitable choice for novice researchers when the purpose dictates it comes from the fact that two of the exemplars are publications that report on dissertation research (i.e., Catallo et al., 2013; Cooper, 2014).

Also worthy of note are two qualities missing in the exemplars. One of these is reflexivity and the second is acknowledgement of mixing at the level of method. Except in the one overtly feminist piece by McMahon (2007), there is very little evidence of reflexivity about paradigm in these texts. This is consistent with Bryman's (2006) conclusion that only 6% of more than 200 mixed methods publications in the social sciences mentioned anything about paradigm. This would be easy to attribute to the practical realities of the peer review process and the limited space available in the typical publication. Others would take the more cynical position that this is more evidence that most authors of mixed method empirical publications that survive the peer review process come from a post-positivist paradigm, where methodological positioning is assumed to be unnecessary (Giddings & Grant, 2007).

There is a level of experimentation with mixing methods in five of the nine of the exemplars. Catallo et al. (2013) and Gasson and Waters (2013), for example, used mixed methods with grounded theory, while Creamer and Ghoston (2012) used a mixed method approach with content analysis. Cooper (2014) and Jang et al. (2008) used case study in their mixed method analytical procedures. This type of experimentation matches newly emerging literature that pursues a more in-depth analysis of the use of mixed method approaches with a method, as can be seen by a book about mixed methods in action research (Ivankova, 2015) and by advocacy for a mixed methods approach to participatory research (Olson & Jason, 2015). A future direction for mixed method research is to invite more conversations about mixing at the level of method.

The diversity of the exemplars and their suggestion that the everyday practice of mixed methods is, at times, at odds with the methodological literature may help to refocus the dialogue away from the binaries that shaped the movement when it was first conceived in the 1980s. Most importantly, it challenges the implicit assumption that permeates much of the methodological literature that mixed methods are best conceptualized as a combination of qualitative and quantitative methods or data. Some of the binary thinking is explored in the next section.

Refocusing the Logic of Combination

Sandelowski (2014) and others, such as Giddings & Grant (2007), have criticized the founding voices in mixed methods from the 1980s for perpetuating a kind of binary logic that they charge derives from positivism. This paradigm is characterized by the assumption that reality is singular and that the goal of research is to discover the "right" answers. After suggesting that it polarizes mixed methods from monomethods as well as exaggerates differences between qualitative and quantitative methods, Sandelowski observed, "Mixed-method research thus not only establishes a new binary—that is, mixed-/mono-method research—but also reinforces an old one, namely QL/QN [qualitative/quantitative] research" (p. 3). Making the same argument about binary thinking and provocatively labeling mixed methods as "positivism in drag," Giddings and Grant (2007, p. 52) charged, "Although it passes for an alternative methodological movement that purports to breach the divide between qualitative and quantitative research, most mixed methods studies favor the form of analysis and truth finding associated with positivism."

No place is a binary logic more apparent than in the discourse that frames mixed methods as the combination of qualitative and quantitative approaches. This logic is particularly prominent in the way priority is conventionally defined (i.e., qualitative, quantitative, or equivalent). It is also evident in the assumption that the quality of mixed methods research rests only on the quality of the qualitative and quantitative strands. The same logic is reflected in the caution that mixed methods researchers be aware that their audience contains qualitative and quantitative researchers. This type of binary thinking neglects the likelihood that audiences increasingly also contain researchers with an interest in mixed methods. It is also refracted in the debate about paradigms and the positioning of qualitative and quantitative approaches as opposing paradigms. The same gap in logic surfaces in yet another way in the advice that is given about how to structure a research team. The recommendation to include at least one researcher with a quantitative expertise and one with a qualitative expertise overlooks the idea that mixed methods is yet a third, distinct area of expertise.

Some of the definitional issues that are often raised as being unresolved share the logic of mixed methods as the combination of qualitative and quantitative approaches. The argument that there are diverse views about how mixed methods research is defined (Johnson, Onwuegbuzie, & Turner, 2007) can be parsed in two different ways. The first distinguishes mixed methods as the combination of qualitative and quantitative data. The second characterizes mixed methods as the combination of inductive and deductive analytical procedures. Both reflect an emphasis on procedural aspects of the design of a mixed methods research study.

Creswell and Plano Clark (2007, 2011) implicitly take the first position that mixed methods involve the combination of qualitative and quantitative data. One way to visualize this combination is shown below:

$$Mixed\ methods = QUAL + QUANT\ data$$

This perspective is compatible with the equation of qualitative research with the collection of words and quantitative research with the collection of numbers. From this vantage point, any study that collects data in the form of both words and numbers is mixed methods. This view matches the priority given to using a combination of approaches for purposes of triangulation. The distinction is muddied by the argument that all researchers mix (Sandelowski, 2014) and transform data (Symonds & Gorard, 2010) and by the proclivity to transform words into numbers by counting the frequency of themes and using this as the basis for further analysis.

A second way that mixed methods have been defined reflects another extension of the combination logic. Instead of situating mixed methods during data collection, this definition locates mixed methods research as a combination of inductive and deductive analytical procedures. This aspect of a study can be visualized in the following manner:

Mixed methods = QUAL (Inductive) + QUANT (Deductive)

This definition is a good match for a study that combines hypothesis testing and generation. It can be compatible with grounded theory. One advantage of this definitional perspective is that it invites the possibility suggested by Morse (2010) and Small (2011) that research involving two qualitative methods (i.e., words) can be mixed methods if inductive and deductive analytical procedures are involved. A limitation of this perspective is that, like other variants of it, this qualitative–quantitative dichotomy does not hold up in practice. Quantitative researchers have their own version of inductive analytical procedures, including exploratory factor analysis where statistical procedures, rather than a conceptual framework or theory, define a set of variables that hang together as constructs.

Applying the Mixed Methods Label

The logic of mixing methods and types of data is inherent in many research approaches (Sandelowski, 2014). It is not unique to mixed methods. The choice to apply the mixed methods label requires deliberation. Rather than to use it to signal the combination of multiple types of data, affixing a mixed methods label to a piece of research is a way to declare that the logic of mixing is central to the reason for doing a study or for understanding its conclusions. This logic foregrounds the intent to mix, especially in the way the purpose of the research is framed and the analysis is pursued, rather than through mechanical functions that have little to do with the interpretive output.

The intent to engage diverse viewpoints is consistent with Greene's (2007) mixed methods way of thinking and reflects a fascination, not with consistency and homogeneity, but with paradoxes that often emerge when different data sources are compared. It is a commitment to weigh multiple competing explanations. This logic extends to a more expansive definition of mixed methods that embraces the idea that a study can be mixed, while one publication extracted from it may not necessarily be so. The logic of mixing can, and often does, occur across projects and publications where the credibility of results is built by replication and the need to substantiate and build on findings. The mixed method label communicates to a reader or audience member an overriding logic of engaging differences.

Despite much rhetoric to the contrary, centering the logic of mixing is tantamount to saying mixed methods is lodged within a distinct paradigm. This paradigm has been characterized as dialectical pluralism (Greene & Hall, 2010; Johnson & Schoonenboom, 2016). This affiliation negates the argument that mixed methods involve a type of paradigm mixing that is intellectually dishonest. As noted in Chapter 3, dialectical pluralism is characterized by belief that reality is multiple, constructed, and ever changing; a respect for diverse viewpoints and ways of knowing; and the motivation to pursue contradictory or unexpected results, including through what in positivist research might be called *outlier* and in qualitative research is called *negative case*.

Research methods and practice are ever changing (Hesse-Biber, 2010a). Adopting the logic that mixed methods produces a synergy or a quality that is unique beyond its qualitative and quantitative elements opens the door to new and innovative approaches to mixed methods research. It invites the possibility of mixing two types of qualitative data, which is different from a mindset that, as Creswell (2011) has suggested, a method such as content analysis cannot be mixed methods because it begins with data that is entirely in the form of words. It also downplays the binary logic that questions the appropriateness of applying a mixed methods label to a report about a set of results that was not planned at the onset of a project. This kind of definitional expansiveness is consistent with Guest's (2012) proposal that it may be helpful to apply the mixed methods label as a way to understand a series of interlinked publications from a larger research project, even when it is not reflected in an individual publication.

New generations of students, whose training makes it possible for them to be less inured in positivism and post-positivism and the type of dualistic thinking that polarizes qualitative and quantitative research approaches, seem to find the idea of mixing methods intuitively appealing and intellectually logical in ways that are quite different from generations shaped by the discourse in the 1980s, when the force of the argument was to distinguish the two as inherently different paradigms. More and more innovative examples of mixed methods have begun to appear in the literature published in an extraordinarily diverse array of journals and international venues and can be seen in research involving new technology and public spaces (for example, Wallenberg et al., 2010), creative uses of methods (for example, a meta-case study of a city through its public spaces by Carmona, 2014), and by applications of data secured through the Internet, including photos and videos. It is difficult to be innovative when repeating the same set of data collection methods (i.e., surveys and interviews) that have been used by countless researchers for decades. Refocusing the dialogue away from a prescribed set of designs and narrow definitions of when the mixed methods label is appropriate and toward expanding the list of strategies to integrate research approaches invites the type of innovation and experimentation that will keep the field vibrant.

The logic of mixing methods and types of data is inherent in many research approaches (Sandelowski, 2014) and, consequently, not a characteristic that is useful to distinguish them. Rather than to use it to signal the combination of multiple types of data when the multimethod label is most apt, affixing a mixed methods label to a publication is a way to communicate to an audience that the logic of mixing is central to the purpose of the study and to the utility of the knowledge produced. This idea brings us back to reimagining the architectural arch as a metaphor not only for the way a study is executed but to frame the value-added of a mixed methods approach in the meta-inferences produced.

We close with a summary of key points from the chapter and suggestions for supplemental activities.

Summary of Key Points

1. Mixed methods research is being utilized in a wide range of largely applied disciplines, including in fields of business, nursing, and education.

2. Specialized and methodologically oriented journals, such as the *Journal of Mixed Methods Research* and the *International Journal of Multiple Research Methods,* are not the only venues for mixed methods research.

3. Two-phase mixed methods designs have conventionally been conceived of in ways that do not promote mixing during analysis.

4. The mixed methods research that is appearing in print today is far too diverse to fit readily into widely used classification schemes about the timing, priority, and the conventionally defined set of purposes for using mixed methods.

5. You do not have to be an expert in mixed methods research to produce a high-quality publication with innovative qualities.

6. Rather than through the features of the design, an unconventional way to evaluate priority is through the inferences and meta-inferences produced.

Supplemental Activities

1. Construct a table that will make it possible to identify similarities and differences in the major controversies identified by Johnson (2015), Creswell (2011), and Tashakkori and Teddlie (2010).

2. Create a template similar to the figures that are used to extract the qualitative and quantitative inferences and the overriding meta-inference from Gasson and Water's (2013) study from Chapter 3 and the study by Catallo et al. (2013) from Chapter 4 and apply it to another one of the chapter exemplars. Consider what additional insight is gained by this frame of reference compared to the templates provided in the respective chapters.

3. Scan the table of contents of science-oriented magazines or journals oriented to a popular audience, such as *Psychology Today, Science,* or *Nature*, to locate a few articles reporting on research that utilized multiple methods. Consider the value-added of this approach by zeroing in on the meta-inferences and the contribution each method made to them.

Key Term

- Inferential transparency

Recommended Reading

Creswell, J. W. (2011). Controversies in mixed methods research. In N. K. Denzin & Y. S. Lincoln (Eds.), *The SAGE handbook for qualitative research* (pp. 269–283). Thousand Oaks, CA: SAGE.

Teddlie, C., & Tashakkori, A. (2012). Common "core" characteristics of mixed methods research: A review of critical issues and call for greater convergence. *American Behavioral Scientists, 56*(6), 774–788.

APPENDIX A

Summary of Key Points by Chapter

CHAPTER 1: DEFINITIONAL ISSUES

1. Just because someone completes a qualitative and quantitative phase does not necessarily mean it is a mixed methods study.
2. Mixed methods are both a research method and a research methodology.
3. A study is not mixed methods if there is no mixing or integration of the qualitative and quantitative strands.
4. Deductive and inductive analytical procedures are required to meet a minimal definition of mixed methods research.
5. The contribution of triangulation to enhancing validity is one of the key rationales for using mixed methods.
6. Because qualitative researchers often use numbers to report their results, the word–number distinction between qualitative and quantitative methods is only marginally useful.
7. One of the challenges researchers face when using mixed methods is to honor the fundamental philosophical assumptions of qualitative and quantitative approaches.
8. Fully integrated mixed methods take place when interaction between the qualitative and quantitative strands occurs at all stages of the study.

CHAPTER 2: CATEGORIZING THE PURPOSES OF MIXED METHODS RESEARCH

1. It is the purpose, not the design, that drives the decision to use mixed methods.
2. A value-added of mixed methods is an invitation to explore unexpected and/or contradictory results that emerge when two types of data or two or more analytical techniques are bought together.
3. Partly because of how broadly it is conceived, the complementarity design is used most frequently.
4. Intentionally setting up a study to pursue competing hypotheses or theoretical explanations is an underdeveloped way of framing the purposes of a mixed method study.

5. The reasons for using a mixed methods approach are often not stated explicitly.

6. Differences between the stated reason for using mixed methods and the actual execution are a testament to how even the most well-designed research project evolves over time as results emerge.

7. Situations where a mixed methods approach is not likely to be the most appropriate methodological choice fall under three categories: nature of the problem, issues of expediency, and matters of expertise.

CHAPTER 3: RECOGNIZING PARADIGMATIC ASSUMPTIONS

1. Paradigmatic views are theories about knowledge and how it is constructed that are shared by members of a community.

2. In addition to views about the nature of reality and knowledge, mental models (Greene, 2007) include personal beliefs, predispositions, and understandings of the social world. Rather than paradigms, these are what have the strongest influence on the research topics and aims that are of greatest interest to us.

3. Identifying yourself as having a preference for qualitative or quantitative methods is not tantamount to revealing the paradigm that is most compatible with your way of thinking.

4. Paradigms are incompatible when they are based on very different views about the nature of reality.

5. Only a few methods are intrinsically linked to a single paradigm.

6. Qualitative and quantitative research can be approached from the perspective of a variety of paradigmatic positions. They are methods for collecting and analyzing data and not paradigms in and of themselves.

7. There are four major strains of paradigmatic thought that provide the architecture to support the logic of mixing methods. These are the pragmatic paradigm, dialectical pluralism, critical realism, and the transformative–emancipatory paradigm.

8. It is possible to mix some paradigms because there is so much overlap in the philosophical assumptions of the paradigms that guide behavioral and social research.

CHAPTER 4: DISTINGUISHING MIXED METHODS DESIGNS

1. Mixed methods designs are most frequently distinguished by timing and priority.

2. There are many possible innovative variations of the basic prototypes of mixed method designs.

3. Timing is more readily distinguished than priority, but priority is more important because it is the key to evaluating the overall logic of the inquiry.
4. The timing of data collection and analysis (i.e., concurrent, sequential, or multiphase) does not determine priority.
5. An effective way to determine priority is through a judgment about the overriding logic of inquiry.
6. One design type does not necessarily produce a higher-quality study than another.
7. There is no generally accepted way to judge priority when it is not explicitly stated in an article.

CHAPTER 5: STRATEGIES FOR MIXING PRIOR TO ANALYSIS

1. Mixing is the design feature that distinguishes a mixed method from a multimethod study.
2. The principal value-added of mixing is its potential to strengthen explanatory power.
3. The value-added of mixed methods is enhanced when mixing occurs at multiple stages of the research process.
4. The greatest potential to enhance explanatory power through mixing is to employ a recursive or iterative approach to analysis, have interlinked qualitative and quantitative research questions, and to have both qualitative and quantitative data for a nested or identical sample of participants or respondents.
5. Well-conceptualized research questions communicate preliminary ideas about how mixing will be accomplished.
6. Opportunities for mixing can never be fully anticipated at the onset.
7. Open-ended, nondirectional language that is largely method neutral is the most compatible with communicating the logic associated with mixed methods.
8. The wording of research questions is one indicator of qualitative, quantitative, or mixed priority.
9. Most mixed methods studies use more than one sampling procedure.
10. A sampling design that is unique to mixed methods is one that combines the feature of a traditional quantitative (i.e., probability) approach to sampling with those of a qualitative (i.e., purposeful) approach.
11. Timing and type are two features that distinguish mixed method sampling.
12. Using either an identical or nested sample of participants is an inherently mixed methods sampling procedure.
13. Statements that explicitly identify the value-added from integrating qualitative and quantitative approaches and that link conclusions to the source of data that supports them are a form of methodological transparency that is unique to mixed methods.

CHAPTER 6: MIXED METHOD ANALYTICAL PROCEDURES

1. Not all mixed methods studies use analytical strategies to integrate qualitative and quantitative data or during analysis.
2. Mixing during analysis can be accomplished without using any analytical procedures that are unique to mixed methods.
3. The potential to link conclusions from qualitative and quantitative strands of a study in a meta-inference is an analytical strategy that is unique to mixed methods.
4. The overall quality of a mixed methods research report rests on the development of a coherent explanation that links inferences that are qualitatively and quantitatively derived.
5. Interpretive transparency makes the principal conclusions of a study and their sources explicit.
6. Separating out the discussion of the results of qualitative and quantitative analyses into different sections without a section devoted to mixing is antithetical to the idea of fully integrated mixed methods.

CHAPTER 7: DATA TRANSFORMATION AND OTHER STRATEGIES FOR MIXING DURING ANALYSIS

1. Many, but not all, mixed methods analytical procedures utilize data transformation.
2. Quantifying qualitative data to report on the prevalence of themes or categories is a type of data transformation, but it involves counting, not mixing.
3. It is not the least unusual to find a case study that links both qualitative and quantitative data, but it is very unusual to find one that qualitizes by exclusively using quantitative data.
4. One way that mixing occurs in case study research is through the synthesis produced by a cross-case analysis.
5. Qualitative and quantitative data can be linked in a case study without either qualitizing or quantitizing.
6. In mixed methods case study research, separate qualitative and quantitative strands are often linked through sampling procedures.

CHAPTER 8: EVALUATING QUALITY IN MIXED METHODS RESEARCH PUBLICATIONS

1. There are many different views about what criteria should be included in a framework to evaluate the quality of mixed methods research.
2. The conventional view is that a framework to evaluate mixed methods research should include a separate set of criteria for the qualitative, quantitative, and mixing strands of the study.
3. An alternate viewpoint is that a framework to evaluate mixed methods research should focus on dimensions that are unique to the approach.
4. There is a strong level of consensus about the centrality of methodological transparency in evaluating research in the social and applied sciences because it is so instrumental to the ability to confirm or replicate the results.
5. There is widespread agreement that any evaluation framework designed to assess the quality of mixed methods research should include a measure of when and how much mixing occurred.
6. There is evidence in the literature to support the link to overall quality of two features of mixed methods studies (a) the amount of mixing and (b) the use of nonparallel or concurrent designs for purposes other than triangulation or confirmation.

CHAPTER 9: DESIGNING AND REPORTING A FULLY INTEGRATED MIXED METHOD RESEARCH PROPOSAL OR DOCTORAL DISSERTATION

1. The credibility of a study rests almost wholly on the way it is reported.
2. The way a mixed method publication is organized reflects the priority awarded to the qualitative, quantitative, and/or mixed method phases.
3. The multimethod label is appropriate for studies that lack research questions that require analysis involving interlinked variables.
4. There are features of the design of a mixed method study that facilitate meaningful mixing.
5. The design features that are most feasible for a mixed method study undertaken by a graduate student include the same or overlapping qualitative and quantitative participants and data collection using publicly available instruments or data.
6. Content analysis is a method that is especially adaptable to a mixed methods approach and to research that a graduate student might pursue.

7. It is common practice in mixed methods to include a figure in a publication that maps the steps taken in the process of data collection and analysis.
8. Visual displays, such as tables and figures, are important tools for the researcher to use to document both the process of and product of the analytical procedures.

CHAPTER 10: CONTROVERSIES AND FUTURE DIRECTIONS

1. Mixed methods research is being utilized in a wide range of largely applied disciplines, including in fields of business, nursing, and education.
2. Specialized and methodologically oriented journals, such as the *Journal of Mixed Methods Research* and the *International Journal of Multiple Research Methods,* are not the only venues for mixed methods research.
3. Two-phase mixed methods designs have conventionally been conceived of in ways that do not promote mixing during analysis.
4. The mixed methods research that is appearing in print today is far too diverse to fit readily into widely used classification schemes about the timing, priority, and the conventionally defined set of purposes for using mixed methods.
5. You do not have to be expert in mixed methods research to produce a high-quality publication with innovative qualities.
6. Rather than through the features of the design, an unconventional way to evaluate priority is through the inferences and meta-inferences produced.

APPENDIX B

List of Supplemental Activities by Chapter

CHAPTER 1: DEFINITIONAL ISSUES

1. Create a table that summarizes similarities and differences in the definitions of mixed methods offered by various researchers in Table 1 in the article by Johnson, Onwuegbuzie, and Turner (2007).

CHAPTER 2: CATEGORIZING THE PURPOSES OF MIXED METHODS RESEARCH

1. Identify a sample of mixed methods articles on the same topic or from the same set of disciplinary journals. Read through the abstract and introduction to each article, focusing particularly on the area of the article describing the purpose of the research, and highlight sentences where the authors provide a reason for using mixed methods. Conduct your own inductive analysis of the reasons given for using mixed methods and see how the categories you generate compare to those of Greene et al. (1989) and Bryman (2006).
2. Follow the steps listed above and try to categorize each article using the typology of purposes proposed in this chapter. How useful is the typology in classifying purposes of the articles in your sample? What are the characteristics of articles that do not seem to fit in any of the categories?
3. Examine Keltner's (1995) article for the value-added of using multiple methods. What conclusions were discovered that would not have been possible with one method alone?

CHAPTER 3: RECOGNIZING PARADIGMATIC ASSUMPTIONS

1. Review the tables that have been presented to delineate the major philosophical positions for each of the paradigms reviewed in this chapter. Go through and circle the statements that match your views. Then use the model presented

in the text to write a paragraph that has a sentence that reflects each of the domains of philosophical thought (e.g., ontology, epistemology, methodology, axiology). Share your statement with a colleague and ask him or her to critique it to identify statements that are inherently inconsistent.

2. Use the blank table presented in Appendix C to identify which statement in each section most represents your point of view. Acknowledge statements where your opinion is not yet fully formed. Then construct a statement following the model presented in the chapter that you could use in situations that call for philosophical transparency.

3. Assume that there are skeptics in the audience for a presentation you are making on the results of a mixed methods study who are in the camp that mixed methods might better be called "mixed up" methods because they blur the lines between qualitative and quantitative approaches. In a couple of sentences, describe the defense you might mount in terms of paradigms for combining qualitative and quantitative approaches.

CHAPTER 4: DISTINGUISHING MIXED METHODS DESIGNS

1. Imagine a study comparing the types of verbal interactions a parent has with preschool children over the course of the day using electronic toys (such as a baby laptop or talking farm) and traditional story books, such as pursued by Sosa (2016). Propose research questions that might be suitable for a mixed methods study seeking data about the frequency and length of parent–child interactions with the toy and that considers the quality or complexity of those exchanges.

2. Take the blank template provided in Appendix C and summarize the key features of the mixed methods grounded theory study by Gasson and Waters (2013) about interaction in online classes featured as the exemplary publication in Chapter 3.

CHAPTER 5: STRATEGIES FOR MIXING PRIOR TO ANALYSIS

1. The approach taken by the exemplar in this chapter (i.e., Young & Jaganath, 2013) could be used to evaluate social media posts for an increase in knowledge about many topics, such as nutrition, mindfulness, or some aspect of interest in or knowledge about math or science. Identify an attitude that interests you that you think is linked in positive ways to an outcome or behavior, such as the association between mindfulness and management of eating. Using the Young and Jaganath article as a model, write one qualitative research question, one quantitative research question, and one research question that requires mixing. Then rewrite these into two questions that involve mixing qualitatively and quantitatively derived data.

2. Do a digital library search using the search terms *mixed methods research AND* [*the current year*]. Eliminate the articles with a methodological purpose and pull out those that explicitly state research questions. Of those, study the research questions to see if any explicitly address the topic of mixing.

CHAPTER 6: MIXED METHOD ANALYTICAL PROCEDURES

1. Look at the discussion and conclusion sections of the exemplars featured in earlier chapters of this textbook to see if you can locate other examples of authors who provide statements that reflect a meta-inference to integrate conclusions drawn from the qualitative and quantitative data or analytical procedures. Look particularly at the Durksen and Klassen's (2012) longitudinal study about the experiences of preservice teachers during student teaching.

2. Researchers have begun to test the effectiveness of using small robots to help autistic children develop more effective social and interactive skills. Draft research questions for a mixed methods observational study with videotapes showing a child alone in a room with a robot. These questions should address the amount of interaction between the child and the robot and create categories for the types of interactions between the child and the robot. See related articles (Salisbury, 2013; Wang, 2013).

CHAPTER 7: DATA TRANSFORMATION AND OTHER STRATEGIES FOR MIXING DURING ANALYSIS

1. Imagine that you are in charge of campus safety at a large urban college and you decide to conduct a mixed methods study to triangulate data about the location of campus crimes in the last three years with students' perceptions about the characteristics of safe and unsafe locations on campus. In small groups, discuss different strategies you could use to collect and analyze data for this kind of study.

2. The critical incident technique is highly adaptable to a mixed methods approach. It has been used to understand types of occupational or workplace stress, the factors related to it, and the types of physical and social symptoms it produces. One of its great advantages as a qualitative method is that the unit of analysis is brief descriptions of real-life events provided by participants that can be collected through interviews or online surveys. Each description of an incident can be coded in ways that allow a comparison of the source of stress and the symptoms associated with it by severity.

    This activity can be done alone or with a small group of other students. Begin by writing a paragraph that describes a stressful event you experienced related to your work that occurred within the last 30 days. Describe how stressful you found the event and explain why you found it stressful. Follow this with a list of three adjectives that describe the emotional and physical reactions, if any, you experienced during the incident. Now repeat this activity by following the same format to describe a second example of a stressful experience at work. Experiment with coding each paragraph you have written, just as you would if you were using the critical incident technique in your own research.

a. Label the type or source of the stress you reported. This might be something such as *interpersonal conflict* or *a too-heavy workload*.
b. Identify the underlying reason for why the event was stressful.
c. Apply a form of intensity coding and rate how stressful the event seemed to be using a scale of 0–5 (0 = not at all stressful, 1 = slightly stressful, and 5 = highly stressful).

CHAPTER 8: EVALUATING QUALITY IN MIXED METHODS RESEARCH PUBLICATIONS

1. Score a mixed methods article that is in the reference list you have been accumulating using the evaluation rubric that is introduced in this chapter. Reflect on what types of judgments you had to make to score the article and what additions you would recommend to make the rubric more effective.
2. Follow the model set by the MMER to create an additional criterion that you can score with between 3 or 4 hierarchical levels of quality. The criterion might be about philosophical transparency or reflexivity about paradigm, for example. It could also be about validity. Pick something that matters to you when you are reading a research article.
3. Work with a partner to use MMER to score two or three of the mixed method articles that have been identified as exemplars in this textbook. Score each article independently and then compare your scores to see where the scores you assigned are similar and different.

CHAPTER 9: DESIGNING AND REPORTING A FULLY INTEGRATED MIXED METHODS RESEARCH PROPOSAL OR DOCTORAL DISSERTATION

1. Apply the guidelines for methodological transparency listed in Table 9.4 to the article by Stemler et al. (2011) about school mission statements to determine if the lack of foundational grounding in the mixed methods literature is reflected in other ways throughout the article.

2. Compare the qualities and what is communicated about mixing in three or four mixed methods publications that include a process-oriented figure that maps steps in the process of data collection and analysis. Compare what is communicated about mixing in these visual displays with the one discussed in the chapter from Jang et al. (2008), which designated a third column to itemize the steps that involved mixing.

CHAPTER 10: CONTROVERSIES AND FUTURE DIRECTIONS

1. Construct a table that will make it possible to identify similarities and differences in the major controversies identified by Johnson (2015), Creswell (2011), and Tashakkori and Teddlie (2010).

2. Create a template similar to the figures that are used to extract the qualitative and quantitative inferences and the overriding meta-inference from Gasson and Water's (2013) study from Chapter 3 and the study by Catallo et al. (2013) from Chapter 4 and apply it to another one of the chapter exemplars. Consider what additional insight is gained by this frame of reference compared to the templates provided in the respective chapters.

3. Scan the table of contents of science-oriented magazines or journals oriented to a popular audience, such as *Psychology Today*, *Science*, or *Nature*, to locate a few articles reporting on research that utilized multiple methods. Consider the value-added of this approach by zeroing in on the meta-inferences and the contribution each method made to them.

APPENDIX C

Blank Template for Article Summaries

Article Title			
Rationale/Purpose			
Priority			
Timing of Data Collection			
Timing of Data Analysis			
Mixing	Fully integrated: Yes or No		
	Design	Yes or No	
	Data collection	Yes or No	
	Data analysis	Yes or No	
	Inferences	Yes or No	
Meta-inference			
	Qualitative conclusion		
	Quantitative conclusion		
Value-added			

APPENDIX D

Templates for Chapter Exemplars

Appendix D.1	Exemplary Article About Preservice Teachers: Summary of Key Features of Durksen and Klassen (2012)		
Rationale/Purpose	Initiation		
Priority	Mixed		
Timing of Data Collection	Concurrent		
Timing of Data Analysis	Concurrent		
Mixing	Fully integrated: Yes		
	Design	✖	Two qualitative and two quantitative research questions
	Data collection	✖	Linked through extreme case sampling
	Data analysis	✖	Qualitative and quantitative data integrated in two case studies
	Inferences	✖	
Meta-inference	Fluctuations in motivation are related to personal qualities and job resources.		
	Qualitative conclusion	Context and personal qualities influenced commitment and engagement.	
	Quantitative conclusion	The pattern of commitment and engagement followed a U-shaped pattern.	
Value-added	• Pursued contradictory data • Used qualitative data to explore differences between the two groups identified through analysis of the quantitative data • Captured complexity and how experiences varied by context		

Appendix D.2	Exemplary Article About the Online Collaborative Behaviors: Summary of Key Features of Gasson and Waters (2013)		
Rationale/Purpose	Initiation		
Priority	Qualitative		
Timing of Data Collection	Multiphase		
Timing of Data Analysis	Quantitative → Qualitative → Qualitative/Quantitative		
Mixing	Fully integrated: No		
	Design	✖	Research question is qualitative
	Data collection	✖	Linked through extreme case sampling
	Data analysis	✖	Blended
	Inferences	✖	Blended
Meta-inference	Identified both visible and invisible learning strategies		
	Qualitative conclusion	Lurkers experienced vicarious learning	
	Quantitative conclusion	Identified level of involvement and opinion leaders	
Value-added	• Developed an innovative substantive theory of action in online learning communities • Disconfirmed some emerging theoretical propositions • Raised new analytical questions • Revealed inconsistencies in the data		

Appendix D.3	Exemplary Article About the Disclosure of Intimate Partner Violence: Summary of Key Features of Catallo, Jack, Ciliska, and MacMillan (2013)		
Rationale/Purpose	Complementarity		
Priority	Equal		
Timing of Data Collection	Separate and sequential		
Timing of Data Analysis	Quantitative → Qualitative → Qualitative/Quantitative		
Mixing	Fully integrated: Yes		
	Design	✖	Qualitative and quantitative research addressed linked but separate phenomenon
	Data collection	✖	Linked at sampling
	Data analysis	✖	Blended
	Inferences	✖	Blended
Meta-inference	Women who experienced the most violence were the least likely to disclose because of fear of judgment from health care providers.		
	Quantitative conclusion: Women who experienced the most violence were the least likely to disclose.		
	Qualitative conclusion: Reluctance to disclose was associated with fear of stigmatization.		
Value-added	• Collected data from various perspectives • Produced a more thorough understanding of a complex phenomenon • Proposed a strategy for adjusting the grounded theory sampling strategy • Offset selection bias by identifying participants for the qualitative phase from the random sample		

Appendix D.4	Exemplary Article About School Effectiveness in Challenging Circumstances: Summary of Key Features of Jang et al. (2008)		
Rationale/Purpose	Complementarity		
Priority	Qualitative		
Timing of Data Collection	Concurrent		
Timing of Data Analysis	Iterative		
Mixing by Stage	Fully integrated: Yes		
	Design	✖	No research questions
	Data collection	✖	Multilevel sample; consolidated qualitative and quantitative data on the same variables
	Data analysis	✖	First analyzed the qualitative and quantitative data separately, then integrated them to create consolidated themes
	Inferences	✖	
Meta-inference	Schools that were successful in the face of challenging circumstances (a) built distributive leadership, (b) supported professional learning, (c) created a welcoming school culture, and (d) fostered students' literacy and numeracy.		
	Qualitative conclusion	There was considerable variation between schools in the way that quantitative factors manifested.	
	Quantitative conclusion	School leaders demonstrated concern for shared leadership, professional development, and student development.	
Value-added	• Identification of both overlapping and unique aspects of the phenomenon • "The recognition of emergent themes and new insights" (p. 241) • Quantitative data did not capture the variability evident in the qualitative data • Pointed to changes required to the survey instrument		

Appendix D.5	Exemplary Article About the Link Between Well-Being and Social Cohesion Among Elderly Men and Women: Summary of Key Features of Elliott et al. (2014)		
Rationale/Purpose	Complementarity		
Priority	Mixed		
Timing of Data Collection	Sequential		
Timing of Data Analysis	Quantitative → Qualitative → Quantitative		
Mixing by Stage	Fully integrated: Yes		
	Design	✖	One qualitative; one quantitative research question.
	Data collection	✖	Nested sample, mixing through critical case sampling
	Data analysis	✖	Mixing through blended variables
	Inferences	✖	
Meta-inference	There is a moderate association between perceptions of neighborhood cohesion, social participation, and well-being among older adults.		
	Qualitative conclusion	Social participation influences well-being.	
	Quantitative conclusion	Neighborhood cohesion is more strongly associated with well-being among older age groups.	
Value-added	• Study of three cohorts allows confirmation of results • Identified weaknesses in the instrument		

Appendix D.6	Exemplary Article Using a Mixed Methods Content Analysis of Mission Statements: Summary of Key Features of Creamer and Ghoston (2012)		
Rationale/Purpose	Complementarity		
Priority	Mixed		
Timing of Data Collection	Concurrent		
Timing of Data Analysis	Quantitative ➜ Qualitative		
Mixing by Stage	Fully integrated: Yes		
	Design	✖	One qualitative, one mixed research question
	Data collection	✖	Stratified random sampling; linked
	Data analysis	✖	Data transformation
	Inferences	✖	
Meta-inference	Acknowledgement of an appreciation for diversity was found significantly more often in colleges of engineering with greater-than-average enrollments of women.		
	Qualitative conclusion	There was a lot of variety in the values endorsed in mission statements.	
	Quantitative conclusion	The diversity coded was significantly correlated to the proportion of male graduates and the number of female graduates.	
Value-added	• Application of mixed methods to conduct a content analysis of mission statements • Identify new or unexpected trends in the values endorsed by colleges of engineering • Consider links between characteristics of the environment and values endorsed in mission statements		

Appendix D.7	Exemplary Article About Teaching Practices That Promote Student Engagement: Summary of Key Features of Cooper (2014)		
Rationale/Purpose	Development		
Priority	Quantitative		
Timing of Data Collection	Sequential		
Timing of Data Analysis	Sequential		
Mixing	Fully integrated: Yes		
	Design	✖	One qualitative, one quantitative research question
	Data collection	✖	Survey data used to select case studies
	Data analysis	✖	Survey data from students integrated into concept maps for each classroom, then into five case studies
	Inferences	✖	Meta-inference
Meta-inference	Characteristics of the teaching approach are much more strongly related to student engagement than to the characteristics of the individual.		
	Qualitative conclusion	Student engagement was not as high in classrooms where connected instruction was not supplemented with academically challenging activities.	
	Quantitative conclusion	Connected learning had a much stronger connection to student engagement than other teaching practices.	
Value-added	<ul><li>"The case study enhances our understanding of the nuanced relationship between teaching practice and student engagement" (p. 392), showed ranges of practice within a single classroom (p. 384)</li><li>"Survey data were integrated into each concept map to situate individual classrooms within school-wide student perceptions, shedding greater light on classroom practice than teaching individually and collectively related to engagement" (p. 384)</li><li>Graphic displays (Venn diagram, concept maps, conceptually clustered matrices) facilitated cross-case comparisons</li></ul>		

Appendix D.8	Exemplary Article About Rape Myths Among Athletes: Summary of Key Features of McMahon (2007)		
Rationale/Purpose	Complementarity		
Priority	Qualitative		
Timing of Data Collection	Qualitative ➔ Qualitative		
Timing of Data Analysis	Qualitative ➔ Qualitative		
Mixing	Fully integrated: No		
	Design	✖	
	Data collection	✖	Qualitative samples overlap
	Data analysis	✖	
	Inferences	✖	Qualitative mixing
Meta-inference	Participants ascribed to subtle rape myths as a strategy to avoid acknowledging vulnerability.		
	Qualitative conclusion	Men and women athletes from all teams expressed victim-blaming beliefs in subtle ways.	
	Quantitative conclusion	Low acceptance of rape myths among student athletes	
Value-added	<ul><li>Qualitative methods captured views about rape myths that are specific to student athlete culture.</li><li>Interviews produced "rich, descriptive data that could not have been discovered from the survey" (p. 368).</li><li>Qualitative methods offset weaknesses in the quantitative instrument.</li></ul>		

GLOSSARY

Axiology refers to the dimension of research paradigms that reflects philosophical assumptions about the place of values in empirical research.

Blending is a strategy for data consolidation where a variable, category, or theme generated from one type of analysis is tested using another type of data or where a variable, category, or factor is created by combining qualitative and quantitative data.

Complementarity argument is a pragmatic assumption that claims that the use of a combination of methods can offset the weaknesses inherent in any method.

Complementarity design seeks to gain a more holistic picture by exploring different aspects of the same phenomenon.

Concurrent mixed methods sampling utilizes a single sample of participants where qualitative and quantitative data are collected simultaneously but not necessarily at a single point in time.

Connecting (or **linking**) is a type of mixing that involves the integration of the qualitative and quantitative strands at the sampling stage by using quantitative data to select participants in the qualitative phase or, more rarely, by using qualitative data to identify the sample for the quantitative phases.

Content analysis is an empirical research method for systematically analyzing data that are in textual or visual form.

Convergent validity states that the confidence or credibility of results is enhanced when two or more methods produce congruent or comparable data (Jick, 1979).

Converting is a strategy for data consolidation where qualitative data are converted to quantitative data or quantitative data to qualitative data so that they can be analyzed together.

Critical realism is a paradigm that views entities as existing independently of being perceived but are only being partially and imperfectly perceived. All knowledge is viewed as partial, incomplete, and uncertain (Maxwell & Mittapalli, 2010).

Cross-case comparison is a mixed method analytical strategy that consolidates qualitative and quantitative data by constructing holistic, internally coherent profiles that are used to test or expand upon qualitatively or quantitatively derived themes for the purposes of comparison.

Data transformation is the conversion of qualitative data into quantitative data or quantitative data into qualitative data for the purposes of analysis.

Design refers to a thoughtfully constructed link between the purposes of a research study and the strategies used to implement it.

Development design uses the results of one method to inform the content or design of the other method. This label applies to two-phase instrument design studies as well as to studies that combine both exploratory and confirmatory phases of analysis.

Dialectical pluralism is a paradigm that reflects what some consider to be the overarching logic of mixed methods: the deliberate engagement with different points of view and ways of achieving knowledge.

Embedding is a type of mixing that occurs during data analysis that strategically brings qualitative and quantitative data together for analysis.

Epistemology is the dimension of research paradigms that reflects philosophical assumptions about the relationship between the knower and reality and the participant and what constitutes credible or warranted conclusions or inferences.

Evaluation research is focused on program development. It "involves the triangulation of qualitative and quantitative methods to examine acceptability, integrity, and effectiveness of intervention methods as both a formative and summative process" (Nastasi et al., 2007, p. 166).

Evaluation/intervention design involves collecting qualitative and quantitative data to evaluate the effectiveness of an intervention, program, activity, class, or workshop.

Expansion design describes studies where data are collected in more than two phases and from respondents at multiple levels of an organization or school (e.g., students, teachers, administrators).

Extreme case sampling is a type of purposeful (rather than representative) sampling and involves selecting cases because they are at the extremes of a sampling distribution (i.e., outliers).

Fully integrated mixed methods research is an approach to mixed methods research where there is the intention to mix or integrate the qualitative and quantitative strands of study throughout each of the stages or phases of the research process.

Incompatibility thesis argues that qualitative and quantitative research are different and incompatible approaches.

Inferences are conclusions or interpretations drawn from the results of the analysis in the quantitative, qualitative, and mixing strands.

Inferential transparency is a type of methodological transparency that explicitly links the contribution of the qualitative, quantitative, and mixing strands to the conclusions drawn from a study.

Initiation design involves exploring extreme or negative cases to test competing hypotheses or to explore unexpected or contradictory findings from earlier studies.

Interpretive comprehensiveness involves the different ways that consideration of more than one viewpoint is incorporated, not only during the process of drawing conclusions but also throughout other phases of the research process.

Interpretive efficacy refers to the degree to which inferences in each strand of a mixed methods study are effectively integrated into a conceptually coherent and substantively meaningful meta-inference.

Interpretive transparency is a type of reflexivity that enhances the credibility of a study by explicitly linking the source of data to a conclusion or inference.

Linking is a type of mixed method analytical procedure where qualitative and quantitative data are interwoven in a case narrative.

Logic of inquiry is the overriding methodological or philosophical emphasis.

Mental models are personal constructions that emerge from the experiences, beliefs, and values that come to pattern our lives (Greene, 2007).

Meta-inferences are inferences that link, compare, contrast, or modify inferences generated by the qualitative and quantitative strands (Teddlie & Tashakkori, 2009, p. 300).

Methodological consistency occurs when rigor is demonstrated by adherence to the philosophical and methodological assumptions of a method (Creswell, 1998).

Methodological foundation refers to the expectation for authors of a mixed methods publication to demonstrate expertise in the research methods employed, including mixed methods.

Methodological transparency promotes replication by providing explicit detail about the steps taken to complete data collection and data analysis as well as in specifying which results came from the qualitative analysis and which came from the quantitative analysis.

Methodology is a coherent framework of philosophical assumptions, methods, guidelines for practice, and sociopolitical commitments (Greene, 2008).

Methods consist of a systematic and coherent set of agreed-upon practices and procedures for conducting empirical research.

Mixed method sampling procedures use various approaches to combine a traditional quantitative (i.e., probability) approach to sampling with a qualitative (i.e., purposeful) approach.

Mixed methods analytical procedures set out to identify, compare, and consolidate thematically similar results by using more than one source or form of data.

Mixed priority mixed method studies award the most attention to results that are produced through mixed methods analytical procedures.

Mixing is the linking, merging, or embedding of qualitative and quantitative strands of a mixed methods study.

Multilevel/expansion designs are studies that have multiple stages of data collection and address different research questions at each stage.

Multimethod studies occur when more than one qualitative approach or more than one quantitative approach is used in a single study.

Ontology is the dimension of research paradigms that reflects philosophical assumptions about the nature of truth and reality and whether it is external or constructed.

Paradigms are not original idiosyncratic constructions but a set of philosophical assumptions that are inherently coherent about the nature of reality and the researcher's role in constructing it that is agreed upon by a community of scholars.

Phases (or **stages**) are steps in the process of completing a research study: planning and design, data collection, sampling, analysis, and drawing inferences.

Philosophical transparency is present when authors or presenters explicitly articulate the philosophical foundations of their work.

Pragmatism is a paradigm with a realist view that acknowledges diversity and complexity and sets aside debates about philosophy in favor of what works in a particular setting or for a particular set of research questions.

Priority has conventionally been defined to distinguish three types of studies: where the qualitative strand is given priority, where the quantitative strand is given priority, and where the qualitative and quantitative strands of a study are given equal priority.

Qualitizing is a mixed methods analytical strategy where measures on quantitative instruments are summarized

in narrative form for the purposes of further analysis and cross-case comparison.

Quantitizing which is when qualitative data is transformed into a quantitative format, often through frequency counts.

Quasi-mixed methods contain both a qualitative and quantitative strand but lack any point of interface between the two (Teddlie & Tashakkori, 2009).

Replication conveys an expectation that others using the same data and methods can duplicate the results of a study.

Sequential mixed method sampling occurs when a subsequent sampling strategy is directly linked to the results of analytical procedures in an earlier strand or study.

Significance enhancement increases the comprehensiveness, cohesiveness, robustness, and theoretical power of inferences and conclusions.

Text-in-context coding is a form of mixing that occurs during the process of qualitative coding of textual or visual data. It is a systematic procedure to flesh out variation in the way a variable or theme is manifested.

Theoretical sampling is a type of purposive sampling used in grounded theory to develop theoretical categories by application to a new sample of participants, sometimes in a different location. It is emergent in the sense that the sample is not determined until after the first phase of the analysis.

Timing generally refers to the timing of the collection of the qualitative and quantitative data. Sequential designs are those in which one phase of data collection leads to another. Multiphase designs have more than two, often iterative, phases of data collection.

Transformative–emancipatory paradigms are distinguished by the overtness of their axiological commitment to address issues of social justice and their commitment to nonhierarchical methods.

Triangulation involves corroboration or verification through multiple data points or multiple types of data about the same phenomenon.

Validity is a term used in both qualitative and quantitative research to refer to strategies that are used during data collection and analysis that confirm the credibility, confirmability, and justifiability of the findings and inferences drawn at the conclusion of a study.

Value-added is an element of methodological transparency where the insight, inferences, or conclusions that are produced by the use of mixed methods are explicitly identified.

REFERENCES

Ahmed, A., & Sil, R. (2012). When multi-method research subverts methodological pluralism—or why we still need single-method research. *Perspectives in Politics, 10*(4), 935–953.

Alise, M. A., & Teddlie, C. (2010). A continuation of the paradigm wars? Prevalence rates of methodological approaches across the social/behavioral sciences. *Journal of Mixed Methods Research, 4*(2), 103–126.

American Educational Research Association. (2006). Standards for reporting on empirical social science research in AERA publications. *Educational Researcher, 25*(6), 33–40.

American Psychological Association. (2010). *The publication manual of the American Psychological Association* (6th ed.). Author: Washington, DC.

Bazeley, P. (2006). The contribution of computer software to integrating qualitative and quantitative data and analyses. *Research in Schools, 13*(1), 64–74.

Bazeley, P. (2009). Integrating data analysis in mixed method research: An editorial. *Journal of Mixed Methods Research, 3*(3), 203–207. DOI: 10.1177/1558689809334443

Bazeley, P. (2012). Integrative analysis strategies for mixed data sources. *American Behavioral Scientist, 56*(6), 814–828. DOI: 10.1177/0002764211426330

Bazeley, P. (2013). *Qualitative data analysis: Practical strategies*. Thousand Oaks, CA: SAGE.

Bazeley, P., & Jackson, K. (2013). *Qualitative data analysis with NVIVO*. Thousand Oaks, CA: SAGE.

Bazeley, P., & Kemp, L. (2012). Mosaics, triangles, and DNA: Metaphors for integrated analysis in mixed methods research. *Journal of Mixed Methods Research, 6*(1), 55–72. DOI: 10.1177/1558689811419514

Beach, K. D., Becker, B. J., & Kennedy, J. M. (2007). Constructing conclusions. In C. F. Conrad & R. C. Serlin (Eds.), *The SAGE handbook for research in education: Engaging ideas and enriching inquiry* (pp. 493–510). Thousand Oaks, CA: SAGE.

Bergman, M. M. (2008). The straw men of the qualitative–quantitative divide and their influence on mixed methods research. In M. M. Bergman (Ed.), *Advances in mixed methods research* (pp. 11–21). Thousand Oaks, CA: SAGE.

Bergman, M. M. (2010). On concepts and paradigms in mixed methods research. *Journal of Mixed Methods Research, 4*(3), 171–175. DOI:10.1177/1558689810376950

Brannen, J. (1992). *Mixing methods: Qualitative and quantitative research*. Aldershot, UK: Avebury Press.

Bryman, A. (2004). *Social research methods* (2nd ed.). Oxford, UK: Oxford University Press.

Bryman, A. (2006). Integrating quantitative and qualitative research: How is it done? *Qualitative Research, 6*(1), 97–113.

Bryman, A. (2007). Barriers to integrating quantitative and qualitative research. *Journal of Mixed Methods Research, 1*, 8–22.

Bryman, A., Becker, S., & Simpik, J. (2008). Quality criteria for quantitative, qualitative, and mixed methods research: A view from social policy. *International Journal of Social Research Methodology, 11*(4), 261–276.

Butterfield, L. D., Borgen, W. A., Amundson, N. E., & Maglio, A.T. (2005). Fifty years of the critical incident technique: 1954–2004 and beyond. *Qualitative Research, 5*, 475. DOI: 10.1177/1468794105056924

Cameron, R., Sankaran, S., & Scales, J. (2015). Mixed methods use in project management research. *Project Management Journal, 46*(2), 90–104.

Capraro, R. M., & Thompson, B. (2008). The educational researcher defined: What will future researchers be trained to do? *The Journal of Educational Research, 101*(4), 247–253.

Caracelli, V. J., & Greene, J. C. (1993). Data analysis strategies for mixed-method evaluation design. *Educational Evaluation and Policy Analysis, 15*(2), 195–207.

Carmona, M. (2014). Re-theorizing contemporary public space: A new narrative and a new normative. *Journal of Urbanism: International Research on Placemaking and Urban Sustainability, 8*(4), 373–405.

Castro, F. G., Kellison, J. G., Boyd, S. J., & Kopak, A. (2010). A methodology for conducting integrative mixed methods research and data analysis. *Journal of Mixed Methods*

Research, 4(4), 342–360. DOI: 10.1177/1558689810382916

Catallo, C., Jack, S. M., Ciliska, D., & MacMillan, H. L. (2013). Mixing a grounded theory approach with a randomized controlled trial related to intimate partner violence: What challenges arise for mixed methods research? *Nursing Research and Practice*, 1–12. DOI:10.1155/2013/798213

Charmaz, K. (2014). *Constructing grounded theory*. Thousand Oaks, CA: SAGE.

Chell, E. (1998). Critical incident technique. In G. Symon & C. Cassell (Eds.), *Qualitative methods and analysis in organizational research: A practical guide* (pp. 51–72). Thousand Oaks, CA: SAGE.

Collins, K. M. T., Onwuegbuzie, A. J., & Jiao, Q. G. (2006). Prevalence of mixed-methods sampling designs in social science research. *Evaluation and Research in Education, 19*(2), 83–101.

Collins, K. M. T., Onwuegbuzie, A. J., & Jiao, Q. G. (2007). A mixed methods investigation of mixed methods sampling designs in social and health science research. *Journal of Mixed Methods Research, 1*(3), 267–294. DOI: 10.1177/1558689807299526

Collins, K. M. T., Onwuegbuzie, A. J., & Johnson, R. B. (2012). Securing a place at the table: A review and extension of legitimation criteria for the conduct of mixed research. *American Behavioral Scientists, 56*(6), 849–865.

Collins, K. M. T., Onwuegbuzie, A. J., & Sutton, I. L. (2006). A model of incorporating the rationale and purpose for conducting mixed-methods research in special education and beyond. *Learning*

Disabilities: A Contemporary Journal, 4(1), 67–100.

Cooper, K. (2014). Eliciting engagement in the high school classroom: A mixed methods examination of teaching practices. *American Educational Research Journal, 51*(2), 363–402. DOI: 10.3102/0002831213507973

Creamer, E. G. (2015). Review of article about teaching practices that promote engagement. *Mixed Methods International Research Association Newsletter No. 2.*

Creamer, E. G. (2016). A primer about mixed methods in an educational context. *International Journal of Learning, Teaching, and Educational Research, 15*(8), 1–13. Retrieved November 2, 2016, from http://ijlter.org/index.php/ijlter/article/view/700/pdf

Creamer, E. G., Edwards, C., & Musaeus, P. (2016, April 10). Developing credible conclusions: Findings from a content analysis of research exemplars. Research paper presentation at the American Educational Research Association Annual Meeting, Washington, DC.

Creamer, E. G., & Ghoston, M. (2012). Using a mixed methods content analysis to analyze mission statements from colleges of engineering. *Journal of Mixed Methods Research, 7*(2), 110–120. DOI: 10.1177/1558689812458976

Creamer, E. G., & Tendhar, C. (2015). Using inferences to evaluate the value added of mixed methods research: A content analysis. *International Journal of Multiple Research Approaches*. DOI: 10.1080/18340806.2015.1129286

Creswell, J. W. (1998). *Qualitative inquiry and research design: Choosing*

among five approaches (1st ed.). Thousand Oaks, CA: SAGE.

Creswell, J. W. (2002). *Educational research: Planning, conducting, and evaluating quantitative and qualitative research*. Upper Saddle River, NJ: Pearson Education.

Creswell, J. W. (2008). *Educational research: Planning, conducting, and evaluating quantitative and qualitative research*. Upper Saddle River, NJ: Prentice Hall.

Creswell, J. W. (2011). Controversies in mixed methods research. In N. K. Denzin & Y. S. Lincoln (Eds.), *The SAGE handbook of qualitative research* (pp. 269–283). Thousand Oaks, CA: SAGE.

Creswell, J. W., & Plano Clark, V. L. (2007). *Designing and conducting mixed methods research* (1st ed.). Thousand Oaks, CA: SAGE.

Creswell, J. W., & Plano Clark, V. L. (2011). *Designing and conducting mixed methods research* (2nd ed.). Thousand Oaks, CA: SAGE.

Creswell, J. W., Plano Clark, V. L., Gutmann, M. L., & Hanson, W. E. (2011). Advanced mixed methods research designs. In A. Tashakkori & C. Teddlie (Eds.), *Handbook of mixed methods in social and behavioral research* (pp. 209–240). Thousand Oaks, CA: SAGE.

Creswell, J. W., Shope, R., Plano Clark, V. L., & Green, D. O. (2006). How interpretive qualitative research extends mixed methods research. *Research in Schools, 13*(1), 1–11.

Creswell, J. W., & Tashakkori, A. (2007). Developing publishable mixed methods manuscripts [Editorial]. *Journal of Mixed Methods Research, 1*(2), 17–111.

Cross, J. E., Dickmann, E., Newman-Gonchar, R., & Fagan, J. M. (2009). Using mixed-method design and network analysis to measure development of interagency collaboration. *American Journal of Evaluation, 30*(3), 310–329.

Curry, L., & Nunez-Smith, M. (2015). *Mixed methods in health sciences research: A practical primer.* Thousand Oaks, CA: SAGE.

Dahlberg, B., Wittink, M. N., & Gallo, J. J. (2010). Funding and publishing integrated studies: Writing effective mixed methods manuscripts and grant proposals. In A. Tashakkori & C. Teddlie (Eds.), *Handbook of mixed methods in social and behavioral research* (pp. 775–802). Thousand Oaks, CA: SAGE.

Dellinger, A. B., & Leech, N. L. (2007). Toward a unified validation framework in mixed methods research. *Journal of Mixed Methods Research, 1*(4), 309–332.

Denzin, N. (1978). *The research act: A theoretical introduction to sociological methods* (2nd ed.). New York, NY: McGraw Hill.

Denzin, N. K. (2010). Moments, mixed methods, and paradigm dialogs. *Qualitative Inquiry, 16*(6), 419–427.

Downe-Wamboldt, B. (1992). Content analysis: Method, applications, and issues. *Health Care for Women International, 13,* 313–321.

Durksen, T. L., & Klassen, R. M. (2012). Pre-service teachers' weekly commitment and engagement during a final training placement: A longitudinal mixed methods study. *Educational and Child Psychology, 29*(4), 32–46.

Eisenhardt, K. M. (1989). Building theories from case study research. *Academy of Management Review, 14*(4), 532–550.

Elliott, J., Gale, C. R., Parsons, S., Kuh, D., & The HALCyon Study. (2014). Neighborhood cohesion and mental well-being among older adults: A mixed methods approach. *Social Science & Medicine, 107,* 44–51.

Ercikan, K., & Roth, W. M. (2006). What good is polarizing research into qualitative and quantitative. *Educational Researcher, 35*(5), 14–23.

Erzberger, C., & Kelle, U. (2003). Making inferences in mixed methods: The rules of integration. In A. Tashakkori & C. Teddlie (Eds.), *Handbook of mixed methods in social and behavioral research* (pp. 457–490). Thousand Oaks, CA: SAGE.

Feilzer, M. Y. (2010). Doing mixed methods research pragmatically: Implications for the rediscovery of pragmatism as a research paradigm. *Journal of Mixed Methods Research, 4*(1), 6–16. DOI: 10.1177/1558689809349691

Feinberg, M., Willer, R., & Keltner, D. (2012). Flustered and faithful: Embarrassment as a signal of prosociality. *Journal of Personality and Social Psychology, 102*(1), 81–97.

Fidel, R. (2008). Are we there yet? Mixed methods research in library and information science. *Journal of Library and Information Science Research, 30,* 265–272.

Freshwater, D. (2007). Reading mixed methods research: Contexts for criticism. *Journal of Mixed Methods Research, 1*(2), 133–146.

Fuentes, C. M. M. (2008). Pathways for interpersonal violence to sexually transmitted infections: A mixed methods study of diverse women. *Journal of Women's Health, 17,* 1591–1603.

Gambrel, L. E., & Butler, J. L. (2013, April). Mixed methods research in marriage and family therapy: A content analysis. *Journal of Marital and Family Therapy, 39*(2), 163–181.

Gasson, S., & Waters, J. (2013). Using a grounded theory approach to study online collaborative behaviors. *European Journal of Information Systems, 22,* 95–118.

Giddings, L. S. (2006). Mixed-methods research: Positivism dressed in drag? *Journal of Research in Nursing, 11*(3), 195–203. DOI: 10.1177/1744987106064635

Giddings, L. S., & Grant, B. M. (2007). A Trojan horse for positivism? A critique of mixed methods research. *Advances in Nursing Science, 30*(1), 52–60.

Graneheim, U. H., & Lundman, B. (2003). Qualitative content analysis in nursing research: Concepts, procedures, and measures to achieve trustworthiness. *Nursing Education Today, 24,* 105–112.

Greene, J. C. (2007). *Mixed methods in social inquiry.* San Francisco, CA: Wiley.

Greene, J. (2008). Is mixed methods social inquiry a distinctive methodology? *Journal of Mixed Methods Research, 2*(1), 7–22.

Greene, J. C., & Caracelli, V. J. (2003). Maxing paradigmatic sense of mixed methods practice. In A. Tashakkori & C. Teddlie (Eds.), *Handbook of mixed methods in social and behavioral research* (pp. 91–110). Thousand Oaks, CA: SAGE.

Greene, J. C., Caracelli, V. J., & Graham, W. F. (1989). Toward a conceptual framework for mixed-method evaluation designs. *Educational Evaluation and Policy Analysis, 11*(3), 255–274.

Greene, J. C., & Hall, J. N. (2010). Dialectics and pragmatism: Being of consequence. In A. Tashakkori & C. Teddlie (Eds.), *Handbook of mixed methods in social and behavioral research* (pp. 119–144). Thousand Oaks, CA: SAGE.

Guba, E. G., & Lincoln, Y. S. (1994). Competing paradigms in qualitative research. In N. K. Denzin & Y. S. Lincoln (Eds.), *Handbook of qualitative research* (pp. 105–117). Thousand Oaks, CA: SAGE.

Guest, G. (2012). Describing mixed methods research: An alternative to typologies. *Journal of Mixed Methods Research, 7*(2), 141–151.

Halcomb, E. J., & Andrew, S. (2009). Practical considerations for higher degree research students undertaking mixed methods projects. *International Journal of Multiple Research Approaches, 3*, 153–162.

Hanson, D., & Grimmer, M. (2007). The mix of qualitative and quantitative research in major marketing journals, 1993–2002. *European Journal of Marketing, 41*(1/2), 58–70.

Hanson, W. E., Plano Clark, V. L., Creswell, J. W., & Creswell, J. D. (2005). Mixed method research designs in counseling psychology. *Journal of Counseling Psychology, 52*(2), 224–235.

Harrison, Y. D., & Murray, V. (2012). Perspectives on the leadership of chairs of nonprofit organization boards of directions: A grounded theory mixed-method study. *Nonprofit Management and Leadership, 22*(4), 411–437. DOI:10.1002/mml.21308

Hart, L. C., Smith, S. Z., Swars, S. L., & Smith, M. E. (2009). An examination of research methods in mathematics education (1995–2005). *Journal of Mixed Methods Research, 3*(1), 26–41.

Hauser, L. (2013). Qualitative research in distance education: An analysis of journal literature 2005–2012. *The American Journal of Distance Education, 27*(155), 155–164.

Hesse-Biber, S. (2010a). Emerging methodologies and methods practices in the field of mixed method research. *Qualitative Inquiry, 16*(6), 415–418.

Hesse-Biber, S. (2010b). *Mixed methods research: Merging theory with practice*. New York, NY: Guilford Press.

Hesse-Biber, S. (2010c). Qualitative approaches to mixed methods practice. *Qualitative Inquiry 16*(6), 455–468.

Hesse-Biber, S., & Johnson, R. B. (2015). (Eds.) *The Oxford handbook of multimethod and mixed methods research inquiry*. Oxford, UK: Oxford University Press.

Heyvaert, M., Hannes, K., Maes, B., & Onghena, P. (2013). Critical appraisal of mixed methods studies. *Journal of Mixed Method Research, 7*(4), 302–327.

Heyvaert, M., Hannes, K., & Onghena, P. (2017). *Using mixed methods research synthesis for literature reviews*. Thousand Oaks, CA: SAGE.

Hites, L. S., Fifolt, M., Beck, H., Su, W., Kerbawy, S., Wakelee, J., & Nassell, A. (2013). A geospatial mixed methods approach to assessing campus safety. *Evaluation Review, 37*(5), 347–369.

Howe, K. R. (1988, November). Against the quantitative–qualitative incompatibility thesis or dogmas die hard. *Educational Researcher*, 10–16.

Howe, K. (2004). A critique of experimentalism. *Qualitative Inquiry, 10*(1), 42–61.

Hunter, A., & Brewer, J. (2015). Designing multimethod research. In R. B. Johnson (Eds.), *The Oxford handbook of multimethod and mixed methods research inquiry* (pp. 185–205). Oxford, UK: Oxford University Press.

Hurmerinta-Peltomäki, L., & Nummela, N. (2006). Mixed methods in international business research: A value-added perspective. *Management International Review, 46*(4), 439–459.

Ivankova, N. (2015). *Mixed methods applications in action research: From methods to community*. Thousand Oaks, CA: SAGE.

Ivankova, N., & Kawamura, Y. (2010). Emerging trends in the utilization of integrated designs in the social, behavioral, and health sciences. In A. Tashakkori & C. Teddlie (Eds.), *Handbook of mixed methods in social and behavioral research* (pp. 581–611). Thousand Oaks, CA: SAGE.

Ivankova, N. W., & Stick, S. L. (2007). Students' persistence in a distributed doctoral program in educational leadership in higher education: A mixed methods study. *Research in Higher Education, 48*(1), 93–135.

Jang, E., McDougall, D. E., Pollon, D., Herbert, M., & Russell, P. (2008). Integrative data analytic strategies in research in school success in challenging circumstances. *Journal of Mixed Methods Research, 2*(3), 221–247.

Jick, T. D. (1979). Mixing qualitative and quantitative methods: Triangulation in action. *Administrative Science Quarterly, 24*, 602–611.

Jimenez-Castellanos, O. (2010). Relationship between educational resources and school achievement: A mixed method intra-district analysis. *Urban Review, 42*, 351–371.

Johnson, R. B. (2012). Guest editor's editorial: Dialectical pluralism: A metaparadigm whose time has come. *American Behavioral Scientist, 56*, 751–754.

Johnson, R. B. (2015). Conclusions: Toward an inclusive and defensible multimethod and mixed methods science. In R. B. Johnson (Eds.), *The Oxford handbook of multimethod and mixed methods research inquiry* (pp. 688–706). Oxford, UK: Oxford University Press.

Johnson, R. B., McGowan, M. W., & Turner, L. A. (2010). Grounded theory in practice: Inherently a mixed method? *Research in the Schools, 17*(2), 65–78.

Johnson, R. B., & Onwuegbuzie, A. J. (2004). Mixed methods research: A research paradigm whose time has come. *Educational Researcher, 33*(7), 14–26.

Johnson, R. B., Onwuegbuzie, A. J., & Turner, L. A. (2007). Toward a definition of mixed methods research. *Journal of Mixed Methods Research, 1*(2), 112–133.

Johnson, R. B., & Schoonenboom, J. (2016). Adding qualitative and mixed methods research to health intervention studies: Interacting with differences. *Qualitative Health Research, 26*(5), 587–602.

Kafir, R. L., & Creamer, E. G. (2014, June 15–18). A mixed methods analysis and evaluation of the mixed method research literature in engineering education. ASEE annual conference proceedings, Indianapolis, Indiana.

Keltner, D. (1995). Signs of appeasement: Evidence for distinct displays of embarrassment, amusement, and shame. *Journal of Personality and Social Psychology, 68*(3), 441–454.

Keltner, D. (2009). *Born to be good: The science of a meaningful life*. New York, NY: Norton.

Keltner, D., & Buswell, B. N. (1996). Evidence for the distinctness of embarrassment, shame, and guilt: A study of recalled antecedents and facial expressions of emotion. *Cognition and Emotion, 10*(2), 155–171.

Kemper, E. A., Stringfield, S., & Teddlie, C. (2003). Mixed methods sampling strategies. In A. Tashakkori & C. Teddlie (Eds.), *Handbook of mixed methods in social and behavioral research* (pp. 273–296). Thousand Oaks, CA: SAGE.

Kitchenham, A. (2010). Mixed methods in case study research. In A. J. Mills, G. Durepos, & E. Wiebe (Eds.), *Encyclopedia of case study research* (pp. 562–565). Thousand Oaks, CA: SAGE.

Krippendorff, K. (2004). *Content analysis: An introduction to its methodology* (2nd ed.). Thousand Oaks, CA: SAGE.

Leech, N. L. (2012). Writing mixed research reports. *American Behavioral Scientist, 56*(6), 866–881.

Leech, N. L., Collins, K. M. T., Jiao, Q. G., & Onwuegbuzie, A. J. (2011). Mixed research in gifted education: A mixed research investigation of trends in the literature. *Journal for the Education of the Gifted, 34*(6), 860–875.

Leech, N. L., Dellinger, A. B., Brannagan, K. B., & Tanaka, H. (2010). Evaluating mixed research studies: A mixed methods approach. *Journal of Mixed Methods Research, 4*(1), 17–31.

Leech, N. L., & Onwuegbuzie, A. J. (2009). *Qualitative Quantitative Journal, 43*, 265–275. DOI: 10.1007/s11135-007-910503

Leech, N. L., Onwuegbuzie, A. J., & Combs, J. P. (2011). Writing publishable mixed research articles: Guidelines for emerging scholars in the health sciences and beyond. *Journal of Multiple Research Approaches, 5*, 7–24.

López-Fernandez, O., & Molina-Azorin, J. F. (2011). The use of mixed methods research in interdisciplinary educational journals. *International Journal of Multiple Research Approaches, 5*(2), 269–283.

Luck, L., Jackson, D., & Usher, K. (2006). Case study: A bridge across the paradigms. *Nursing Inquiry, 13*(2), 103–109.

Makel, M. C., & Plucker, J. A. (2014). Facts are more important than novelty: Replication in the education sciences. *Educational Researcher, 43*(4), 304–315.

Mason, J. (2006). Mixing methods in a qualitatively driven way.

Qualitative Research, 6(1), 9–25. DOI: 10.1177/1468794106058866

Mathison, S. (1988). Why triangulate? *Educational Researcher, 17*(2), 13–17.

Maxwell, J. A. (1992). Understanding and validity in qualitative research. *Harvard Educational Review, 62*(3), 279–299.

Maxwell, J. A. (2004). Causal explanation, qualitative research, and scientific inquiry in education. *Educational Researcher, 33*(2), 3–11.

Maxwell, J. A. (2010). Using numbers in qualitative research. *Qualitative Inquiry, 16*(6), 475–482.

Maxwell, J. A., & Mittapalli, K. (2010). Realism as a stance for mixed methods research. In A. Tashakkori & C. Teddlie (Eds.), *Handbook of mixed methods in social and behavioral research* (pp. 145–168). Thousand Oaks, CA: SAGE.

Mazzola, J. J., Walker, E. J., Schockley, K. M., & Spector, P. E. (2011). Examining stress in graduate assistants: Combining qualitative and quantitative survey methods. *Journal of Mixed Methods Research, 5*(3), 198–211.

McFerran, K., Roberts, M., & O'Grady, L. (2010). Music therapy with bereaved teenagers: A mixed method perspective. *Death Studies, 34*, 541–565.

McGill, L. T. (1990). Doing science by the numbers: The role of tables and other representational conventions in scientific journal articles. In A. Hunter (Ed.), *The rhetoric of social research: Understood and believed* (pp. 129–141). New Brunswick, NJ: Rutgers University Press.

McMahon, S. (2007). Understanding community-specific rape myths. *Affilia: Journal of Women and Social Work, 22*(4), 357–370.

McTavish, D. G., & Pirro, E. B. (1990). Contextual content analysis. *Quality and Quantity 24*, 245–265.

Mertens, D. M. (2007). Transformative paradigm: Mixed methods and social justice. *Journal of Mixed Methods Research, 1*(3), 212–225. DOI:10.1177/1558689807302811

Miles, M. B., & Huberman, A. M. (1994). *Qualitative data analysis: An expanded sourcebook* (2nd ed.). Thousand Oaks, CA: SAGE.

Miles, M. B., Huberman, A. M., & Saldana, J. (2014). *Qualitative data analysis: A methods sourcebook.* Thousand Oaks, CA: SAGE.

Miller, S. (2003). Impact of mixed method and design on inference quality. In A. Tashakkori & C. Teddlie (Eds.), *Handbook of mixed methods in social and behavioral research* (pp. 423–488). Thousand Oaks, CA: SAGE.

Molina-Azorin, J. F. (2010). The application of mixed methods in organizational research: A literature review. *The Electronic Journal of Business Research Methods, 8*, 95–105.

Molina-Azorin, J. F. (2011). The use and added value of mixed methods in management research. *Journal of Mixed Methods Research, 5*(1), 7–24. DOI: 10.1177/1558689810384490

Molina-Azorin, J. F. (2012). Mixed methods research in strategic management: Impact and applications. *Organizational Research Methods, 15*, 33–56.

Molina-Azorin, J. F., López-Gamero, M. D., Pereira-Moliner, J., & Pertusa-Ortega, E. (2012). Mixed methods studies in entrepreneurship research: Applications and contributions. *Entrepreneurship & Regional Development, 24*, 425–456.

Morgan, D. L. (2007). Paradigms lost and pragmatism regained: Methodological implications of combining qualitative and quantitative methods. *Journal of Mixed Methods Research, 1*(1), 48–76. DOI: 10.1177/2345678906292462

Morse, J. M. (1991). Approaches to qualitative–quantitative methodological triangulation. *Nursing Research, 40*, 120–123.

Morse, J. (2010). Simultaneous and sequential qualitative mixed methods designs. *Qualitative Inquiry, 16*(6), 483–491.

Morse, J. M. (2003). Principles of mixed methods and multimethod research design. In A. Tashakkori & C. Teddlie (Eds.), *Handbook of mixed methods in social and behavioral research* (pp. 189–208). Thousand Oaks, CA: SAGE.

Morse, J., & Niehaus, L. (2009). *Mixed method design: Principles and procedures.* Walnut Creek, CA: Left Coast Press, Inc.

Nastasi, B. K., Hitchcock, J. H., & Brown, L. M. (2010). An inclusive framework for conceptualizing mixed method design typologies. In A. Tashakkori & C. Teddlie (Eds.), *The SAGE handbook of mixed methods in social and behavioral research* (2nd ed., pp. 305–338). Thousand Oaks, CA: SAGE.

Nastasi, B. K., Hitchcock, J., Sarkar, S., Burkholder, G., Varjas, K., & Jayasena, A. (2007). Mixed methods in intervention research: Theory to adaptation. *Journal of Mixed Methods Research, 1*(2), 164–182.

Newman, I., & Hitchcock, J. H. (2011). Underlying agreements between quantitative and qualitative research: The short and tall of it. *Human Resource Development Review, 10*(4), 381–398. DOI:10.1177/1534484311413867

Newman, I., Ridenour, C., Newman, C., & DeMarco, G. M. (2003). A typology of research purposes and its relationship to mixed methods. In A. Tashakkori & C. Teddlie (Eds.), *Handbook of mixed methods in social and behavioral research* (pp. 167–188). Thousand Oaks, CA: SAGE.

O'Cathain, A. (2009). Reporting mixed methods projects. In S. Andrew & E. J. Halcomb (Eds.), *Mixed methods research for nursing and health sciences* (pp. 135–158). Oxford, UK: Blackwell Publishing.

O'Cathain, A. (2010). Assessing the quality of mixed methods research: Toward a comprehensive framework. In A. Tashakkori & C. Teddlie (Eds.), *The SAGE handbook of mixed methods in social and behavioral research* (pp. 531–555). Thousand Oaks, CA: SAGE.

O'Cathain, A., Murphy, E., & Nicholl, J. (2007a). Integration of publications as indicators of 'yield' from mixed methods studies. *Journal of Mixed Methods Research, 1*(2), 147–163.

O'Cathain, A., Murphy, E., & Nicholl, J. (2007b). Why, and how, mixed methods research is undertaken in health services research in England: A mixed method study. *BMC Health Services Research, 7*(1). DOI: 10.1186/1472-6963-7-85

O'Cathain, A., Murphy, E., & Nicholl, J. (2008). The quality of mixed methods studies in health services research. *Journal of Health Services Research and Policy, 13*(2), 92–98.

O'Cathain, A., Murphy, E., & Nicholl, J. (2010). Three techniques for integrating data in mixed methods studies. *BMJ: British Medical Journal, 341*, 1147–1150.

Odom, S. L., Li, S., Sandall, S., Zercher, C., Marquart, J. M., & Brown, W. H. (2006). Social acceptance and rejection of preschool children with disabilities: A mixed method analysis. *Journal of Educational Psychology, 98*(4), 807–823.

Olson, B. D., & Jason, L. A. (2015). *Participatory mixed methods research.* In S. Hesse-Biber & R. B. Johnson (Eds.), *The Oxford handbook of multimethod and mixed methods research inquiry* (pp. 393–405). Oxford, UK: Oxford University Press.

Onwuegbuzie, A. J. (2003). Effect sizes in qualitative research: A prolegomenon. *Quality and Quantity, 37*, 393–409.

Onwuegbuzie, A. J., & Collins, K M. T. (2007). A typology of mixed methods sampling designs in social science research. *The Qualitative Report, 12*(2), 281–316.

Onwuegbuzie, A. J., & Frels, R. K. (2013). Introduction: Toward a new research philosophy for addressing social justice issues: Critical dialectical pluralism. *International Journal of Multiple Research Approaches, 7*(1), 9–26.

Onwuegbuzie, A. J., & Johnson, R. B. (2006). The validity issue in mixed research. *Research in Schools, 13*(1), 48–63.

Onwuegbuzie, A. J., & Leech, N. L. (2004). Enhancing the interpretation of significant findings: The role of mixed methods research. *The Qualitative Report, 9*(4), 770–792.

Onwuegbuzie, A. J., & Leech, N. L. (2006). Linking research questions to mixed methods data analysis procedures. *The Qualitative Report, 11*(3), 474–498.

Onwuegbuzie, A. J., Slate, J. R., Leech, N. L., & Collins, K. (2007). Conducting mixed analyses: A general typology. *International Journal of Multiple Research Approaches, 1*, 4–17.

Open Science Collaboration. (2015, August 28). Estimating the reproducibility of psychological science. *Science, 349*(6251). DOI: 10.1126/science.aac4716

Pace, R., Pluye, P., Bartlett, G., Macaulay, A. C., Salsberg, J., Jagosh, J., & Seller, R. (2012). *International Journal of Nursing Studies, 49*, 47–53.

Palinkas, L. A., Aarons, G. A., Horwitz, S., Chamberlain, P., Hurlburt, M., & Landsverk, J. (2011). Mixed method designs in implementation research. *Journal of Administration and Policy in Mental Health, 38*, 44–53.

Plano Clark, V. L. (2010). The adoption and practice of mixed methods: U.S. trends in federally funded health-related research. *Qualitative Inquiry, 16*(6), 428–440.

Plano Clark, V. L., Anderson, N., Wertz, J. A., Zhou, Y., Schumacher, K., & Miaskowski, C. (2014). Conceptualizing longitudinal mixed methods designs: A methodological review of health sciences research. *Journal of Mixed Methods Research,* 1–23.

Plano Clark, V. L., & Badiee, M. (2010). Research questions in mixed methods research. In A. Tashakkori

& C. Teddlie (Eds.), *The SAGE handbook of mixed methods in social and behavioral science research* (2nd ed., pp. 275–304). Thousand Oaks, CA: SAGE.

Plano Clark, V. L., Huddleston-Casas, C. A., Churchill, S. L., Green, D. O., & Garrett, A. L. (2008). Mixed methods approaches in family science research. *Journal of Family Issues, 29*(11), 1543–1566.

Plowright, D. (2013). To what extent do postgraduate students understand the principles of mixed methods in educational research? *International Journal of Multiple Research Approaches, 7*(1), 66–82.

Pluye, P., Gagnon, M. P., Griffiths, F., & Johnson-Lafleur, J. (2009). A scoring system for appraising mixed methods research, and concomitantly appraising qualitative, quantitative and mixed methods primary studies in mixed studies reviews. *International Journal of Nursing Studies, 46*(4), 529–546.

Pluye, P., & Hong, Q. N. (2014). Combining the power of stories and the power of numbers: Mixed methods research and mixed studies reviews. *Annual Review of Public Health, 35,* 29–45.

Poth, C. (2014). What constitutes effective learning experiences in a mixed methods research course? An examination from the student perspective. *International Journal of Multiple Research Approaches, 8*(1), 74–86.

Powell, H. S., Mihalas, A. J., Onwuegbuzie, S. S., & Daley, C. E. (2008). Mixed methods research in school psychology: A mixed methods investigation of trends in the literature. *Psychology in Schools, 45,* 291–309.

Rauscher, L., & Greenfield, B. H. (2009). Advancements in contemporary physical therapy research: Use of mixed methods design. *Journal of American Physical Therapy Association, 89,* 91–100.

Ray, D. C., Hull, D. M., Thacker, A. J., Pace, L. S., Swan, K. L., Carlson, S. E., & Sullivan, J. M. (2011). Research in counseling: A 10-year review to inform practice. *Journal of Counseling & Development, 89*(3), 349–359.

Ridenour, C. S., & Newman, I. (2008). *Mixed methods research: Exploring the interactive continuum.* Carbondale: Southern Illinois University Press.

Ross, A. A., & Onwuegbuzie, A. J. (2012). Prevalence of mixed methods research in mathematics education. *Editorial Staff, 22*(1), 84–113.

Rossman, G. B., & Wilson, B. L. (1985). Numbers and words: Combining quantitative and qualitative methods in a single large-scale evaluation study. *Evaluation Review, 9*(5), 627–643.

Sale, J. E. M., & Brazil, K. (2004). A strategy to identify critical appraisal criteria for primary mixed-methods studies. *Quality and Quantity, 38,* 351–364.

Sale, J. E. M., Lohfeld, L. H., & Brazil, K. (2002). Revisiting the quantitative-qualitative debate: Implications for mixed-methods research. *Quality and Quantity, 36,* 43–53.

Salisbury, D. (2013, March 23). Humanoid robot helps train children with autism. *Vanderbilt University: Research News at Vanderbilt.* Retrieved October 15, 2016, from http://news.vanderbilt.edu/2013/03/robot-helps-children-with-autism

Sandelowski, M. (2001). Real qualitative researchers do not count:

The use of numbers in qualitative research. *Research in Nursing and Health, 24,* 230–240.

Sandelowski, M. (2003). Tables or tableaux? The challenges of writing and reading mixed methods studies. In A. Tashakkori & C. Teddlie (Eds.), *Handbook of mixed methods in social and behavioral research* (pp. 321–350). Thousand Oaks, CA: SAGE.

Sandelowski, M. (2008). Reading, writing, and systematic review. *Journal of Advanced Nursing, 64*(1), 104–110.

Sandelowski, M. (2014). Guest editorial: Unmixing mixed-methods research. *Research in Nursing and Health, 37,* 3–8.

Sandelowski, M., Voils, C. I., & Knafl, G. (2009). On quantitizing. *Journal of Mixed Method Research, 3*(3), 208–223. DOI: 10.1177/1558689809334210

Sandelowski, M., Voils, C. I., Leeman, J., & Crandell, J. L. (2012). Mapping the mixed methods-mixed research synthesis terrain. *Journal of Mixed Methods Research, 6*(4), 317–333. DOI: 10.1177/1558689811427913

Sapolsky, R. M. (2013, July 27). The appeal of embarrassment. *Wall Street Journal.*

Schram, A. B. (2014). A mixed methods content analysis of the research literature in science education. *International Journal of Science Education, 36*(15), 2619–2638.

Schuessler, J. (2016, January 6). New York public library invites a deep digital dive. *The New York Times.* Retrieved October 21, 2016, from http://www.nytimes.com/2016/01/06/books/new-york-public-library-invites-a-deep-digital-dive.html?

smprod=nytcore-ipad&smid=nyt-core-ipad-share

Shannon-Baker, P. (2015). "But I wanted to appear happy": How using arts-informed and mixed methods approaches complicate qualitatively driven research on culture shock. *International Journal of Qualitative Methods*, *14*(2). Retrieved October 21, 2016, from http://ejournals.library .ualberta.ca/index.php/IJQM/article/ view/23018/0

Sheehan, M. D., & Johnson, R. B. (2012). Philosophical and methodological beliefs of instructional design faculty and professionals. *Education Technology Research Development*, *60*, 131–153. DOI:10.1007/s11423-011-9220-7

Small, L. S. (2011). How to conduct a mixed methods study: Recent trends in a rapidly growing literature. *The Annual Review of Sociology, 37*, 57–86.

Sollaci, L., & Pereira, M. (2004). The introduction, methods, results, and discussion (IMRAD) structure: A fifty-year survey. *Journal of the Medical Library Association, 92*(3), 364–371.

Song, M-K., Happ, M. B., & Sandelowski, M. (2010). Development of a tool to assess fidelity to a psycho-educational intervention. *Journal of Advanced Nursing, 66*, 673–682. DOI: 10.1111/j.1365-2648.2009.05216.x

Sosa, A. V. (2016). Association of the type of toy used during play with the quantity and quality of parent–infant communication. *JAMA Pediatrics, 170*(2), 132–137.

Stake, R. (2003). Case studies. In N. Denzin & Y. S. Lincoln (Eds.), *Strategies for qualitative inquiry* (2nd ed., pp. 134–164). Thousand Oaks, CA: SAGE.

Stemler, S. E., Bebell, D., & Sonnabend, L. A. (2011). Using school mission statements for reflection and research. *Educational Administration Quarterly, 47*(2), 383–420.

Stentz, J. E., Plano Clark, V. L., & Matkin, G. S. (2012). Applying mixed methods to leadership practice: A review of current practices. *The Leadership Quarterly, 23*, 1173–1183.

Stenvoll, D., & Svensson, P. (2011). Contestable contexts: The transparent anchoring of contextualization in text-as-date. *Qualitative Research, 11*(5), 570–586. DOI: 110.1177/1468794111413242

Stoecker, R. (1991). Evaluating and rethinking the case study. *The Sociological Review, 39*(1), 88–112.

Strauss, A., & Corbin, J. (1998). *Basics of qualitative research: Grounded theory procedures and techniques* (2nd ed.). Newbury Park, CA: SAGE.

Symonds, J. E., & Gorard, S. (2010). Death of mixed methods? Or rebirth of research as craft. *Evaluation and Research in Education, 23*(2), 121–136.

Tashakkori, A., & Teddlie. C. (2008). Quality of inferences in mixed methods research: Calling for an integrative framework. In M. M. Bergman (Ed.), *Advances in mixed methods research* (pp. 101–119). Thousand Oaks, CA: SAGE.

Tashakkori, A., & Teddlie. C. (2010). Epilogue: Current developments and emerging trends in integrated research methodology. In A. Tashakkori & C. Teddlie (Eds.), *The SAGE handbook of mixed methods in social and behavioral science research* (2nd ed., pp. 803–826). Thousand Oaks, CA: SAGE.

Teddlie, C., & Tashakkori, A. (2009). *Foundations of mixed methods research: Integrating qualitative and quantitative approaches in the social and behavioral sciences.* Thousand Oaks, CA: SAGE.

Teddlie, C., & Tashakkori, A. (2012). Common 'core' characteristics of mixed methods research: A review of critical issues and call for greater convergence. *American Behavioral Scientists, 56*(6), 774–788.

Teddlie, C., & Yu, F. (2007). Mixed methods sampling: A typology with examples. *Journal of Mixed Methods Research, 1*(1), 77–100. DOI: 10.1177/2345678906292430

Torres, V. (2006). A mixed method study testing data model fit of a retention model for Latino/a students at urban universities. *Journal of College Student Development, 47*(3), 299–318.

Truscott, D. M., Swars, S., Smith, S., Thornton-Reid, F., Zhao, Y., Dooley, C., Williams, B., Hart, L., & Matthews, M. (2010). A cross-disciplinary examination of the prevalence of mixed methods in educational research: 1995–2005. *International Journal of Social Research Methodology, 13*(4), 317–328.

Van der Roest, J. W., Spaaij, R., & van Bottenburg, M. (2015). Mixed methods in emerging academic subdisciplines: The case of sport management. *Journal of Mixed Methods Research, 9*(1), 70–90.

Wallenberg, L. J., Ashbolt, R., Holland, D., Gibbs, L., MacDougall, C., Garrard, J., Green, J. B., & Waters, E. (2010). Increasing school playground physical activity: A mixed methods study combining environmental measures and children's perspectives. *Journal of Science and Medicine in Sport, 13*, 210–216.

Walsh, I. (2014). A strategic path to study IT use through users' IT culture and IT needs: A mixed-method grounded theory. *Journal of Strategic Information Systems, 23*, 146–173.

Wang, S. (2013, May 1). Robot aids in therapy for autistic children. *Wall Street Journal*. Retrieved October 15, 2016, from http://www.wsj.com/articles/SB10001424127887324582004578456681984219240

Weber, R. P. (1985). *Basic content analysis*. Beverly Hills, CA: SAGE.

Weber, R. P. (1990). *Basic content analysis* (2nd ed.). Beverly Hills, CA: SAGE.

Wesely, P. M. (2010). Language learning motivation in early adolescents: Using mixed method research to explore contradiction. *Journal of Mixed Methods Research, 4*(4), 295–312.

Wisdom, J. P., Cavaleri, M. A., Onwuegbuzie, A. J., & Green, C. A. (2012). Methodological reporting in qualitative, quantitative, and mixed methods health services research articles. *Health Research and Educational Trust: Health Services Research, 47*(2), 721–745.

Wolcott, H. F. (1994). *Transforming qualitative data: Description, analysis, and interpretation*. Thousand Oaks, CA: SAGE.

Yin, R. K. (2006). Mixed methods research: Are the methods genuinely integrated or merely parallel? *Research in the Schools, 13*(1), 41–47.

Young, S. D., & Jaganath, D. (2013). Online social networking for HIV education and prevention: A mixed-methods analysis. *Sexually Transmitted Diseases, 40*(2), 162–167.

NAME INDEX

SUBJECT INDEX

Note: In page references, f indicates figures and t indicates tables.